# VIETNAM

## *Yesterday and Today*

Ellen Hammer

HOLT, RINEHART and WINSTON, Inc.

New York

*Contemporary Civilizations Series*

THE MOTIF on the title page and at the beginning of each chapter is the legendary and distinctively Vietnamese dragon fish.

Library of Congress Catalog Card Number: 65–26445

# Preface

It is difficult to write about Vietnam during this cruel period of its history. No foreign country is easy to know, least of all one so remote from American experience and so closed against the intrusion of outsiders as this ancient Asian land. The assumptions of Western political analysis do not offer much guidance within the Vietnamese context, and the firm conclusions drawn by observers one day are often denied by the next day's events.

But no one can fail to be moved by the tragedy of these brave people: they fought for and in 1954 won their independence after a long struggle only to be plunged into internecine war. Today their very survival as a nation is at stake. The inability of their leaders and their institutions to achieve and preserve peace has been a Vietnamese problem for centuries. Now this problem has been aggravated by the international tensions of the twentieth century.

This book attempts to describe the complex background of recent developments in Vietnam. The friends of the Vietnamese nation can only hope that the Vietnamese people will find in their proud history comfort and incentive for evolving, by themselves, the right solutions to their apparently inextricable problems. But the past history of civilizations and nations shows only too clearly that satisfactory solutions are not necessarily the outcome of human endeavor.

ELLEN J. HAMMER graduated from Barnard College and holds a Ph.D. in Public Law and Government from Columbia University where she specialized in International Relations. For several years she was a member of the research staff of the Council on Foreign Relations in New York. She has investigated Vietnamese problems during a number of extended sojourns in that country. In the course of these visits she had far-reaching exchanges of views with many of the participants in the Vietnamese crisis and acquired firsthand knowledge of crucial events described in this book. She is the author of *The Struggle for Indochina,* a 1954 History Book Club selection, several monographs, and numerous articles on Vietnamese affairs.

VERA MICHELES DEAN, general editor of the Contemporary Civilizations Series, is professor of international development at the Graduate School of Public Administration, New York University. Mrs. Dean was research director and editor of the Foreign Policy Association, 1928–1961, and served as director of the Non-Western Civilizations Program at The University of Rochester, 1954–1962.

With the assistance of Harry D. Harootunian, Mrs. Dean prepared the anthology WEST AND NON-WEST: NEW PERSPECTIVES which is the basic reader in the Contemporary Civilizations Series.

# Contents

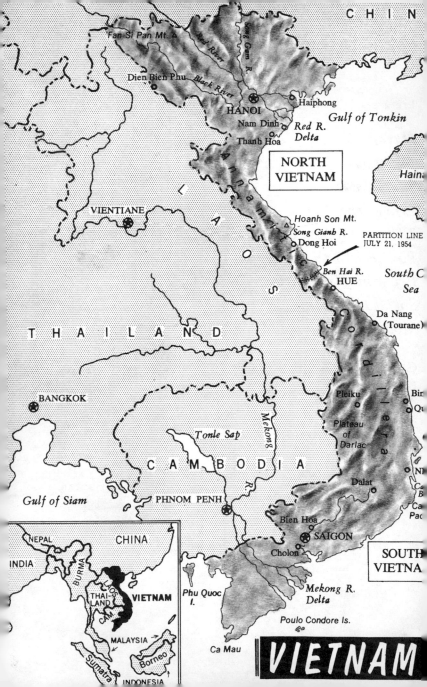

# VIETNAM

E ARLY in the fifteenth century, Vietnam's national hero Le Loi, who liberated Vietnam from Chinese rule, issued a proclamation composed by the great Vietnamese scholar and poet Nguyen Trai in which it is written: "Our people long ago established Vietnam as an independent nation with its own civilization. We have our own mountains and our own rivers, our own customs and traditions, and these are different from those of the foreign country to the north [China] . . . We have sometimes been weak and sometimes powerful, but at no time have we suffered from a lack of heroes."

These words are as true today as when they were written, and as they were a thousand years before then. The Vietnamese are an ancient people with a complex society, who were building temples and writing works of poetry and prose more than fifteen centuries ago. They were profoundly in-

1

fluenced by Chinese civilization, but their struggle against the imperialism of China is almost as old as the Vietnamese nation itself.

In the nineteenth century, the country became part of another empire—that of France. The French opened Vietnam to the West. Although they occupied the country for less than a century, they too left their imprint on it, although to a lesser extent than China.

But the Vietnamese proved, as always, to be stubborn opponents of foreign rule. The long war which finally ended the French colonial era in 1954 was the culmination of nationalist agitation which had prevailed, in one form or another, since Frenchmen first arrived in force during the nineteenth century.

Nationalism and communism made common cause to achieve independence for Vietnam in 1954. But that uneasy alliance was never a complete one, for if some nationalists were also Communists, many were not. The breach between these two groups led to civil war and was the direct cause of the division of the country into two separate and opposing states.

North and South Vietnam are inhabited by a single people who share the same history and the same traditions. This is not the first time their country has been divided. Early in the seventeenth century Vietnam was split into two antagonistic parts, and they remained separate for more than one hundred and fifty years.

Ravaged by war and divided by politics, the Vietnamese have not yet found their place in the twentieth century. It is part of their tragedy that the country has been caught up in the struggle between the Communist world and the West while, at the same time, it has been undergoing a painful period of social revolution.

# The Land

Vietnam stretches southward along the sea at the edge of the great land mass of China. Much of the country is mountainous and little inhabited. The people are crowded into the lowland areas in the deltas of rivers, where they grow their rice. The country is endowed with natural riches—raw materials of the densely populated north complement the agricultural wealth of the south whose population is more dispersed. But politics has split Vietnam in two, leaving each half poor and dependent for survival either on extreme measures at home or aid from abroad.

From the southern boundary of China, Vietnam extends for more than 1,200 miles along the eastern coast of the Indochinese peninsula, which juts out into the South China Sea and curves into the Gulf of Siam. Vietnam's history has been intimately involved with that of its immediate neighbors to the west, Cambodia and Laos, and historical accident far more than geographical logic has drawn the frontiers between them. Vietnam's border with Cambodia passes through swamp and jungle as it meanders across the southern plains and highlands. Further north, the border with Laos is difficult to discern and even more difficult to guard, for it traverses the mountains and high plateau regions called the Annamitic Cordillera.

This area came to be known as Indochina, because here two great civilizations meet—the Indian and the Chinese. Laos and Cambodia, like neighboring Thailand and Burma, are links in the chain of states bearing the imprint of the Indian civilization which once extended into what is now central and southern Vietnam. But the Vietnamese people, during the many centuries when they were concentrated in the northern delta regions of the peninsula, were more directly subject to influences from China. Vietnam's mountain chains and major rivers run from northwest to southeast, and these geographic features, while erecting a barrier against penetration from the Indian world, created a permanent invasion route for the peoples from the north. These features opened the country to China, and for more than two thousand years the Vietnamese have been subject to the civilization and the pressure of their powerful northern neighbor.

The Vietnamese themselves, when they began to expand from the Red River Delta in the north—the ancient home of their people—used this network of valleys and rivers to travel southward. They carried with them their complex agrarian culture that centered on the growing of rice. Shunning the mountainous back country, regarded by them as the land of "bad water" (*nuoc doc*) and evil spirits, they kept to the flat coastal areas and the deltas of small rivers. They settled wherever they found land suitable for planting and sowed their rice in irrigated plots. They colonized the narrow plains of central Vietnam and continued their steady advance into the fertile delta of the Mekong River in the south which they reached in the seventeenth century. There they have remained ever since—in the deltas of the Red River and the Mekong River and in the long strip of territory between the two deltas.

That the Vietnamese have succeeded in maintaining their identity as a nation is remarkable in view of the astonishing geographic diversity of the country. Not only is it divided between mountain and plain, but both lowlands and highlands are themselves broken up into a patchwork of separate regions, marked off one from the other by natural barriers, and each stamped with its own distinctive character and its own special climate.

# The Plains

The string of plains, beginning at the Red River Delta in the northernmost part of the country (which the Vietnamese call the Bac Bo), continues into central Vietnam (called by Vietnamese the Trung Bo), through the fertile province of Thanh Hoa and the poorer provinces of Nghe An and Ha Tinh. This northern half of the country, which is rather uniform in terms of climate and geography, ends at a mountain called the Hoanh Son, just south of which flows a river called the Song Gianh. A thousand years ago this river was the southern frontier of Vietnam. When, for almost two hundred years ending in 1788, Vietnam was divided between two ruling families, the same river border separated them.

Old chronicles tell of how, in the sixteenth century, a famous scholar named Nguyen Binh Khiem told a young man who wanted to flee the north and was later to found a new dynasty of princes in the south, "The Hoanh Son can shelter ten thousand generations."

In 1954 the Geneva Conference drew a demarcation line at the seventeenth parallel between Communist North Vietnam and Nationalist South Vietnam, not at this geographic and historic frontier but over sixty miles to the south at the obscure Ben Hai River. This line left some 61,000 square miles to the north and 66,000 to the south, dividing Vietnam once again between two leaders who, although both from central Vietnam, were born on opposite sides of the Hoanh Son—Ho Chi Minh from Nghe An to the north, and Ngo Dinh Diem from Quang Binh to the south.

South of the Hoanh Son the chains of mountains and plateaus of the Annamitic Cordillera close in toward the coastline. The plains are narrow here, and the old Vietnamese imperial capital of Hue lies on one of them, immured behind lagoons and dunes which discourage contact with the outside world. South of the breathtaking Pass of Clouds between Hue and Da Nang, where the mountains end in the sea and fishermen spread their nets in the blue-green water far below, the plains broaden to form the most important rice fields of central Vietnam. The plains narrow again farther south, and the mountains join the sea once more at Cape Varella. The small plains which edge the lower central Vietnamese coast are separated by a series of mountain promontories, of which the most southerly is Cape Padaran.

Central Vietnam is thus turned eastward toward the sea by the steep slopes of the Annamitic Cordillera which lies parallel to the coast and bars the way to the west. Only the narrow coastal corridor which begins south of Nha Trang links the people of central Vietnam with their countrymen who live beyond the Cordillera in the southern part of the country (the Nam Bo or Cochin China). This part of Vietnam shares the great rice- and rubber-bearing delta of the Mekong River with Cambodia.

North, central, and south Vietnam were known as Tonkin, Annam, and Cochin China for less than a century. It is therefore historically inaccurate to use these terms except during that relatively short time, from about 1884 to 1954, when Vietnam was a part of the French Empire. But with the country now divided into the states of North and South Vietnam, the foreigner, to avoid confusion, is forced to make use of this convenient terminology.

# The Highlands

The plains extend over only one fifth of Vietnam. They are densely populated, widely cultivated, and they have provided virtually all the food that the Vietnamese have lived on for centuries. The mountains and plateaus, which loom above them, are covered by jungle, forests, or scrub and seem to belong to a different country. These are the home of dispersed ethnic minority groups who often cultivate their food, notably rice and corn, by the *ray* system. Under this system, the people, indifferent to the dangers of unplanned deforestation, clear an area by felling the trees and burning the vegetation left on it, plant their crops there for a few seasons, and then move on. They rotate a series of fields, returning to each when enough time has elapsed for new vegetation to grow and restore the earth's fertility. For a long time these minority groups were unchallenged in their domain, for the Vietnamese of the lowlands until recently made little attempt to colonize these large areas. Only the adventurous went to

*In North Vietnam a sampan sails on the placid waters of*
*Ha Long Bay which is surrounded by huge limestone rocks.*

seek their fortune in the highlands. There kings and political leaders sought refuge in times of national crisis, and the
highlands have always been a zone of operations for revolutionaries.

In Tonkin two distinct mountainous regions are separated
from each other by the Red River as it flows from the
province of Yunnan in southern China to the Gulf of
Tonkin. To the east of the Red River the mountains are
relatively low; they fan out in a series of arcs converging at
the Tam Dao Mountain, 5,219 feet high, which overlooks
the hilly so-called Middle Region above the delta, and a
number of valleys leading into China. Most of the considerable mineral wealth of Vietnam lies in these northern moun-

tains—iron, zinc, tin, wolfram, and manganese—and thus is at the exclusive disposal of the North Vietnamese government. The immense deposits of coal, which stretch to the sea at the Gulf of Tonkin, add to this wealth. To the west of the Red River the land is more forbidding. The mountains are high and less accessible, and are dominated by the Fan Si Pan; at 10,308 feet the highest point in Vietnam.

Further south the Annamitic Cordillera thrusts past the seventeenth parallel across the length of Annam and ends in a series of high plateaus—Kontum, Pleiku, Darlac, Lang Bien, Djiring. Plantations of coffee, tea, and rubber flourish in this region. They benefit from the rich red soil, the remnant of volcanic activity which now occurs in Vietnam only off the southern Annamese coast under the sea. Finally the High Plateaus, so difficult to approach from the east, slope gently westward into the low plains of the Mekong River Delta.

## The Seacoast

The Vietnamese seacoast, its length impressive in proportion to the narrowness of the country, adds still another dimension to the landscape. It was on these shores that migrating peoples from across the water arrived and added their numbers to the primeval population of Vietnam. The accessibility of the sea helped the Vietnamese in their movement toward the south. And it is the sea which furnishes one of the basic ingredients in the Vietnamese diet, *nuoc mam,* the sauce produced from salt-water fish with which the Vietnamese season their food.

Between the deltas of the Red River in the north and the Mekong River in the south lies an almost uninterrupted chain of beaches bordered by coconut trees and *filaos* (a variety of

*On one of South Vietnam's many beaches workmen load equipment on a typical Vietnamese cargo boat.*

pine that serves to hold the sand dunes). The sand from these beaches is used in the glass industry. In many areas the beaches are interrupted by an elaborate system of lagoons off which lie sites for the production of the salt that is highly important to the economy of Vietnam.

The southern Annamese coast is lined with protected natural bays, among them Cam Ranh Bay, in the Nha Trang area, which is one of the finest natural harbors in Asia. In 1905 the Russian fleet anchored in this port on the eve of its defeat by the Japanese in the first great modern victory of an Asian country over a European power. This victory raised hopes of nationalists in Vietnam and the rest of Asia.

The configuration of the coast changes farther north. It

varies from the area between Qui Nhon and Haiphong, where the only real shelter for ships is in the Bay of Tourane, to the very irregular northern Tonkinese coast. Here the most striking view is Ha Long Bay, where hundreds of limestone rocks jut up out of the sea like strange animals. This is supposed to be the haunt of a mysterious sea serpent which may resemble the legendary dragon omnipresent in Vietnamese traditions and symbolism.

Off the central Vietnamese coast lie the groups of islands called the Paracel and the Spratley, the subject of a dispute for ownership between South Vietnam and Nationalist China. There sea swallows go to make their nests, which are carefully gathered and used as an expensive delicacy in both Vietnamese and Chinese cooking. More intimately involved in Vietnamese history are the islands to the extreme south. On Poulo Condore is situated the largest penitentiary of Vietnam where, under French rule, many who fought for independence were imprisoned by the colonial authorities. The biggest Vietnamese island is Phu Quoc, in the Gulf of Siam, where mother-of-pearl and tortoise shell are collected to be made into objects of art and utility by Vietnamese artisans. This is the place where the Emperor Gia Long, founder of the last dynasty to rule in Vietnam, took refuge when, during his fight to assert his claim to the throne, he and his followers were expelled from the mainland. He later fled to Poulo Condore before returning to the mainland. Still other offshore islands are claimed by Cambodia as well as by Vietnam.

## Monsoons and Climate

In this hot and humid country, which lies between the Tropic of Cancer and the Equator, the cycle of the monsoons sets the tempo of life. For six months in the year, from November to

April, these winds originate in the northeast above the cold and dry Central Asian continent and blow in a southwesterly direction. The process reverses itself during the other six months of the year as changes in pressure cause the water-laden winds from above the sea in the southwest to blow toward the northeast, bringing a season of rain to the sun-baked land.

The diverse pattern of Vietnam's mountains and plains is reflected in its climate. The effect of the monsoons changes with the latitude as well as according to the size and position of the highlands. In the Mekong River Delta, which is open to the south, six months of rain alternate with six dry months in the classic fashion of the monsoon region. There is an endless enervating summer, with only small variations of temperature; the hottest months are in the spring, and the periodic storms which punctuate the months between May and October offer little relief from the perpetual heat. In Saigon, the capital of South Vietnam, the average monthly temperature ranges between 78° and 84°.

Seeking a respite from the heat, the well-to-do population of the capital goes to Dalat in the Annamese highlands, where the monthly average varies between 63° and 70° and the only climatic disadvantage is excessive humidity. The site of Dalat was chosen in 1893 by a great French scientist, Dr. Alexandre Yersin, discoverer of the plague bacillus, to whom Vietnam also owes the introduction of rubber- and quinine-producing trees, as well as its first medical school.

In the small plains of Annam which are closest to the Mekong River Delta, the summer months are hottest. The rainy season comes here later than in Cochin China and reaches its height at the beginning of the winter monsoon. The precipitation is, of. course, heaviest near the highlands, where the monsoons release their burden of water. And Hue,

*The peasant in his fields with his team of water buffaloes is a familiar sight in the Vietnamese countryside. Throughout Vietnam the work of plowing, planting, and reaping the rice harvest is done by hand.*

because of its proximity to the mountains, is one of the most rain-soaked spots in the country. But, if the peasant knows in what period he can expect the rains, nowhere in Vietnam can he be sure they will come in the amounts he requires for his rice fields. The rainfall has been known to double from one year to the next, running the gamut from drought to flood, and the farmer lives in constant fear of both.

As one moves north the difference between summer and winter, already apparent in Hue, becomes more perceptible. In Tonkin, the dry and rainy seasons are less sharply separated and the Red River Delta has a clearly defined winter. In Hanoi, the capital of North Vietnam, the temperature, which may reach more than 100° on a June day, can fall well below 50° in winter. February to April is a time of drizzle, when mist blankets the delta for weeks on end, providing sufficient moisture for the peasants to grow a second annual crop of rice. Along the coast facing the China Sea, the period between June and December not infrequently brings typhoons —violent winds accompanied by extremely heavy rains— which ravage one area or another practically every year.

The regularity of the monsoons and the ensuing determination of the seasons inevitably affected the course of Vietnamese history. Late in the eighteenth century the Emperor Gia Long, in his protracted struggle to unite Vietnam under his rule, planned his military campaigns according to the monsoons, sailing his ships northward along the coast with the summer winds and recalling them to his southern base when the winds blew southward; this has been recorded in history as the Monsoon War. The Franco-Spanish fleet which more than half a century later launched the attack that led eventually to the French occupation of Vietnam, anchored at Da Nang (Tourane) in 1858. Its commanders decided against risking the uncertainties of the north and took advantage of the monsoon that was blowing from the northeast to turn southward instead. It was in Cochin China that they won their first victories against the Vietnamese, and thus acquired a foothold in the country more than twenty years before they finally arrived in Tonkin. In the late 1940's, during the long years of war between the French and the Communist-led Vietminh, artillery and aircraft were able to operate effectively only during the dry season. When the rains turned the rice paddies of the delta into a muddy lake, guerrillas were able to move about freely in sampans. They used the cover of the rains to strengthen their forces and to tighten their grip on the countryside. Today the subversive war fought by the Communist Vietcong forces in South Vietnam follows this same pattern.

But, above all, the monsoons establish the rhythm of agriculture—the season to sow the rice and the season to harvest it—which since time immemorial has set the pattern of Vietnamese life.

## Rice and Water

The growing of rice in irrigated fields profoundly influenced the evolution of the Vietnamese people. It provided their staple food in quantities which enabled them to live together in densely populated settlements and to spread out along the length of the coastline. But it also confined them almost entirely to the plains.

The Vietnamese peasants in most areas still cultivate their rice as they have done for many centuries, planting it first in the mud where it sprouts in a few weeks into a rich yellow-green carpet, then transplanting it by hand to fields which have already been ploughed with the aid of water buffalo and which are drained by rudimentary tools. To irrigate this land, the Vietnamese carry water from one field to the next by means of a variety of simple devices, ranging from wheels called *norias* to waterproofed baskets attached to long ropes. Modern machinery for farming and irrigation has been introduced only recently, and is limited to certain sections. The dates of the harvesting vary according to the region. In the north, where the teeming population can barely manage to raise enough food for its own needs, two annual rice crops are now common.

The needs of rice culture helped to shape the organization of Vietnamese society but also profited from its strong collective character. Vietnamese history is marked by the peasants' unending battle to control the recalcitrant waters, their greatest benefactor if regulated but their most dangerous enemy when unchecked. Official records give the date of 1108 for the first mention of a dike against floods in the northern delta, but others may well have preceded it, for problems of hydraulics have been a primary concern of every responsible government which has ruled the country.

## THE NORTHERN DELTA

The northern delta (also called the Red River Delta) is, in fact, not one delta but two. It is formed primarily by the Red River, its waters swelled by the Clear and Black Rivers, in conjunction with the much smaller Thai Binh River. A tributary of the Thai Binh connects Haiphong, the major port of the north, to the Gulf of Tonkin. The city of Hanoi on the Red River is centrally located at the heart of a network of streams along which boats travel regularly to the principal delta towns and northward beyond the delta, through the valleys of the high regions. So useful is this disposition of rivers and valleys that for well over a thousand years there has been a city on or near this key geographic site.

The Vietnamese people have farmed the northern delta soil for more than twenty centuries, and have achieved there one of the densest concentrations of agricultural population in the world. By World War II some seven and a half million people were already crowded together in these 5,790 square miles of territory. In this region the Red River, when swollen by rains, rises higher than the plain through which it flows and in the summer may rise as much as thirty feet higher than the level of the city of Hanoi itself. Its powerful floods are irregular; they come several times in a season, rapidly and without notice.

To protect themselves against the dual danger of flood and

drought, the Vietnamese have crisscrossed the land with dikes and canals, turning it into a vast checkerboard. Under the Vietnamese emperors the peasant was required to spend some sixty days a year, and sometimes twice that time, laboring on these indispensable public works. Only during the sowing and the harvesting seasons and in periods of great heat or rain could this *corvée,* or forced labor, be avoided. The peasants worked with little more than their hands, carrying the earth in baskets dangling from both ends of a long pole hung across their shoulders—Vietnamese peasants still carry most of their burdens this way. Each man thus contributed his share to a task which was never finished because the dikes were always in danger of breaching when the waters rose. In periods of flood a guard was stationed on the dikes day and night to sound a gong if they appeared to be on the point of giving way, and the people of the village would rush out to try to strengthen the weak spot. Periodically such breaks occurred, bringing devastation in their wake. Then the peasant, with dogged persistence, waited only for the waters to subside to return to his labor of Sisyphus, going to work with his fellow villagers in rebuilding the dike, and repairing as best he could the damage to his rice field.

The network of canals connects the different branches of the rivers which cross the delta, although not all these canals are man-made. They break the force of the flood when it comes, and they provide fresh water to irrigate the plains as well as to remove the salt deposited by the sea which in many areas blights the earth and renders it unfit for cultivation. In 1829 one of Vietnam's most distinguished writers, Nguyen Cong Tru, directed the building of a number of dikes and drainage canals to win back from the sea considerable areas which are still parts of the provinces of Thai Binh and Ninh Binh. And this effort to reclaim more land from the sea has continued to the present time, as has that to maintain and improve the dikes.

Dikes enclose the canals as well as the rivers. These great levees rise high above the monotonous flatness of the northern delta and are often wide enough to be used as roads along which cars travel with ease. In the shelter of the dikes lie the villages and rice fields of the delta. In the course of centuries the land was divided and subdivided by inheritance among families until it was broken up into tiny holdings, each tended with painstaking care. "Dry" crops like corn, sweet potatoes, and manioc are grown to supplement the rice, and help fill the gap when rice reserves are exhausted and the new crop of rice is not yet ready for reaping. Even so, the danger of starvation is never very far off, and a few bad rice harvests are sure to plunge the delta into disaster.

The same picture of rice fields and the struggle of the population to maintain them against the elements persists in the large Thanh Hoa delta on the southern border of Tonkin, as it does, with local variations, in the smaller deltas along the Annamese coast.

## THE SOUTHERN DELTA

In Cochin China the Vietnamese had to adapt their hydraulic techniques and agriculture to different conditions. They arrived in the south in any considerable number only during the last two hundred years, and by the time they had won independence from France, the southern delta (also called the Mekong River Delta) still had a population of under five million in a region much larger than the northern delta.

Much of the land in Cochin China is richer than that in the north; not only because the south, until recently, was virgin territory—some of it still is—not exhausted by many centuries of intensive cultivation without adequate use of fertilizers, but partly because of the intrinsic quality of the soil. Its richness, however, is due largely to the nature of the great Mekong River which, along with the lesser Dong Nai and Vaico Rivers, forms the southern delta.

The Mekong originates in Tibet. From the Falls of Khone at the Cambodian-Laotian frontier southward through the plains, where Cambodians and Vietnamese live under its placid influence, right up to the sea, it is almost continually navigable. Unlike the Red River, it carries rich alluvial deposits. The waters, lowest in March, increase at the beginning of June when the rains come. They rise slowly, in large part because so much of the water drains off into the Cambodian great lake, the Tonle Sap, and the Mekong reaches its height only around October, after the period of maximum rainfall is past. Then as slowly as the Mekong has risen, it falls. With such a system, as simple and unchanging as the seasons, the southern peasant was able to regulate the cycle of his agricultural life according to the Mekong, without fear. It was not necessary to reproduce the massive dikes of the north in the southern delta.

Because the south is not burdened by population pressure, as is the north, the land is rarely used for rice culture during the dry season; nor is it worked with the same thorough care—as if it were being gardened rather than farmed—as in the north. Most of the southern rice is harvested in November or in January, in the so-called half-season. In very low areas a kind of "floating rice" is grown, which is not transplanted but is sown, before the floods come, directly in the fields where it is to grow.

Cochin China is literally a region of water and earth. It is not only crossed by large rivers and their tributaries, but is covered with an elaborate lattice of streams and canals which link small remote villages with each other and with the

*Nearly all of South Vietnam's rice crop is transported to market by sampan on the vast network of canals which lace the southern delta region.*

metropolitan area of Saigon-Cholon, to which junks carry surplus rice and corn. A significant fact about Cochin China is that in normal times such surpluses did exist. In good years before World War II, this area was able to export more than a million tons of rice; and before the recent division into the two Vietnams, 250,000 tons were shipped to the underfed millions in the northern deltas.

Although Saigon is the largest port in Vietnam, it lies some forty-two miles from the sea on the right bank of a river which bears its name. Like Hanoi, Saigon is a political capital and with Cholon, its Chinese suburb, forms the metropolis of a large delta. But, unlike Hanoi, it is also a seaport. The granite rocks rising above the long white beaches of Vung Tau (which the French called Cape Saint

Jacques) signal the entrance to the estuary, and the tide flows upstream twice a day, facilitating the entry of ships. The greatest concentration of population in South Vietnam is in the area of Saigon which even before the war was the largest Vietnamese city. To the east, in the direction of the Annamese highlands, the forested areas are sparsely inhabited except for wide stretches of rubber plantations which, since the French colonial period, have produced, along with rice, one of Vietnam's two major exports.

Much of western Cochin China was opened up during the colonial period when the French speeded up the program, initiated by the Emperor Gia Long at the beginning of the nineteenth century, for the development of what was then virtually uninhabited country. A great many canals were cut and the land was drained, and as a result the area under rice quadrupled between 1870 and 1930. Vietnamese settlers traveled in sampans along these waterways, carrying their family possessions with them, to make their homes in the west; and villages and towns grew up along their banks. Although built primarily to transport men and produce, the canals brought the tides far inland, and were thus especially useful for irrigation and drainage.

The rice fields of Cochin China, which take the form of large estates in the west, now cover the flat delta plains. This is extremely fertile land, thinly settled and still in the early stages of development. Extensive areas of swampy jungle and mangrove forest, like the Ca Mau peninsula and the Plain of Reeds, are not yet drained; and the soil is still plagued by a high alum content and by deposits of salt which testify to the short time elapsed since the land emerged from the sea. These regions, made particularly unattractive by swarms of malaria-carrying mosquitoes and other insects, have long been a sanctuary for guerrilla fighters of all kinds.

# A Country Divided

Overpopulated in the northern deltas, Vietnam is barely developed in the highlands; and Cochin China has far to go if it is to be exploited to its fullest capacity. Even if the country were not divided, a more equitable distribution of population could be achieved only with difficulty because of the special nature of Vietnam's population problems (see Chapters II and VI). Under present conditions, Saigon and Hanoi have no choice but to try to deal with the situation within the geographic limits set by the seventeenth parallel, at which Vietnam is divided, as they must also deal separately with their agricultural and industrial development.

The country's considerable agricultural riches are most abundant in South Vietnam, and as a result of the country's division, hard-pressed North Vietnam has been barred from the southern "rice bowl" on which it used to depend for part of its food. By contrast, the greater part of Vietnam's raw materials, enough to supply an industrial base for the entire country, are found in Tonkin, while South Vietnam has only a small supply of coal.

The drawing of a political frontier at the seventeenth parallel cut off all direct contact between North and South Vietnam, with the exception of the political refugees who left the north for the south in 1954 and 1955 and later the Communist infiltrators who came south along the "Ho Chi Minh trail" and by sea. Thus, this complementary economy, that would have been a notable asset in a united country, has been transformed into a severe handicap, leaving North and South Vietnam in a state of extreme economic unbalance. Forbidden access to vitally needed national resources across this frontier, North and South Vietnam have been compelled to devise artificial means of meeting their basic needs.

# The People

The Vietnamese lead a Spartan existence in a difficult land. The character and behavior of both peasants and officials—the only two important classes in Vietnam during most of its history—were shaped by the harsh conditions of daily life. The agricultural nature of their civilization combined with the strong influence of Confucianism to favor the growth of a collective society in which the interests of the individual were strictly subordinated to those of the group.

In the course of centuries the Vietnamese encountered a number of other peoples, some of whom they assimilated, but many of whom they did not. And there is an impressive variety of ethnic minorities in the country today. But they are not the only source of diversity in the population of Vietnam.

23

The original Vietnamese themselves changed as they moved southward. Facts of geography and history made this development inevitable. The nationalism which swept the country from the Chinese frontier to the Point of Ca Mau during the long struggle for independence from France impressed the world, but it was never synonymous with uniformity. Regional differences between lowland Vietnamese can be very real, and Vietnamese are keenly sensitive to them.

## A Nation of Rice Farmers

There are about 34 million Vietnamese—18 million in the north and 16 million in the south—and the population is increasing at the startlingly fast rate of some 3.4 per cent a year.

Since the beginning of their recorded history the Vietnamese have built their lives around their rice fields. Rice was not only their daily food but was one of the ritual offerings which the Vietnamese made to their gods and ancestors. From it they distilled the alcohol which they used in religious ceremonies. They measured their wealth by the size and produce of their rice fields and paid their taxes accordingly, often in rice. Even in the twentieth century the rich continued to invest their holdings in rice fields, a practice which helped to slow down the development of Vietnamese industry and left it almost entirely in the hands of foreigners.

The traditional methods of growing rice became an essential part of peasant life. Around these time-honored practices, geared to the changing seasons, an elaborate ritual developed in which festivals and religious ceremonials each had their place. The entire country used to celebrate the sowing of the first rice of the year: until the end of the

Vietnamese Empire, after World War II, the emperor himself dug the first symbolic furrow during a solemn ceremony. Other ceremonies marked each stage of planting and harvesting. The year was punctuated by agrarian festivals like those at mid-autumn and the arrival of spring. Tet, the first week of the first month of the lunar calendar, is still the most important holiday in the year. It is a time of feasting—under the empire the only holiday when the peasant rested—when the Vietnamese set off fireworks, decorate their homes with flowering branches, and pay reverence to their ancestors. Thus the people herald the renewal and rejuvenation of nature after its death during the winter.

The Vietnamese tended to neglect the high seas, as they did the mountains, in order to concentrate on their rice fields and the movement of their people southward. However, the country also has maritime traditions. There are a number of nautical terms in the language, and many people still live as fishermen. The impetus for sea travel may have been limited, but the Vietnamese sailor was skilled and coastal trade prospered. The Vietnamese emperors, for their part, built up war fleets, expecially in the period of Gia Long. Today coastal traffic, both legal and illegal, is still carried on by junks as well as by motor-propelled ships.

At home the peasant spends much of his time fishing in the fresh water on or near his rice fields. Fish provides most of the protein in the Vietnamese diet. It is eaten fresh, dried, or fermented, as well as in the form of *nuoc mam*, the fish sauce, whose preparation is the principal food industry in Vietnam.

## THE STRUGGLE FOR EXISTENCE

Only by unremitting labor under a blazing sun can the peasant find enough food to nourish his family. To the basic

*At the local markets in North Vietnam
Tonkinese women sell crabs strung on sticks.*

rice and fish he adds a variety of beans and, at rare intervals, poultry and pork. He uses little sugar, and although tropical fruits are plentiful (ranging from a wealth of varieties of the common banana to the highly esteemed lichee in the north and the mangosteen in the south), those which are particularly rich in vitamins, like the citrus fruits, are neither widely grown nor eaten.

Even this meager ration can be taken from the peasant at any time by drought or flood. He owns so little and has so few reserves that a single bad harvest can wipe him out. In the past, he was often compelled to borrow seed and work buffalo, and as a result fell easy prey to the usurer who might be Chinese or Indian or, not infrequently, one of his own more fortunate countrymen. Even when he succeeded in maintaining legal title to his plot of land, which he was by no means always able to do, he remained at the mercy of the moneylender who forced him to pay exorbitant rates out of his scanty crops.

This cruel, uncertain existence has bred a race of men who are inured to physical and moral suffering and who expect little of life in the way of pleasure or comfort. In addition to chronic malnutrition, public sanitation is rudimentary and disease is endemic. When disease does not kill outright, it tends to debilitate and lowers the productivity of labor. Outbreaks of plague and cholera occur with terrifying suddenness, and tuberculosis, malaria, and leprosy are common scourges, as are a large variety of intestinal parasites. But despite considerable infant mortality, families are large, and the high rate of population increase adds to the drain on already gravely inadequate food supplies and public health services.

## THE VIETNAMESE CHARACTER

The rigorous conditions of life and the formal patterns of behavior which the Vietnamese are taught as children, reinforced by influences of Buddhism and Taoism, have created an outwardly sober restraint among the people. Their profound fatalism has been nourished by religion and by personal experience. Death is an exit which they not infrequently choose for themselves deliberately, sometimes for motives of honor but sometimes also for surprisingly futile reasons. Life is all the less valued because the Vietnamese believe in the survival of the individual after death; and the dead are not secure from the daily solicitations of their descendants, or sometimes even from punishment. For example, even after his death, General Le Van Duyet, one of Emperor Gia Long's companions in the early nineteenth century, was condemned to imprisonment by Gia Long's successor, and a chain was put on the General's tomb.

At one extreme, in order to have an enemy haunted by the ghost of a suicide, people have been hired to hang themselves outside the homes of individuals (whom they may not even know) in exchange for payment to the suicide's needy family. At the other extreme, many of Vietnam's heroes have killed themselves when the battle turned against them. Notable victims of this practice were the Trung sisters who drowned themselves when they were defeated after launching a revolt against Chinese rule during the first century. In 1801 General Vo Tanh, facing defeat in battle, composed a poem describing his plight before he burned himself to death. Sometimes, as in the case of Hoang Dieu, last governor of Hanoi before the French took over toward the end of the nineteenth century, hanging was preferred to death by fire or water. In 1963, during the crisis between the Buddhist hierarchy and the government, a number of Buddhists burned themselves alive. This wave of suicides, once begun, proved difficult to stop, and even when that government was overthrown and replaced by another which favored the Buddhists, people continued to immolate themselves by fire.

The average Vietnamese has never been in a position to control his own environment, and he is reluctant to act on his own initiative. (The virtue of free will, as Westerners understand it, is not recognized.) Over the centuries he has been taught to accept authority at every stage of his existence: from his father, his teacher, his elders, and government officials. At the same time, in an attempt to find some security in the unpredictable and often menacing world of nature in which he lives, he worships a variety of spirits in natural objects and phenomena, ranging from trees and rocks to thunder. Due respect is paid to such beasts of the jungle as the tiger and the elephant, who are given the title of "Mister." Fishermen worship the whale. The Vietnamese relies heavily on astrology and divination, as well as on ritual and magic, in his daily life.

This description of the Vietnamese character applies primarily to the peasants who constitute the great majority of the population of the country. But the educated elements, even those who are superficially Westernized, have naturally also been shaped by the same background. One reason for the blunders and frustrations of many Westerners in their political dealings with Vietnamese is their failure to look beyond a veneer of Westernization in language and education to more fundamental aspects of the national character. Thus the system of logic used by most Vietnamese sometimes bears little relation to that found in the West. Even when translated into French or possibly English by the educated person, this logic retains the influence of the Vietnamese language in which it was first expressed, and which is often very imprecise in the expression of abstract ideas. The adoption of the Roman alphabet liberated this monosyllabic language from dependence on the elaborate characters derived from the Chinese in which it used to be written, and favored the introduction of new words based on modern and Western experience. But despite improvements brought about by the efforts of Vietnamese scholars like Pham Quynh, Nguyen Van Vinh, and Hoang Xuan Han, this language remains inadequate for the diffusion of science and philosophy.

The evaluation and expression of facts by most Vietnamese is not only more subjective than in the West, but is conditioned by the speaker's purpose in presenting a particular fact, by the person he is addressing, and even by the taboos of his language, which may prevent him from saying exactly what he thinks even if he wishes to do so. Communication with foreigners in Vietnam, as in other countries influenced by Chinese culture, is made even more difficult by the existence of certain rules of courtesy which preclude telling a stranger what he might not like to hear. And out of the kindness of his heart, the Vietnamese often adapts his answers to what he believes to be the desires of his interlocutor. In such an environment it seems unjust for foreigners who have been given what turns out to be inaccurate information to consider that they were deliberately misled.

## National Origins

For many centuries tribes related to the Indonesians lived unchallenged around the delta of the Red River until strangers speaking a Thai language (the term is a linguistic one and should not be confused with the inhabitants of present-day Thailand) wandered across the northern mountains from China. The Vietnamese race evolved from the encounter of these groups during the Neolithic Age. It is believed that the Muong people, who today inhabit areas of North Vietnam, are the direct descendants of the original Vietnamese race. Some tribes that did not merge with the newcomers were driven back into the highlands.

The Vietnamese have a legend of how the nation was founded. They tell the story of a man born in the mountains of the union between a wood nymph (*tien*) and a descendant of a genie of agriculture, who married the daughter of the dragon, the lord of the waters. Their son then became the hero who presided over a golden age. His wife, Au Co, so tradition has it, bore one hundred sons whom their parents divided between them. Fifty followed their mother into the mountains where they elected their eldest brother as king. He became the first ruler of the Hong Bang dynasty which ruled over the earliest Vietnamese kingdom, called Van Lang. The years of this kingdom's existence are as uncertain and legendary as Van Lang itself. But behind the symbolic poetry of the story can be seen an actual historical process: the meeting and mingling of people who came from the sea and the mountains to form the Vietnamese nation.

The culture of these ancient Vietnamese was that of monsoon Asia, and many of their practices have survived to the present. They blackened their teeth, chewed betel, and painted the eyes or heads of monsters from the sea on their boats to protect themselves against these creatures, as some Vietnamese still do today. Their practice of tattooing also persisted in the country for a very long time. The ancient popular religion, in spite of the rise of organized religions, has retained its influence as the Vietnamese have clung to the worship of stones and trees, the ancestor cult, and the earth god.

The tools of the ancient inhabitants were of polished stone, for the use of metal came late to the Vietnamese. They emerged from the Neolithic Age at a date which is usually given as between the fourth and third centuries B.C. This Bronze Age has been called the Dong Son civilization, after the site where a number of objects in bronze were found. The use of iron also dated from this time although iron began to replace bronze only about the time of the birth of Christ. Probably the Vietnamese learned the use of both from the Chinese, whose civilization was much more advanced at the time.

The Vietnamese language bears witness to the intermingling of peoples which took place in the delta of the Red

River. Its base is Indonesian or Mon-Khmer overlaid with Thai. Later on, Chinese elements were added to the race and to the language.

## Ethnic Minorities

In more recent centuries other peoples crossed the northern frontier into Vietnam. Unlike the vanquished tribes of Indonesian stock, who had been forced to take refuge in the mountains, they did not struggle for possession of the delta regions, nor did they lose their identity by mixing with the indigenous Vietnamese population. They settled apart from it, in the back country beyond the northern delta, in their own self-perpetuating ethnic communities. South of the seventeenth parallel are other such ethnic islands. These are composed of peoples whose ancestors had lived in the region long before the Vietnamese ever arrived there. Under Indian influence they achieved a high level of civilization, until the power of their kingdoms was broken by the Vietnamese.

Today the ethnic minorities living in the northern part of Vietnam have been estimated at as many as two and a half million. The areas in which they live are often demarcated by boundaries drawn not across the flat surface of the earth, but according to altitude, for they settled at different heights depending on the order in which they arrived in the country and on their own special requirements. In the valleys and on the lower slopes of the hinterland are the most numerous of the northern minorities—the Tho (now called Tay by the Hanoi government), who speak a Thai language; the Muong; and the Thai. The society of all three is feudal, their religion is primarily the worship of spirits and ancestors, and they grow rice either in flooded rice fields or on the dry highlands. The Nung inhabitants of the north are closely related to the Chinese: some fifteen thousand of them fled the Communist regime of North Vietnam after the division of the country in 1954 and settled in the south. Higher up are the Man, and perched still closer to the sky, the Meo. These nomadic peoples crossed the high valleys from China in relatively recent times, the Man around the sixteenth century and the Meo early in the nineteenth century.

Further south, on both sides of the seventeenth parallel, the peoples of Indonesian origin make their home in the highlands of the Annamitic Cordillera; their number is estimated at one million. The Vietnamese used to group them together indiscriminately as Moi, a term which is synonymous with barbarians. They are, in reality, a number of separate tribes, each with its own distinctive character- istics, some more advanced than others, and often with little in common except, perhaps, a history of intertribal warfare. Some, like the Jarai and the Rhade, speak languages of the Malayo-Polynesian type; the Sedang and the Bohnar, among others, speak Mon-Khmer tongues. Their religions range from animism to Christianity.

Only in recent years has the problem arisen of integrating the ethnic minorities of north and central Vietnam into the Vietnamese state. The Vietnamese emperors, before the French arrived in the country, tended to leave these high- landers in virtual independence as long as their leaders recognized the sovereignty of the Vietnamese and paid them tribute and taxes. The French, in their turn, generally re- spected the traditions of the mountain people, and as France extended its control over the highlands, these were adminis- tered separately from the lowland areas. A curious episode in the history of the colonial period was the brief adventure of one Frenchman who exploited the stubborn sense of inde- pendence of the Sedang tribe to set himself up as their king.

Some French missionaries devoted their lives to the mountain people and worked to improve their conditions of life and health and to establish schools. When Frenchmen tried to enlist the highlanders as forced labor in the High Plateaus of central Vietnam, there were sometimes clashes between them, but eventually these minorities came to regard the French as their only protection against the encroachments of the Vietnamese from the lowlands.

But in the 1940's another force emerged to compete with the French for the loyalty of the mountain populations. This force was the Vietminh, the Communist-led movement which drew many of its best jungle fighters from these ethnic minorities during the war against France that led to the independence of North and South Vietnam in 1954. North Vietnam never underestimated the numerical and political importance of the ethnic minorities. The regions they occupy have been organized into two autonomous zones, each with limited self-administration and with a sizable representation in the National Assembly in Hanoi. Written alphabets have been devised for some of these minorities, and members of the different tribes have been trained as teachers, medical personnel, and political organizers.

When the Communists evacuated the highlands south of the seventeenth parallel in 1954, they brought many of their recruits among the mountain people back to Hanoi, where they were given further training. A few were even sent to the U.S.S.R. for advanced education. When the time came, Hanoi-trained tribesmen returned secretly along jungle trails across the seventeenth parallel with promises of autonomy for their fellow tribesmen in South Vietnam, to rally them on behalf of the Communist north.

The Saigon government, from the start, was at a disadvantage in dealing with this infiltration. Unlike the Hanoi regime, which had been working with the ethnic minorities since the 1940's, the newly formed government, led by Ngo Dinh Diem, had exercised no previous authority over any part of the country and had no capital of goodwill to draw on among the mountain population. At the same time, Saigon was confronted with the urgent necessity of resettling northern refugees from the coastal areas and people from the overcrowded central plains. The government sought to relocate them in the High Plateaus. However, the mountain tribes had traditionally regarded the High Plateaus as their own, and they resented the newcomers. Unfortunately, Saigon was late in becoming aware of this resentment. By the time the government did become aware of the political necessity of trying to win over the highland population which occupies the strategic northern frontier region of South Vietnam, many tribesmen had been alienated by the arrival of numerous settlers whose more advanced farming methods clashed with the ancestral way of life of the mountain people.

## THE CHAM AND THE KHMER

In South Vietnam are also the remanants of once vigorous peoples who were compelled to give way before the relentless southward drive of the Vietnamese: the Cham and the Khmer. All that remains materially of the kingdom of Champa are deserted brick towers like those in the hills around Nha Trang and Phan Rang, reminiscent of miniatures of temples in South India; further north, the once majestic but now almost completely destroyed ruins of My Son in Quang Nam province; and, above all, the beautiful antiquities in the Cham Museum in Da Nang which testify to the profound impact of India in this part of the world. Ethnically, some 35,000 impoverished people survive who

*The only remains of the once flourishing Cham civilization are the ruins of temples like this one in central Vietnam.*

have preserved a smattering of the old Indian ways. Most of them are now Muslims and they have not lost touch with the Muslim world. Before Saigon broke off diplomatic relations with Indonesia in 1964, citizens of the Republic of Indonesia had entered into contact with the Cham; this author even encountered one such Indonesian living in a Cham village.

Unlike the Cham, whose villages are found in central

Vietnam as well as further south, the half million Khmer, who are of Cambodian stock but live on Vietnamese soil, are concentrated in the Mekong River Delta close to the Cambodian border. The Khmer practice a form of Buddhism. Their presence under Vietnamese sovereignty has been one cause among many of the strained relations between Cambodia and South Vietnam.

## THE CHINESE

Most powerful of the ethnic minorities in South Vietnam are the Chinese, who have been able to achieve a stranglehold on the southern economy. This hold has enabled the economy to function with relative ease but it has also allowed the Chinese to reap disproportionate profits for themselves. The bitterness of the Vietnamese over this state of affairs has tended to obscure the considerable contribution of the Chinese to the growth of the nation. Trieu Da, king of "Nam Viet" in the third century B.C., had been a Chinese general before he achieved his place in the Vietnamese pantheon of empire, and successive waves of Chinese have arrived in the country at intervals ever since that time. Chinese immigrants came to escape political crises in China and a number were ultimately assimilated into the Vietnamese population. In 1679, several thousand refugees who had left China after the Manchus overthrew the Ming Empire arrived to settle in the region that was to become Cochin China. In the 1950's, the valiant priest, Father Nguyen Lac Hoa, escaped from the Chinese Communist regime and built up a settlement in the swamps of Ca Mau. There he organized the villagers into a group called the "Sea Swallows" to defend the region, located in the heart of Communist-held territory, against the Vietcong.

Before the French took over the country, as well as later

when Vietnam became a French possession, the Chinese grouped themselves in congregations, each led by one of their own people to whom they paid their taxes. When they intermarried with the Vietnamese population, the children of these mixed marriages were known as Minh Huong who, since the time of the Emperor Minh Mang (1820–1841), were given a special legal status outside the Chinese community. The examinations leading to jobs in the government were open to them, and by the second generation they could be completely assimilated.

But in recent times the great majority of the Chinese inhabitants of Vietnam—who number more than one million and are estimated to be less than 1 per cent of the population of the north, but more than 6 per cent of the southern population—tended to live apart from the Vietnamese in separate Chinese communities, to keep their Chinese nationality, and to act as foreigners in an alien land. Under Ngo Dinh Diem, the Chinese in the south were more or less forcibly integrated into the Vietnamese population, at least on paper. However, despite mass adoptions of Vietnamese citizenship, they remain as Chinese as ever, faithful to their own language, their own schools, and above all to their own loyalties, which have yet to be identified with those of the Vietnamese nation. It should be added that in the present-day disintegrating society of South Vietnam, the Vietnamese themselves have so far displayed little devotion to any concept of nationhood which might prove attractive to the Chinese or to any other ethnic group. Cholon, "the great market," long a separate town on the outskirts of Saigon and now administered as part of it, remains a predominantly Chinese city.

One other element must be mentioned in the ethnic patchwork which is modern Vietnam—and that is the French.

Like other Latin people in their colonies, the French have mingled widely with the local population. Tens of thousands of Eurasians left the country at the time the French army evacuated it, if not before, but a minority remained behind and became citizens of Vietnam.

## Philosophy and Religion

The Vietnamese people have been profoundly marked by four great philosophies and religions, all of them imported from abroad: Confucianism, Taoism, Buddhism, and Christianity. However, the forms the first three of these have assumed in the country are not necessarily those which their founders knew or intended. Not only were these philosophies and religions altered by being grafted onto popular Chinese beliefs and then onto the ancient and primitive animist beliefs of the Vietnamese people, but Confucianism, Taoism, and Buddhism also interacted with each other, further transforming themselves in the process. Thus Confucianism, which in essence was a system of social and political morality, eventually took on many religious aspects. And Taoism, which had originated as an esoteric philosophy for scholars, became a popular religion and intermingled with Buddhism among the unschooled peasantry.

Most Vietnamese find no difficulty in assimilating elements of each of these doctrines and paying their reverence to all: in the same day a man may go to a Taoist temple and a Buddhist pagoda while not neglecting the various rites and practices ordained by Confucius. Only Catholicism (Protestant missionaries, although active, have had but limited impact on Vietnam), the latest arrival and the most doctrinally rigid, has remained unaltered and apart and has established a fairly closed and compact religious community. The minority status of Catholics and the temporal character assumed by certain of their religious leaders contributed to the militant role Catholics sometimes played in their dealings with the rest of the population. At the time of the division of the country into the two Vietnams, the Catholics numbered about two million.

Despite this multiplicity of religious practices, the average Vietnamese is not an especially religious man. The rites he observes have lost much of their original meaning, and religious conflict, although certainly not unknown, has generally had non-religious roots. But Confucianism, Taoism, and Buddhism have combined to form a way of life. Together they impregnate the daily existence of the Vietnamese, determining much of his behavior, not only before his gods, but also in his relations with his fellowmen.

## CONFUCIANISM

Few doctrines in history have been interpreted in so many different ways by their proponents as the original teachings of Confucius, to the point where the authority of the Chinese sage has been invoked to justify both revolution and despotism. The political system into which Confucianism finally degenerated has been discredited in Vietnam as it has been in the rest of the Chinese-influenced world, but even so the Confucianist influence on social relations and social organization remains far-reaching.

Confucius, who was born in China around 551 B.C., viewed men as primarily social beings formed by society and themselves capable of shaping that society. He drew up an ethical code grounded on social virtue to guide the individual through the maze of his social and political relations. This code laid down man's specific duties—to his family, to society, to the state. The code brought all of these duties into harmony with the world of nature through the rites practiced by the emperor, the Son of Heaven, who alone could intercede for the nation with the powers of Heaven and Earth.

Confucianism reached Vietnam under the aegis of the Chinese, who governed the country until the tenth century. It was an urbane, moderate philosophy: in the *Analects* of Confucius it is written, "The Master said to go too far is as bad as not to go far enough." Virtue could be acquired only by learning, and civilian officials were accorded precedence and control over the military. This doctrine was in a real sense democratic: education, not birth, made a scholar out of a man and a ruler out of a scholar. Therefore, education had to be widespread to inculcate the desirable principles of moral and rational behavior in all the people. Only virtue justified the wielding of political power, which was sanctified by the entire natural order—a "mandate of heaven." From this it followed that the absence of virtue resulted in the withdrawal of this "mandate" and hence authorized revolt against an unjust ruler. Either a natural or a military disaster could be interpreted as a sign that the "mandate of heaven" had been withdrawn.

But if "democratic" is taken to imply a society in any way resembling that with which we are familiar in the West, then the word is misleading. Fundamental to the whole system was the emphasis on duty and hierarchy. Ideas of equality and individual rights had little place in the Confucianist world. In this densely populated society a man who wanted to cultivate his own personality had to retire to the mountains and there live the life of a hermit. Many examples of this behavior are found in China and Vietnam, in mythology and literature. In ordinary life, according to Confucius, the individual existed only in and for society, which minutely prescribed his obligations of form and substance, as well as his privileges, according to his rank in the community. Included were the signs of respect he owed to his superiors and expected of his inferiors, and even the rites he had to perform to maintain social harmony at the level of the family and the village.

Any consideration of the need for the individual development of every mind was further discouraged by the excessive influence of Confucius' famous disciple Mencius (373–288 B.C.) and the scholars who followed him in insisting on the preeminent importance of tradition. The reformist aspects of Confucianism were gradually neglected in favor of a backward-looking conservatism which developed into the neo-Confucianism which spread across the Chinese frontier to become state dogma in Vietnam in the fifteenth century. This trend suited the despotic rulers who ignored the necessity of popular consent implied in the doctrine of the "mandate of heaven" and concentrated instead on their divine right to rule.

But much as Confucianism was used or abused by individual sovereigns, its hold over Vietnam was tenacious because, until the second decade of the twentieth century, it was rooted in the country's educational system. Education was expected to be primarily moral and was almost entirely limited to the study of the Confucianist classics. A system of examinations, sponsored by the government, selected from among the most proficient students the administrators of the country—the officials or mandarins who were the non-hereditary governing class of Vietnam. Although few people ever reached the highest levels of government, education was, and is, prized as the means to social and governmental advancement. As a result, the Confucianist classics were taught, if only at the most elementary level, in villages throughout the country. This curriculum did not encourage independent thought, nor did it educate the scholar in science or stimulate his interest in philosophy. But generation after generation of teachers indoctrinated village children in their duties to their family and to their community, and taught them about the social hierarchy in which each man had to know his place and to behave accordingly.

## TAOISM

Only a small elite in Vietnam or China has ever been familiar with the philosophy of Lao-Tse, which emphasized contemplation and primitive simplicity. Its ideal was the return to the Tao—the essence of which all things are made. This philosophy helped to pave the way for the coming of Buddhism. But Taoism, because of its unusually abstract character, passed into the daily life of the Vietnamese peasant only as a collection of superstitions and animistic beliefs.

From the Taoist heaven, the Emperor of Jade, Ngoc Hoang, rules over a horde of gods and genies, a world of spirits and demons in which the forces of nature are incarnated in supernatural beings and the great men of the past have become divinities. One famous Taoist adaptation is the cult to Tran Hung Dao, a hero and scholar who in the thirteenth century led the Vietnamese in their historic defeat of the Mongols. The Taoist influence led to the practice of sorcery and magic on a large scale, and a number of Taoist priests were mediums.

Although corrupted Taoism brought an element of magic into the dreary life of the Vietnamese peasant, and Confucianism was useful in building Vietnamese society, a large vacuum was left to be filled by a new religion—Buddhism —which swept through Vietnam in the second and third centuries. It was spread mostly, although not entirely, by the Chinese, but it had originated in India.

## BUDDHISM

The Buddhist looked at family ties and responsibilities with very different eyes from the disciples of Confucius. To him they were insignificant and transient, as well as a source of suffering; for the world of matter was evil and cruel, and the transmigration of souls condemned man to return to it again and again. The faithful Buddhist had to withdraw as much as he could from the world. He had to live ascetically, practicing the virtues of renunciation and passing his time in prayer and contemplation. Only in this way could he ultimately free himself from the burden of countless reincarnations and unending pain to achieve final liberation from matter and feeling in the eternal, unchanging state of Nirvana.

The pessimism and fatalism of Buddhist doctrine echoed the deepest feelings of many Vietnamese, and pagodas and monasteries sprang up throughout the country. Their religion did not prevent some Buddhist monks from playing a prominent role in Vietnam's national affairs, as in the affairs of other Buddhist countries. But for numerous men and women the Buddhist pagodas and monasteries represented a spiritual and physical refuge from an uncertain world afflicted with bloody civil conflicts and natural disasters. Many Confucianists, convinced that man fulfilled himself only in serving society, deplored the ideas and practices of Buddhism. They believed that the Buddhists were shirking their responsibilities to raise families and carry on the family cult, grow rice, pay taxes, and perform military service. And when the Confucianists became all-powerful in Vietnam, as they did by the fifteenth century, they passed laws limiting the number of Buddhist pagodas and monasteries, sometimes forbidding the building of new ones and even imposing examinations on their occupants to ensure that they met the religious qualifications of monks.

In time, however, the Vietnamese people assimilated Buddhism into their local religious practices as they had done earlier with Taoism, and in this adulterated form it intermingled with popular Confucianism. Ancestor worship, practiced by the Vietnamese long before they had ever heard of Buddhism or Confucianism, has absorbed elements of both.

The process of assimilation was all the easier as the form of Buddhism most common in Vietnam was the Mahayana ("Great Vehicle"), which had come from China and was distinguished from the Hinayana ("Little Vehicle") by its host of Bodhisattvas—beings who, although qualified to enter Nirvana, had chosen to remain among the backward masses to help them on their way to enlightenment. The reassuring concept of such godlike protectors gave full rein to the polytheistic and superstitious inclinations of the people, which were already stimulated by similar Taoist influences.

Educated Buddhist leaders struggled to maintain some semblance of orthodoxy and doctrinal purity, at least among an enlightened minority. Even so, the Mahayana divided into a number of sects which were to be found mostly in the north and center of the country. In the south the prevailing form of Buddhism is the Hinayana, which came to Vietnam directly from India, as it did to neighboring Cambodia and Laos, and which in its simplicity is closer to the original Buddhist doctrine. After the country was divided in 1954 into Communist North Vietnam and non-Communist South Vietnam, the north kept Buddhism only as a facade, with an organization headed by known Buddhists but geared more to propaganda in Asian countries than to religious practices. In the south, by contrast, Buddhism is today in full renaissance. South Vietnamese Buddhist leaders set about the unification of the various sects belonging both to the Hinayana and the Mahayana and formed a common central organization. One of the most interesting developments of the past few years has been the increasing Indian influence over Vietnamese Buddhism, which represents both a return to the sources of the religion and a revulsion against the Chinese. Although Buddhist doctrine does not encourage the faithful to concern themselves with the problems of others, these years have also seen the opening of Buddhist schools, dispensaries, and infirmaries in South Vietnam.

The guardians and promoters of Buddhism, the shaven-headed brown- or yellow-clad monks and the nuns in their plain gray cotton robes, are rarely to be seen in numbers on the streets or in the countryside. Unlike the monks of neighboring Cambodia and Laos, they do not roam about begging, but live in monasteries and pagodas. In such cities as South Vietnam's capital Saigon, the pagodas used to be islands of peace amid street traffic and busy crowds. Hue, the center of Vietnamese Buddhism, is a city of pagodas: these austere edifices are scattered through the outskirts of the city in the peaceful hills where the tombs of the faithful contribute to the prevailing melancholy atmosphere. In the extraordinary Marble Mountains near Da Nang, massive figures of Buddha have been carved out of marble in grottoes high above the plain, and pagodas have been built where monks keep watch and sound the familiar gong which punctuates their prayers.

Among the devout Buddhist elite, children are given a Buddhist name at birth in addition to their own, testifying to their allegiance to the religion. Even families among the majority of the population, which has at best only a vague idea of the true Buddhist credo, invite Buddhist priests to conduct such ceremonies as those commemorating the burial of relatives and the death of ancestors.

But Buddhism does not exert its influence only through these orthodox channels. The politico-religious sects which have flourished in the south during the last thirty years have also borrowed heavily from Buddhist beliefs.

## THE POLITICO-RELIGIOUS SECTS

The southernmost part of Vietnam was the French colony of Cochin China for some eighty years. Subjected to more intensive French influence than the other parts of the country, Cochin China was especially aware of the failure of the ancient Asian philosophies and religions to meet the challenge from the West. Actually, the old ways had not had much opportunity to take root in the south because it had been settled only recently and because the scholars and officials who might have established these beliefs in the south had fled at the coming of the French. Many people there turned to Catholicism. Others, during the 1920's and 1930's, were attracted to a new religious blend which combined parts of the traditional religions with elements from the West to create Cao Daism, an exceptionally eclectic faith even in this eclectic land.

Cao Daism worshipped god (represented by an eye), established a priestly hierarchy headed by a pope, borrowed religious figures from East and West alike, bestowed sainthood on such eminent secular figures as the French poet Victor Hugo, and was heavily infused with spiritualism. It took on a strong nationalistic and anti-colonial coloration, allied itself with other groups, and became a refuge for many political revolutionaries. As a result, its pope, Pham Cong Tac, was exiled by the French for several years to an island off the coast of Madagascar and was later banned from Vietnam by Ngo Dinh Diem. At one time Cao Daism claimed two million adherents in Cochin China and in some provinces of central Vietnam. Its feudal army played a prominent role, under the nationalist general Trinh Minh The, at the time of the departure of the French and the consolidation of the Ngo Dinh Diem regime in 1954–55.

Another important sect, the Hoa Hao, is less eclectic and more doctrinally Buddhist. Divided into several sub-sects, it was founded just before World War II by Huynh Phu So. It exists exclusively in the western provinces of Cochin China where, before its clashes with the Ngo Dinh Diem government in 1955, the sect claimed more than one million followers and also had its own army.

## CATHOLICISM

There have been Catholics in Vietnam for well over three hundred years. The first Catholic mission was founded in the country early in the seventeenth century. The Europeans who established this mission were followed with more or less regularity by other priests—Portuguese, Italians, Spaniards, and Frenchmen—and in the hundred and fifty years preceding the French colonization of Vietnam, the creed spread among the people. The number of Vietnamese persecuted for embracing the new faith may have been exaggerated by their fellow Catholics in Vietnam and abroad, but it is certain that many suffered and died on orders of the imperial court, and several of them have been beatified for their martyrdom by the Holy See.

Early in the course of its development, the Catholic cause exerted a profound influence on Vietnamese history and culture. Portuguese Jesuit priests started the enormously important process of Romanizing the Vietnamese alphabet. This process resulted, in 1651, in the publication by Father Alexandre de Rhodes of a dictionary in Latin, Portuguese, and *quoc ngu,* which is Vietnamese transcribed in Roman characters. (Until that time the Vietnamese had used only Chinese characters in writing their language.) *Quoc ngu*

*Catholic influences can be seen throughout Vietnam. This is the cathedral at Phat Diem, in a largely Catholic region in North Vietnam. In 1954 thousands of people fled the area.*

greatly eased the spread of education and opened up new intellectual horizons to the people. At the same time it served the cause of Catholicism by facilitating the dissemination of holy books and catechisms. Another churchman, Pigneau de Béhaine, the Bishop of Adran, was also to play a vital role in Vietnamese history through his friendship and association with the Emperor Gia Long. The conquest of the country by France, "the Elder Daughter of the Catholic Church," understandably increased the influence of Catholicism throughout Vietnam.

At the time of the division of Vietnam in 1954, most of the 860,000 refugees who fled to the south were Catholics, largely from the northern dioceses of Phat Diem and Bui Chu, led by their two bishops and their priests. However, despite this exodus many Catholics remained with their own bishops in the north, where they constitute a substantial community. And it has not been North Vietnamese government policy to force the Catholic hierarchy to break with Rome nor has there been a policy to create a national Catholic church as China has done.

In the south, a considerable part of the Cochin Chinese propertied class was Catholic even before the division, and large Catholic communities existed there. They were strengthened by the influx from the north and by the privileged position Catholics were unofficially accorded by their coreligionists, who occupied important positions in the regime of Ngo Dinh Diem, himself a Catholic. Catholic schools, generally created by foreign missions, were among the best in the country, and they have been very popular among students of various religions.

The religious tolerance which had been a fact of Vietnamese life during the French colonial period, and the uneasy religious peace which prevailed during the nine years of the Ngo Dinh Diem administration, degenerated into strained relations between the government and the Buddhists during the last few months of the Diem regime. This regime ended in 1963 when Diem was assassinated. Since that time South Vietnam has experienced bloody clashes between the two organized religious communities—the Buddhists and the Catholics. This bitter hostility, however damaging it may prove to the immediate future of South Vietnam, may be expected to decline only with the reduction of the basic political tensions on which it feeds.

# Regional Differences

After the Communist takeover of North Vietnam in 1954, whole villages felt forced to pull up their roots and begin their communal life anew in the south. Some of the refugees were resettled in the High Plateaus, raising problems for the mountain peoples who felt themselves threatened by this new and alien influx of population. The others were distributed in Cochin China and along the central Vietnamese coast. Since 1954 northern refugees have been important in South Vietnam in the government as well as in the army. In the north, a comparable process occurred in reverse. People from the half of the country lying south of the seventeenth parallel had played an active part in the army and administration of the Communist Democratic Republic of Vietnam since its foundation in 1945, and they remained with it when Ho Chi Minh established his government in Hanoi in 1954. In the tightly controlled society of the north, conflicts between Vietnamese from different regions were subordinated to ideological discipline and, in any case, were not publicized. In the south, by contrast, these strains became painfully obvious.

It is difficult to generalize on this subject, for as in most generalizations—however necessary they may be—complexity can only be suggested. Although Vietnamese society is characterized by great uniformity, the length of the country, difficulties of communication, and interaction with local conditions have created regional differences. These differences may be perceived in the language, which Vietnamese from separate regions speak with varying intonations, pronunciations, and vocabularies; in the way they build their houses and prepare their food; and in more significant things.

Thus, the people from the overpopulated northern delta, where the struggle for survival is intense and the cool winters are invigorating, have the reputation for being especially hardworking and energetic. As a group they are far more skilled as artisans and traders than the rest of the population. Indeed, other Vietnamese often regard them in much the same way as Vietnamese in general are apt to regard the Chinese who live among them—for they tend to be more enterprising than their other countrymen, more competitive, and often, for precisely these reasons, not very popular. It is not accidental that, although the Chinese under the French maintained thriving communities in such northern cities as Hanoi and Haiphong, they even then preferred the south as a sphere for their economic activities.

The central Vietnamese population north of the Hoanh Son shares certain traits with the Tonkinese, although the accent of the language varies from province to province, and a man from the rich plain of Thanh Hoa was shaped by a very different environment from that of the peasants of Nghe An whose arid soil has long been a breeding ground for revolutionaries, scholars, and politicians.

The speech of Hue in central Vietnam has its own special characteristics, with a chanting accent which both Tonkinese and Cochin Chinese find difficult to understand (not that they can always communicate with each other without effort). But such regional differences, often mocked by the Vietnamese themselves, should not obscure to the foreigner the powerful sense of unity in the Vietnamese nation. Many of the artisans who once flourished around the Vietnamese imperial court have died out. Today the people of Hue, even the most favored of them, are poor and their life is austere. Nevertheless they are closer than elsewhere to the literary and scholarly traditions that were evolved in this old capital.

In the southern delta, life is easier and the torrid climate discourages people from engaging in intense physical activity. The Cochin Chinese face neither the overpopulation nor the exhausted soil which force northerners into such prodigious activity and have so far condemned the Hue area to poverty. Traditions are less firmly embedded in the south, and French culture penetrated deeper here than in older, longer settled areas, especially among the urban propertied class. Understandably, the southern population resented the post-1954 influx of strangers from the north—not simply those who came from the territory now included in North Vietnam, but also their countrymen from the region of central Vietnam lying south of the seventeenth parallel, many of whom flocked to Saigon to participate in the government

Strains have been particularly evident in rural southern areas where islands of northern refugees remain as isolated from their environment as they were the day they first from their envrionment as they were the day they first arrived in the south. The antagonism between southerners and northerners in South Vietnam has also heightened the tensions between Buddhists and Catholics. It has vastly complicated the administration of the country. These difficulties are further aggravated by the subversive Communist movement in the south which, although directed and supported by Hanoi, is handled locally by southerners.

# Life in the Past

The early history of the Vietnamese people is shrouded in legend. But if this oral tradition is necessarily vague and inaccurate, it nonetheless remains a rare source of knowledge for a period which has left few other sources. Much of the documentation for the history of later periods when the country was under Chinese domination is not only in the Chinese language—which during most of their history was the written language of the Vietnamese—but actually is the work of Chinese. Also helpful are the memoirs of travelers of different nationalities who came to Vietnam over the centuries.

A Chinese scholar once wrote, "The people of Vietnam do not like the past" (*Viet nhon bat hieu co*). But it must also be said that the task of learning about their past has not been an easy one for the Vietnamese. Their archives have been destroyed in the course of frequent political upheavals, and in the fifteenth century when the Chinese took over Vietnam for the second time, they carried away the archives and prevented the Vietnamese from studying their own history. After World War II the Vietnamese imperial library in Hue was demolished during a brief period of lawlessness which attended a local Communist takeover. At that time old documents were scattered on the ground like discarded wastepaper, and the distinguished Vietnamese historian Hoang Xuan Han has told how he went to the marketplace to rescue documents of inestimable value which were being used to wrap food and other articles on sale. Other invaluable papers dealing with the contemporary period were destroyed in the burning of the presidential palace during the coup which overthrew Ngo Dinh Diem in 1963. The material which remains is not always reliable, and much of it has been falsified either for personal reasons or out of ideological bias.

# Vietnam and History

Violence born of social injustice and political ambition is endemic to Vietnamese history. So, too, is opposition to foreign rule. During a thousand years as a Chinese colony, the Vietnamese moved out of the legendary past into the historical era. They emerged from the Chinese Empire in the tenth century united by the memory of a series of leaders who had fought for freedom against the Chinese, and by the possession of a civilization which, although it owed much to China, was distinctively Vietnamese. Thereafter—except for a brief period under Chinese rule in the fifteenth century—the Vietnamese were independent under their own sovereigns until the mid-nineteenth century. They grew as a nation by staving off a number of invasions from China, and strengthened their patriotism in this struggle against the Chinese menace.

At the same time the Vietnamese pushed steadily southward along the peninsula, winning new territory at the expense of the Indianized lands of Champa and the Khmer Empire. The Vietnamese pursued a policy of colonization which enabled them not merely to extend the authority of the ruling dynasty over the central and southern parts of the country, but to reproduce with an astonishing fidelity practically the same conditions of life as those which prevailed in the north. This colonization policy, which was directed primarily at increasing the areas under rice cultivation, was not especially imaginative. It made few allowances for changes in terrain, for the contribution which other civilizations might have made to the Vietnamese nation, or for new crops or industries they might have introduced into the Vietnamese economy. The Vietnamese "march to the south" resulted in the establishment of a chain of similarly organized villages which eventually stretched from the Red River to the Mekong River Delta, and in the blanket imposition of the Vietnamese way of life on any indigenous inhabitants who remained in the lowland areas after the Vietnamese had moved in.

Vietnamese had not yet set foot in the southern delta when their country was divided at the Song Gianh River between two princely rulers early in the seventeenth century. But the settlement of the south went on. And two hundred years later, when national unity was achieved in 1802 by Emperor Gia Long, Vietnam extended from the Chinese frontier to the Gulf of Siam.

The Nguyen dynasty founded by Gia Long inherited almost nine hundred years of independence which had been marked by a persistent attachment to the theory and practice of Confucianist government and complete indifference to the advantages of technological progress. The rice farmer remained at the base of the pyramid of government and society. He had never lived in isolation from the significant events and developments of his time: frequent wars, changes in the central government which had repercussions on local administration and even on the pattern of land ownership, the shifting importance of Buddhism and the introduction of Catholicism, and the growth of popular education. But the physical conditions of his existence varied remarkably little because they were determined by agricultural techniques which had not advanced since the days of his remote ancestors.

The Nguyen carried out one of the periodic land reforms which punctuate Vietnamese history. They also consolidated and improved the institutions of Confucianist government. In these policies they were following the example of other strong sovereigns who had achieved power in Vietnam— although never over so extensive an area—after a period of weak central government and lengthy warfare. But little in the experience of the Nguyen or of the country at large had prepared them to meet the challenge that came from the West in the nineteenth century.

# 1,000 Years of Chinese Colonization

The exact date when the people who lived in the Red River Delta first made contact with the more advanced civilization of China is not known. But it can be assumed that they were in touch with their neighbors to the north before they were conquered by them. They were, in any case, using both bronze and iron by the time they were incorporated into the Chinese Empire. They hunted and fished, their agriculture was primitive, and they cleared the land by burning away the vegetation. This was a feudal society not unlike that which survived until the twentieth century among the mountain people of Tonkin. The inhabitants owed their first loyalty to their local lords, who in turn accepted the suzerainty of the hereditary king.

Legend tells of how the earliest Vietnamese kingdom, Van Lang, was conquered by King An Duong Vuong and annexed to his own realm to form the country of Au Lac. *Lac* is the oldest name for the Vietnamese people, and Vietnamese in a poetic mood still like to refer to themselves as *con Hong chau Lac,* "the children of Hong and the grandchildren of Lac."

This king is said to have retained his throne, thanks to the gift of invisibility bestowed on him by a golden tortoise, until his daughter betrayed him to the enemy. The man who eventually defeated him had more precise historical attributes. This was the Chinese general Trieu Da who, in 208 B.C., having joined Au Lac to the province of Southeast China which he governed, declared himself king of the entire region which he named Nam Viet. (*Nam* means "south"; *Viet,* like *Lac,* is a name for the Vietnamese people.) The issue on which Trieu Da finally broke with China was a decree of the Chinese empress that neither "agricultural and metal tools nor horses, cattle and sheep" should be delivered to the Vietnamese.

The independent dynasty of the Trieu remained in power until 111 B.C. Conquered in that year by China under the Han dynasty, the country was transformed into the province of Giao Chi and Chinese culture was opened more generously to the Vietnamese. At first they lived under a protectorate which left their traditional institutions more or less untouched. However, Chinese settlers arrived in considerable numbers along with officials and scholars. They established schools in which they taught their own language and civilization, and imposed their practices and rites on the indigenous population. Wide expanses of land were taken over by these new rulers for their own needs. They raised a militia among the local inhabitants and enlisted them as workers and lesser officials.

All of these developments struck at the roots of the feudal privileges of the old Vietnamese nobility. Thus, in 40 A.D., when a high-ranking Vietnamese was assassinated, his wife and her sister launched a revolt against the Chinese, and their countrymen flocked to join them. These women were the Trung sisters, who proclaimed themselves queens and led their troops into battle. But they were defeated by an illustrious old warrior, Marshal Ma Yuan, in 43 A.D. Following this defeat, the Trung sisters killed themselves. The explanation of historians that this revolt was the last stand of a feudal nobility nostalgic for the past has not prevented the Vietnamese from regarding Trung Trac and Trung Nhi as their first national heroines. A cult to their memory developed in many northern temples. Today, in North Vietnam, the Communists punctiliously honor the Trung sisters. But in the south, the attempt of Madame Ngo Dinh Nhu to use the anniversary of their death as the occasion for a national holiday commemorating patriotism and the virtues of feminism met with little popular response. After the overthrow of Ngo Dinh Diem in 1963, the statue raised in honor of the Trung sisters was demolished.

With the power of the hereditary feudal lords broken, Ma Yuan destroyed most of the local institutions which had insulated the people from the direct impact of the Chinese administration, and these early Vietnamese were forcibly integrated into the Chinese world. It is probable that only such drastic measures, cruel as they may have been, saved the Vietnamese from extinction as a separate people. Their conquerors inadvertently provided them with the social and administrative institutions which were to give them the strength they needed to survive—even against the Chinese themselves. This alone would have been insufficient, if it had not been for the new technological horizons opened to them by the Chinese which altered their manner of living in a way far removed from what they had known before the conquest. They learned to use the metal plow and work animals and to improve and extend both their dikes and their rudimentary system of irrigation. Thus they adopted the way of life which was to be theirs until the present day—that of the rice farmer. As their agriculture produced more for them than ever before, they expanded over wider areas. As a result their population grew, and this growth forced them to seek still more rice land in the Red River Delta and along the sea. This was the beginning of the Vietnamese quest for new plains on which to plant rice—a quest which would one day bring them across the length of the peninsula all the way to the Gulf of Siam.

## IMPACT OF ASIAN CULTURE

Under Chinese rule the Vietnamese were introduced to the great philosophies and religions of Asia. Confucianism and Taoism were spread by the many Chinese scholars who came among them as administrators or as refugees fleeing from civil war in their homeland. Giao Chi—in the first few centuries A.D. before it was supplanted by Canton—was a key port of call on the trade route which linked India and China and extended as far west as the Mediterranean. Indian merchants arrived on Vietnam's shores and from the second century on were often accompanied by Buddhist monks. Other monks from China stopped off to preach in the country on their way to the holy places in India. Thus from both Indians and Chinese the Vietnamese learned of Buddhism. In the sixth century the Indian monk Vinitaruci founded the first *Thien* (Zen) Buddhist sect in the Red River Delta. The Buddhist bonzes, or monks, carried with them not only their religion, but also the science and medicine of India and China, and the time came when Vietnam counted among its own Buddhist monks men who were doctors, botanists, and scholars. Even a few Europeans appeared in the delta of the Red River. The first mention of them was made in 166 A.D., when the Chinese annals report the visit of travelers from the Rome of Marcus Aurelius.

By the third century the Chinese governor of Giao Chi was ruling with the aid of a Sino-Vietnamese upper class. It included landed proprietors descended not only from Chinese settlers but also from the indigenous inhabitants—perhaps the remnants of the feudal aristocracy—who had been wholly assimilated by the Chinese and held high posts in the governing bureaucracy. This class relished the autonomy it had acquired under a remarkable governor, Si Nhiep (187–266). He was one of the handful of excellent governors whose achievements stand out against the bleak background of exploitation and cruelty which characterized the greater part of Chinese colonial rule. When the Chinese government abruptly reversed his liberal policies after his death, a woman, Trieu Au, led a revolt against them in 248. This revolt lasted six months, and when she was defeated at the age of twenty-three she killed herself as the Trung sisters had done two hundred years earlier. Her suicide added another tragic chapter to the history of Vietnamese resistance to foreign rule. A few years after Trieu Au died, an administrative reform separated the territory inhabited by Vietnamese from most of the Chinese regions to the north, and restored the frontiers of the province to dimensions very like those of the legendary kingdom of Au Lac. This reform proved to be an additional factor in rallying the people to future revolts.

## OPPOSITION TO CHINESE RULE

As assimilation progressed, some Vietnamese scholars were given high offices at the imperial court of China. But their native land remained at the mercy of Chinese governors whose rule—on the outskirts of the Chinese Empire and unchecked by any popular control—often degenerated into tyranny and insatiable demands for tribute. The Chinese governors pitilessly imposed forced labor and great suffering on the population to strip the country of its natural resources for the benefit of its foreign masters. In the sixth century Ly Bon, a Vietnamese of Chinese ancestry, rose against one such governor and proclaimed himself emperor of an independent country stretching southward to the Hoanh Son. But he proved unable to hold out against the Chinese any longer than the Trung sisters had done: his army was defeated and he was assassinated in 547. His was only one of a succession of revolts which broke out sporadically among the landed upper classes. As each revolt in its turn was brutally repressed, it contributed to the awakening of a national consciousness among all those who traced their ancestry back to the hundred sons of Queen Au Co.

In the sixth century the Chinese moved the Vietnamese capital to the site where Hanoi now stands. Another Ly, a cousin of Ly Bon, made a bid for independence in 602 and failed. In 679 the Chinese declared the region the Protectorate General of Annam, and thereafter the Chinese customarily designated the country as Annam ("Pacified South"). The lowland areas were submitted to direct Chinese administration, but in the mountain regions the tribes were permitted to maintain autonomy under their own leaders—a practice continued by the Vietnamese after they finally won their freedom. In 791 another Vietnamese rebel, Phung Hung, seized the capital, only to die several months later. The sorrowing people who had followed him built a temple in his honor in which they inscribed his titles as "great king, father and mother of the people."

The Annam protectorate prospered materially, the Buddhist religion flourished and was reflected in the art—where Chinese, Indian, and Indonesian influences mingled—which flowered between the ninth and the eleventh centuries. But the Chinese were no more inclined than in the past to relax their hold on the country. As the burden of their colonial administration became more intolerable under the T'ang dynasty (which had taken over the Chinese throne in 618), the population grew increasingly restive. The peasants, who passed on the legends of the golden age the Vietnamese had known before the coming of the invader, and the Sino-Vietnamese upper classes were gradually forged into a nation. They had only to wait for a situation that would make a successful revolt possible. When it came, it was the same situation that enabled them, a thousand years later, to declare their independence from France in 1945—the weakening of a colonial empire.

This weakening of Chinese rule came about early in the tenth century when the T'ang dynasty collapsed; and in the ensuing anarchy, the Annam protectorate ousted its foreign governor, replaced him with a rich Vietnamese notable, and won Chinese recognition of the son and the grandson who succeeded him. A Chinese army subjugated Annam once again in 923, only to be expelled eight years later. The Vietnamese leader who took over in the wake of the Chinese departure was assassinated by one of his officers after just a few years of power, but another leader emerged to avenge him and conduct a victorious defense against the invading Chinese. He was Ngo Quyen, and in 939 he succeeded in establishing an independent Vietnamese state with its capital at Co Loa—seat of the government of ancient Au Lac which had lost its freedom to the Chinese more than ten centuries before.

## Independence, 939–1408

Having proclaimed the ideals of independence and national unity, the Vietnamese faced the problem of translating them into effective government. This problem, however, the rulers who now passed through Vietnamese history in rapid succession were unable to meet. Ngo Quyen died prematurely, and his son was helpless before the rise of the Twelve Su Quan—feudal lords who carved out fiefs in the Red River Delta and the Middle Region of the north and who warred among themselves. Beginning in 945, this country of farmers, who wanted only peace so that they could tend their rice fields and feed their families, was subjected to more than twenty years of virtual anarchy.

Only in 968, when the country was faced with a new threat from the north, did Dinh Bo Linh compel the ambitious nobles to submit to him as king. He made an arrangement with China whereby the latter agreed to accept the independence of Vietnam in exchange for the triennial payment of tribute by the Vietnamese and their acknowledgement of China's overall sovereignty. For the various small countries along China's borders, like Vietnam (called at this time Dai Co Viet), this arrangement amounted to a form of recognition under the peculiar system of Chinese-dominated international law which prevailed in the region. This arrangement set the pattern for Sino-Vietnamese relations until the arrival of the French in the nineteenth century.

Dinh Bo Linh—the first truly independent Vietnamese king—had undoubted talents as a ruler and a soldier. But he also had a faculty for making enemies. This failing was heightened by his bad judgment in granting his five wives equal status as queens and his choice of his youngest son (instead of the eldest) as heir to the throne. Dinh Bo Linh died at the hand of an assassin—the first of many Vietnamese rulers to do so—and the dynasty he founded did not long survive him. It was overthrown in 980 by a general of the Le family, Le Dai Hanh. He repulsed the Chinese when they attempted to take advantage of the power vacuum caused by Dinh Bo Linh's murder. The first war against Champa (the Indianized kingdom to the south whose boundary with Vietnam was marked by the Hoanh Son) also dates from this period. Placing his trust exclusively in members of his family, Le Dai Hanh divided the administration of the country among his sons who waited only for his death to dispute the succession among themselves. This Early Le dynasty (so called to distinguish it from the dynasty founded by the national hero Le Loi in the fifteenth century) was overthrown in 1009.

Seventy years of independence had passed, and the nation was still struggling for survival. But the era of short-lived dynasties had come to an end. The next four hundred years were divided between two dynasties, the Ly dynasty and the Tran dynasty, each of which knew periods of greatness before it ended in decadence and bloodshed. These dynasties, too, witnessed a dreary succession of local revolts, disputes over the throne, and sordid political murders. But the achievements of the Ly and the Tran kings were nonetheless great. They laid the foundations of an independent Vietnamese state, and under their leadership Vietnamese society and civilization developed and reaffirmed their national character.

## THE LY DYNASTY, 1010–1225

Confucianist scholars, with their close cultural ties to China, had fallen out of favor in the early years of independence, and by the time the Ly dynasty assumed power, almost all the scholars in the country were Buddhist monks. The Buddhist clergy was organized in a hierarchy headed by the "Master of the Kingdom," who prayed with the king and doubtless advised him as well. The Ly had come to power with Buddhist support, and the genuine piety of the dynasty coincided with political necessity. The first Ly kings relied on the monks, the only educated group in Vietnam, for help with the secular business of state, and much of the conduct of foreign affairs was placed in the hands of these bonzes, notably with respect to China.

The faithful gathered to worship Buddha in temples throughout Hanoi (or Thang Long, the "City of the Rising Dragon"), which had become the national capital. The bells of numerous temples also sounded across the rice fields in the countryside where the pagodas were often wealthy institutions endowed with extensive lands on which serfs labored. Many religious schools were constructed, and there was a rich Buddhist literature. But this great epoch of Buddhism began to decline slowly but inexorably as Buddhism blended with the traditional religious practices of the Vietnamese and was altered by them. A number of Buddhist monks even came to be regarded as magicians.

There had been a time when the only way to acquire an official post was to win the support of influential monks. But after a few decades of Ly rule, the government broke this Buddhist monopoly, and in 1070 the Van Mieu, the Temple of Literature, was erected in Hanoi. Statues of Confucius and his principal disciples, flanked by lesser sages, decorated the temple, and scholars and students came regularly to the Van Mieu to carry on the cult to Confucius. Although the original material of its walls has long since been replaced, the Van Mieu has survived into the twentieth century.

In 1075 the first literary examinations—the keystone of the Confucianist edifice of government—were held for the recruitment of officials who were to be known by Westerners as mandarins. Of the ten scholars who sucessfully passed these particular examinations, the man who came out on top was named prime minister. The government made a point of favoring secular education, and the following year a National School (Quoc Tu Giam) was opened on the grounds of the Van Mieu for the sons of officials. When these men were graduated, they too were named to posts in the administration. In this early period only members of the upper class were admitted to the National School and to the examinations.

In 1089 the broad outlines of the mandarinal hierarchy were laid down as they were to remain in future centuries. The division between civil and military officials and the organization of each into nine distinct ranks are practices which date from this period. The network of officials appointed by the Ly kings reached down to the lowest administrative level, the *xa,* which the French translate as *commune* and which—if understood as possibly including several separate hamlets—can also be translated approximately as *village.* The Vietnamese villages achieved autonomy only in the eighteenth century. Each village had its register where the names of all male citizens were inscribed. Those who had neither mandarinal rank nor other titles and did not belong to such special groups as monks, actors, and healers were subject to military service and gave the national army the broad popular base it had hitherto lacked. Men from the ethnic minority groups in the mountains were organized in separate battalions.

The Ly rulers recognized the basic importance of agriculture and decreed that soldiers would perform their military service during only six months of the year and that they would spend the other six working the land. It was a Ly sovereign who, after he conquered the Champa, declared himself Emperor of Dai Viet ("Dai" means great)—the name by which the country was known to its own people until the nineteenth century. His successor attempted to obtain books from China which dealt with military science. However, his attempt was rebuffed, for the Chinese were consistently reluctant to release to foreigners the secrets of their encyclopedias and manufacturing processes, or samples of the plants which grew on their soil. Over the centuries Vietnamese ambassadors had to smuggle these home whenever they could.

Ly Thai To, the founder of the dynasty, instituted the first taxes Vietnamese had ever paid to a government of their own. These taxes were levied on land owned by the village in common and on other sources of income which, from then on, were also to provide revenue for the tax collector. Among these were customs fees—collected on internal trade as well as on foreign commerce—and a tax on salt. Taxes were lowered in time of famine or when the army returned from a victorious and profitable expedition. The government practice of maintaining stores of rice not just to feed the army, but also to distribute among the population in time of famine, began under the Ly.

To extend their authority throughout the country, the Ly undertook the building of roads and dispatched royal couriers in relays to carry the post to remote areas. They arranged for the construction of dikes, and in general encouraged the development of agriculture and the extension of cultivated land—as every Vietnamese government worthy of the name was to do from then on.

Even the wars in the days of the Ly established a pattern that later generations would follow. At home the Ly put down revolts, notably that of the Nung minority in the eleventh century. They struggled with the Chinese until late in the twelfth century, when China recognized a Ly ruler as king and gave the Vietnamese a century of peace on their northern frontier. In the south the Ly pushed forward into the coastal plains beyond the Hoanh Son and displaced the Cham inhabitants. They did so peacefully where possible, relying on the natural superiority of their system of irrigated rice fields and on their cohesive social organization, but by force if they were opposed. A victory over the Cham in the eleventh century brought the southern frontier of Vietnam slightly below the seventeenth parallel, and a royal edict invited the Vietnamese people to settle the newly won provinces. Provincial administrators followed on the heels of these colonists to complete the process of assimilation. In the west the Ly also successfully fought the Khmer Empire.

But by the end of the twelfth century the Ly dynasty had passed its peak. Heavy taxes and levies were imposed on the people to pay for the king's pleasures, which preoccupied him more than the business of government: bandits roamed the country; the province of Nghe An rose in revolt; and another uprising took place in the royal capital itself. It was repressed by the powerful Tran family, which was related to the Ly king by the marriage of the crown prince. This young man, when he succeeded to the throne, became best known for his bouts of madness and drunkenness. He finally retired to a pagoda, leaving the throne to his younger daughter whom the Tran—when they had promptly married her to a member of their family—forced to abdicate in her husband's favor. To secure the Tran succession the uncle of the new king had recourse to ruthless measures: the retired king was driven to suicide in his pagoda; other members of the royal family were murdered; and all Vietnamese who bore the name of Ly were ordered to replace it with the name of Nguyen.

## THE TRAN DYNASTY, 1225–1400

Buddhism, which was believed to have had a deeply humanitarian influence on the Ly (although a Vietnamese historian was still able to report the killing of more than fifty thousand men when one of the Ly armies seized a Chinese citadel in 1076), retained a privileged position under the succeeding dynasty, even though it had come to power through violence. The early Tran rulers protected the Buddhist religion, and one Tran king after his abdication founded a Buddhist sect known as "the Forest of Bamboo," and left his mountain retreat followed by ten disciples to preach among the people. However, Buddhism continued to change through contact with other beliefs and practices. In addition, it was attacked by Confucianists for its antisocial aspects and its indifference to the needs of the state.

The growing power of the Confucianist scholars corresponded to the needs of the administration, for the Tran revived the examination system to recruit new officials so that they could perfect and extend the structure of government inherited from the Ly. At a banquet, the king himself honored the successful candidates who achieved one of the three doctoral degrees and personally conferred on them the robe and insignia which accompanied the title. As a corollary, inevitable in a state whose goals were Confucianist, secular education continued to increase as new schools were founded. Even the National School began to admit a few outstanding students from the lower classes.

To ensure the continuity of the regime, the Tran introduced the custom of transmitting the crown from the ruler while he was still alive to his heir. This arrangement, which gave a special title to the retired king and left him with considerable power even though he ceased to carry on the day-to-day business of government, had the desired effect of avoiding the bitter and often bloody quarrels over succession which had dogged previous dynasties. However, the existence of two kings instead of one left an opening for a clever and ambitious man to play them against each other for his own benefit, and this in fact happened in the end to bring about the downfall of the Tran dynasty.

The Tran devised new ways of extending the land under cultivation in order to feed the growing population. Their government was strong enough to enable them to deal with large-scale problems of hydraulic engineering, and provincial governors were ordered to build dikes along the Red River reaching to the sea. People whose land was seized for this purpose were to be compensated. In 1266 a royal decree authorized nobles to make slaves of wanderers or of the unemployed and to put them to work clearing land and transforming it into rice fields which could then be incorporated into the private holdings of their lords. This measure increased the area under rice cultivation, as it was meant to do, but at the same time it upset the social equilibrium by establishing domains worked by landless peasants who, with no property or other rights of their own, had no stake in

*These stone mandarins, ancient servitors of the Vietnamese emperors, stand guard outside one of the imperial tombs, ready to serve the emperor in death as in life.*

preserving the status quo. It was a development that could only prove to be a source of future disorders, which eventually came to threaten the country's stability.

From the time the Tran dynasty was founded, the danger from the Mongols in China was one of its chief preoccupations. The first war against the Mongols occurred in 1257. But it was only after Kublai Khan had completed his conquest of China and demanded the right to cross Vietnamese territory in order to attack Champa that the situation became serious. The Vietnamese refused to allow the Mongols to pass. But the Mongols came anyway—500,000 strong. The Vietnamese could put less than half that number in the field—some 200,000 men—but they were led by Tran Hung

Dao, and this prince of the house of Tran had the people behind him.

In 1284 the Vietnamese fell back under the shock of the Mongol attack, suffering one defeat after another. But the people remained faithful to the national cause, and guerrillas harried the Mongols behind their own lines. Tran Hung Dao carried on a brilliant defense, and was finally able to vanquish the invader in a crucial battle on the banks of the Bach Dang River. This was the same place where, 350 years earlier, Ngo Quyen, using a similar strategy, had defeated the Chinese to win independence for Vietnam. Tran Hung Dao's proclamation to his troops on the eve of battle is a classic of Vietnamese literature which is traditionally studied in Vietnamese schools.

The Vietnamese had thus accomplished a feat of historic magnitude. Outnumbered and unaided, they had halted the Mongol armies whose advance had spread terror throughout the civilized world. Long afterward, when Tran Hung Dao lay dying and the king came to ask him what to do should the invasion by the enemy from the north be resumed, he expounded on the problem of dealing with an adversary whose numbers were vastly superior to one's own and said, "The army must have one soul like the father and son in the family. It is vital to treat the people with humanity, to achieve deep roots and a lasting base." Vietnamese generals in later centuries who acted on this advice proved successful; those who failed to study the lessons of their own history lived to regret it.

The Vietnamese paid for the devastating Mongol invasions long after they were over. Nature took its revenge for the fields which had been neglected in wartime, and famine resulted. The Tran continued to extend their territory. The marriage of the Tran king's sister, Huyen Tran ("Pearl of

Jet''), to the king of Champa in 1307 brought the Tran land which was to extend their southern frontier to the Pass of Clouds near where Da Nang now stands. (A year later, on her husband's death, the princess had to be spirited away from Champa to save her from being burnt alive on her husband's funeral pyre in the Indian practice of *suttee*.) But more than additional land, the peasants needed peace to achieve a regular pace of life and agriculture. Instead they underwent an interminable series of wars, mostly with Champa, during which they lost their newly won southern territory and once saw their own capital burned by the Cham.

As the calibre of the Tran rulers declined, their administration deteriorated with them. The peasants were pushed to the breaking point by the burden of wars and natural disasters, and insecurity spread throughout the countryside. In theory each villager had an inalienable right to a share in the lands owned by the village in common, in exchange for which he owed taxes, military service, and labor on public works. But harvests were poor and starvation threatened. Many villagers sold their share in the land despite the fact that they were legally forbidden to do so. They were even compelled to sell their wives and children. A number of men went to work for the big landowners who had been steadily building up their holdings since they had first won the right to take over all the rice land they could find workers to clear for them. The men who served them were no longer registered as citizens of any village. They had become serfs, dependent on the goodwill of feudal lords.

Across the northern frontier, the new Ming dynasty in Peking demanded an increase in the amount of the usual tribute paid by Vietnam. The Ming also considered what else they could do to exploit this explosive social situation. But as the Chinese watched, a Vietnamese emerged to deal with it.

HO QUI LY, 1400–1408

By the end of the fourteenth century Vietnam was ruled by the Tran only in name, for they had lost effective control to one of their ministers, Ho Qui Ly. He played the ruling king and the retired king off against each other, had one king strangled, forced another to abdicate, and was knee-deep in the blood of mandarins loyal to the Tran by the time he made himself regent. In 1400 he declared himself king and after a few months put his son on the throne while keeping power in his own hands.

In the few years he managed to govern, Ho Qui Ly, however unscrupulous, proved nonetheless to be one of the most far-sighted rulers Vietnam had known. He limited the size of agrarian holdings and claimed all land in excess of a prescribed amount for the state, which in turn rented it to peasants at a moderate rate. To help the poor, he opened free schools in the provinces, and the best students went on to take examinations in the capital. It was Ho Qui Ly's idea to issue paper money and open the ports to trade. Most important, he recognized the necessity— as few of his Confucianist-reared contemporaries did—of dealing with the modern world as it had evolved in the two thousand years since the birth of Confucius. He worked out a program calling for radical reforms in the examination system which would have required candidates to have some knowledge of peasant life, and submitted them to examinations not just on Confucianist literature and philosophy, but also on simple mathematics and current events. Such reforms as these were to appear in the programs of secret Vietnamese nationalist groups five centuries later.

But the Chinese were not idle during this time. They had been in touch with the numerous dissident elements within

Vietnam—royalists who remained faithful to the Tran dynasty, which the Chinese promised to restore, and all those whose privileges were threatened by Ho Qui Ly's drastic reform program. When the Chinese were ready to strike, they had a massive fifth column in Vietnam. As soon as the Ho troops were defeated in battle by an army from China, a group of Vietnamese officials who were already collaborating with the invaders petitioned for the removal of the Tran dynasty to ease the Chinese takeover of the country. The Ming Emperor was only too glad to oblige these officials by removing the Tran rulers from power.

## A Chinese Province, 1408–1427

Vietnam had now taken a giant step backward to become once again the Chinese province of Giao Chi. The conquerors removed Vietnamese literary and historical works to China— an irreplaceable loss because these works existed only in their original handwritten form—and a number of the country's intellectuals and technicians were also carried off to China. Chinese culture and habits were imposed on the local population who were made to dress and to wear their hair in the Chinese fashion. Students were compelled to study certain Chinese works and no others. In order to subjugate the country further the Chinese also forbade the Vietnamese to import, study, and write treatises on all scientific and technical subjects.

The people were subjected to a regime as cruel as any they had known during their long experience of Chinese rule. Taxes were heavy, and forced labor enslaved the Vietnamese, driving them as far as the mountains to mine gold and to the sea in search of pearls. The great Vietnamese writer Nguyen Trai wrote of the Chinese: "Were the water of the Eastern

Sea to be exhausted, the stain of their ignominy could not be washed away; all the bamboo of the Southern Mountains would not suffice to provide the paper for recording all their crimes."

Some officials and scholars whose training, we must recall, had been in Chinese Confucianism, cooperated with their new masters. Many others, however, refused and fled to the mountains. According to a contemporary saying, "He who wants to live joins the resistance, he who wants to die accepts service under the Ming." And so it turned out, for those who collaborated with the Chinese were killed after the Vietnamese regained control of their country.

## Return to Independence

In the year 1418 a man from the province of Thanh Hoa named Le Loi started a resistance movement against the Chinese. On the mountain of Lam Son he gathered together a band of patriots determined to expel the invader. Here Nguyen Trai, the writer, came to find him and became his companion in arms, expressing the ideas of the rebels in language which stirred those who heard it, rallying them to Le Loi, and transforming him into a hero of legend.

Following the precepts of Tran Hung Dao, who defeated the Mongols in 1284, Le Loi in the beginning attacked only outlying posts and supply columns, falling back so that the enormous numerical superiority of the Chinese could not be turned against his handful of men. On three separate occasions he was forced to seek refuge in the mountains, but each time he returned to fight. Even when his troops were starving he forbade them to pillage, and he maintained absolute discipline among them so that the population received Le Loi's men as their natural protectors. Memories of freedom, made more compelling by the brutality of the Ming, prepared the ground for the rebellion. The remarkable personality of Le Loi and the quality of his followers did the rest. After nine years of guerrilla war, their numbers were swelled by many new recruits. Supplied by the population, they were able to open an offensive against the Chinese in the Red River Delta. By the end of 1427 Le Loi had seized the delta, and the entire country was free.

The peace terms called for Chinese recognition of Vietnamese independence in exchange for the return to the throne of a member of the Tran family, who accepted the customary Chinese suzerainty and dispatched an ambassador bearing tribute to the court of Peking. Having accomplished this formality, the last of the Tran had outlived his usefulness to his countrymen. He committed suicide, leaving his title to Le Loi, who became king in 1428 under the name of Le Thai To and founded the Le dynasty.

## THE LE DYNASTY

As a result of the long war against the Ming, Le Loi found himself king of a devastated land. Wide stretches of rice land had been abandoned, the people were left starving, and the country was afflicted with social disorder and banditry. Knowing the weaknesses of his compatriots, Le Loi imposed a rule of puritanical austerity, with drastic penalties for infringement of his laws. He also undertook a vast program of agrarian reform. Excess land, including that which had been amassed by people who had collaborated with the Chinese, was redistributed among the population. It was sometimes taken from one village and given to another so that nowhere would fields be left uncultivated. Land taxes continued to be levied only on lands owned in common by the village. The creation of large private holdings was forbidden. Village-owned land—then as in later centuries—was to be regularly redistributed among the registered citizens of the village according to their position in the social hierarchy. Le Thanh Ton, Le Loi's outstanding successor, took additional measures to protect agriculture, and he also renewed the prohibition against uncultivated land.

The Le dynasty launched a determined campaign to dislodge the Cham from their lands to the south. They formed militarized agricultural colonies, the *don dien,* to fight for the land, clear it, and convert it into irrigated rice fields so that new villages could be founded. (A similar policy was followed in the north in the Middle Region of Tonkin.) By 1471, the Vietnamese had taken over all but two districts of Champa, and the territory extending to Cape Varella was made into a province of Vietnam. With the *don dien* came Vietnamese schools which then completed, on the cultural level, the policy of assimilation followed in the conquered areas.

Doubtless in reaction against the former Chinese rulers, the Vietnamese language gained favor at this time among many scholars who had hitherto disdained it in favor of Chinese, and a number of outstanding literary works were produced in *chu nom* (which is the transcription of the Vietnamese language by means of characters derived from the Chinese). The Hong Duc legal code, drawn up under the Le, represented another attempt to emphasize the specifically Vietnamese aspects of the country's civilization. This attempt was especially obvious in provisions relating to private property and to the status of women who, in their domestic sphere, were considered almost the equal of men. The code was reminiscent of the Ly period in its relative humanity. But two groups were excluded from full civil rights—slaves and actors. Slaves had no rights of any kind. They were recruited among foreign prisoners of war and from families of men condemned for serious crimes—for punishment could be extended to the family of a wrong-doer down to the third generation. Actors were forbidden to improve either their own social position or that of their families. The girls of actors' families were not permitted to marry nobles or officials, and all examinations were closed to the boys.

But the expulsion of the Chinese could not restore to Vietnam the cultural heritage of which it had been despoiled, and the neo-Confucianism (see Chapter II) which the Chinese had imposed on the country survived them and triumphed under the Le. The Le rulers made themselves defenders of the Confucianist social and political morality that was taught in district and provincial schools. Outstanding graduates went to the capital to study at the National School, which was enlarged under the Le, and to take the literary examinations held regularly every three years. The Le era was notable for its cultural achievements, but it also marked the decline of Buddhism, even though that religion profited from government favor in the latter years of the Le dynasty. Monks no longer had the education to maintain the purity of the doctrine, and many laymen used the pagodas to escape their obligations to the state. Under the Le, therefore, examinations—which had once been a matter of course for Buddhist monks but had long since been abandoned—were again imposed on the monks, as on Taoist priests, by the state, and the building of new temples was forbidden.

Despite the remarkable achievements of these years, this period saw its share of brutality and betrayal, as has every other period of Vietnamese history to the present. Le Loi himself had to put down a revolt in the mountain regions in the course of which he ordered the murder of two of his own generals. Le Loi died a natural death after reigning just six years. But the son who succeeded him died under suspicious circumstances at the age of twenty. This latter death had the horrifying effect of causing the execution of Le Loi's old friend and comrade, the brilliant Nguyen Trai. The passage of power from one ruler to another was often accompanied by bloodshed.

By the early sixteenth century, the Le dynasty had fallen into decay, and from 1527 to 1592 Vietnam was ruled by the Mac family. Many Vietnamese, however, remained loyal to the memory of Le Loi, and a number of high mandarins killed themselves rather than accept Mac rule. But other loyalists preferred to fight, and under General Nguyen Kim resistance organized against the Mac.

# ✳ The Nguyen and the Trinh

Nguyen Kim—whose descendants were to become the Nguyen emperors of Vietnam—died by poisoning in the middle of the sixteenth century, leaving his son-in-law, a member of the Trinh family, to carry on the struggle. He carried it on so effectively that, by the time the war was over and the Mac had been forced to withdraw to the Cao Bang region on the northern frontier (where they remained as obscure puppets of the Chinese for three generations), the Trinh had gained control of the country. In 1593 the Le dynasty was finally restored to the throne, which it retained until late in the eighteenth century; but the true rulers in Hanoi during all those years were the Trinh.

Strained personal relations between a surviving son of Nguyen Kim and his ambitious Trinh brother-in-law caused the former to put as much distance as he could between the royal court and himself. In 1558, at his own request, he was named governor of the Hue area which lay south of the

Hoanh Son. He found conditions in the southern regions of the country invitingly ripe for an autonomy movement. The soldier-farmers who had settled these outlying lands lived isolated in their own small villages. They felt no strong ties to the north because their memories of it were simply not enough to bridge the distance which separated them from their birthplace. Thus, they had no difficulty in following their Nguyen ruler when he cut the administrative ties which subordinated him to Hanoi and finally, in 1620, refused to send any further taxes to the royal court.

From the beginning of the seventeenth century Vietnam was thus split in two at the Song Gianh River. The Trinh ruled as hereditary princes in the north under the aegis of the Le, while the Nguyen—who also proclaimed their loyalty to the Le kings—were masters of the south. The country remained divided between north and south for almost two centuries, until 1788.

The Trinh did not easily resign themselves to the loss of the population south of the Song Gianh and, starting in 1627, they sent seven expeditions against the Nguyen to restore unity. These periodic campaigns, each of which ended in failure, drained the country of manpower and riches, and ravaged it for fifty years. Both the symbol and the cornerstone of the defense system constructed by the Nguyen was the great wall of Dong Hoi, eleven miles long (reinforced by the six miles of the wall of Truong Duc), which cut across the narrow plain at the Nhat Le River north of the seventeenth parallel. Thanks to Portuguese aid, the Nguyen also had a clear-cut superiority in armament, which outweighed the help the Trinh received from the Dutch. The Trinh—who despite their nominal allegiance to the Le had usurped everything except the Le title—could not inspire much fervor in their troops, who were fighting far from their home bases in a harsh climate and a region foreign to them. The Trinh troops fell back before the determined southerners—trained professional fighters who were defending their own rice fields.

After a final defeat in 1672, the Trinh abandoned the struggle. Free at last of the terrible burden of this protracted civil war, they and the Nguyen set about building up their separate realms—the Trinh in the north and the Nguyen in the south.

Writers and artists were active during the next hundred years, particularly in the north where printing was introduced during the eighteenth century—before 1734, printed books had to be imported from China. The northern gold, silver, zinc, and tin mines were exploited in this period, largely by Chinese. The city of Hanoi had already become a commercial center. Whole streets were devoted to a single type of commerce such as silk or pottery, and they were divided between one or several villages which alone had the right to open shops there.

But by the mid-eighteenth century the Trinh had fallen on bad days. The royal treasury had been depleted by their expenditures, and they needed money so badly that, in defiance of the basic precepts of Confucianism, they abandoned the examination system and put state offices on sale to the highest bidder. The power of the central government weakened, and by 1732 it had lost the right to nominate village headmen—leaving the peasants to the tender mercies of whatever persons managed to gain control of each Council of Notables, the group which ruled the village. Large estates grew up, hampering the development of a broadly based system of land ownership. Even a 1723 decree which for the first time provided for the taxation of private lands could not reverse this trend. The resulting social crisis, intensified by extremes of flood and drought, precipitated a popular revolt which the Trinh managed to suppress only in 1769.

While the Trinh were dealing with the problems of an old country in the north, the Nguyen were occupied in building a new one south of the Song Gianh River. During the seventeenth century they absorbed what was left of Champa and stood poised at the edge of the Mekong River Delta. The delta was still nominally under the rule of the Khmer Empire, but the period of Khmer greatness was past. Vietnamese politicians had begun to intervene in their domestic affairs, and by the mid-seventeenth century the Khmer had accepted the suzerainty of the Nguyen lords to whom they paid tribute. Two colonies of Vietnamese already existed in the eastern region of the southern delta, around Bien Hoa. They were refugees from the misery caused by the long vendetta between the Nguyen and the Trinh. These refugees had been joined by exiles, deserters, and wanderers. In 1679 three thousand Chinese refugees, escaping from the Manchu dynasty which had taken over their native land, also settled in the delta. The Nguyen, having first assumed the right to protect all these colonists, later moved to more direct action, and by the end of the century had seized the region outright. They organized it into the provinces of Bien Hoa and Gia Dinh and two districts, one of them the city of Saigon.

To increase the number of these 200,000 inhabitants, the Nguyen collected people from the more populated areas of their realm and dispatched them southward to form new villages. The villages then drew up registers of their inhabitants and their rice fields and began to pay taxes on both. The land a man cleared was recognized as his own private property.

In western Cochin China, Mac Cuu, another Chinese who had rejected Manchu rule, organized a considerable region

*The Ngo Mon, or Midday Gate, in Hue is a perfect example of Nguyen period architecture. Beyond this gate lie the courts and buildings of the Imperial City.*

which he placed under the protection of the Nguyen who named him governor of the frontier land of Ha Tien on the Gulf of Siam. Mac Cuu and the son who succeeded him established a prosperous administration, and Vietnamese Buddhist monks and Chinese scholars came to help them. Ha Tien survived wars with the Khmer and with Thailand, only to be absorbed ultimately into the domains of the Nguyen, a circumstance which brought Nguyen authority to the tip of the peninsula and thus delivered the southernmost portion of the Mekong River Delta into Vietnamese hands.

As the territory under their control spread southward, the Nguyen moved their capital in the same direction and finally established it at Hue, equidistant between the deltas of the

Red River and the Mekong River. The Nguyen then appealed to the Chinese for recognition as independent sovereigns. When this was refused, they resigned themselves to the theoretical sovereignty of the Le, and in 1774 took the title of hereditary princes which the Trinh had assumed long before. Of the twelve provinces under Nguyen rule at this time (excluding Ha Tien which was still under a separate regime), half had been conquered from other countries—three from Champa, and three from the Khmer.

To rule this territory, old and new, the Nguyen set about reproducing the type of administration their ancestors had developed in the north. Their desperate need for personnel did not alter their Confucianist conviction that only education could qualify a man to hold official position and that this education must be both moral and literary. Barely had they taken over their new domain than they began to hold the standard examinations to recruit the men they needed. They could not afford to exclude worthy candidates simply because of social prejudice, however sanctified by tradition, and thus for the first time in the history of Vietnam the examinations were open to all inhabitants regardless of class or nationality. Even the son of an actor was now able to become prime minister.

Schools were created throughout the territory of the Nguyen, and the national language was widely used in literature and in official documents. At the end of the seventeenth century a Temple of Literature in honor of Confucius, modeled after the Van Mieu in Hanoi, was erected in Hue. Buddhism enjoyed the support of the Nguyen, as of the Trinh: pagodas sprang up throughout Hue, and even a number of Confucianist scholars turned to Buddhism. But this was no longer the religion of earlier centuries. It had been diluted by intermingling with peasant beliefs and practices ranging from animism to popularized Taoism. Buddhism remained an integral part of the Vietnamese heritage, but a number of people, especially the poor and the uneducated, sought consolation elsewhere. They turned to Catholicism, the first religion to be brought to Vietnam by Europeans.

## Early Relations with the West

In the early years of the Christian era, while the Vietnamese nation was taking shape in the Red River Delta as the Chinese colony of Giao Chi, traders from the West had anchored far to the south on the Cochin Chinese coast. On the site of Oc Eo—at that time a port of the ancient Indianized kingdom of Fu Nan which antedated Champa—recent excavations have uncovered relics of the Greco-Roman period. There is little information about contacts between the West and the regions lying south of the Red River Delta in intervening centuries, but by the time the first Portuguese sailor arrived in the Bay of Tourane in 1535, these regions had long since become Vietnamese territory. Five years later the Portuguese began to trade with the area.

TRADE AND MISSIONS

The Portuguese did their trading at the port of Fai Foo near the Bay of Tourane, where they found colonies of Chinese and Japanese merchants already installed, each group in its own part of the city, living according to its own laws and customs. After Vietnam had been divided at the Song Gianh early in the seventeenth century, the traders of Fai Foo lived under the jurisdiction of the Nguyen lords. When Japan was closed to the outside world in the 1630's, the Japanese colony was cut off from its homeland, and the

*In 1651 Father Alexandre de Rhodes published the first
dictionary in Latin, Portuguese, and* quoc ngu.

Portuguese—who also made regular trips to the northern
part of Vietnam—were left in control of most of the country's foreign commerce. The Dutch, who came next, preferred to settle in the north, where in 1637 the Trinh
authorized them to open a trading post at Hung Yen and
eventually in Hanoi itself. One of the Le kings even took a
Dutch woman as one of his six wives. Later the English,
whose first attempt at opening commercial relations with the
Vietnamese had ended with the murder of an agent of the
East India Company in 1613, also arrived in Hanoi.

But by the end of the seventeenth century both the English
and the Dutch had withdrawn from Vietnam, disappointed
in their expectations of profitable trade. The early eighteenth

century witnessed a decline in commerce with the West. The Europeans were occupied with their own wars and saw no future in a Vietnamese market which was not only limited in demand, but hedged about with obstacles placed in the way of equitable trading relations by the courts and the mandarinates of the north and the south. The one type of Western merchandise Vietnam had bought in any substantial amount had been arms and munitions, and the demand for these decreased during the century of peace between the Nguyen and the Trinh.

Although most of the foreign traders had gone, they left behind missionaries who played an important role in Vietnamese history. Just as Buddhist monks had arrived in the country in the ships of Indian merchants more than a thousand years earlier, so Portuguese traders had helped to introduce Catholic priests to the Vietnamese. The success of the first Catholic mission, founded at Fai Foo in 1615, led to the decision to send another mission to the north. And in 1627 Father Alexandre de Rhodes, the exponent of *quoc ngu* (Romanized Vietnamese script), was received by the Trinh prince. The Vietnamese proved to be highly receptive to Catholicism then and in the centuries which followed, but mass conversions were impeded by Catholic intolerance of polygamy and by the hostile position taken by the Vatican to ancestor worship.

The clash between the Confucianist rulers of Vietnam and European and native Catholicism dates from the seventeenth century. The Confucianist made little distinction between government and society, and regulated both by the same rules, so that the father in his family's world had absolute religious and secular authority similar to that of the king in the larger world outside. Catholicism, with its transcendental doctrine, struck at the roots of this established order. It created communities obedient to men who were not mandarins, and who, in the beginning, were not even Vietnamese. What is more, the Catholic faith worshipped a god who came from the remote West.

## FEAR OF CHRISTIANITY

Fearing the revolutionary social and political implications of Christianity, the Vietnamese rulers resorted to persecution of the missionaries and all who followed them. The gulf between the Confucianist court and the Catholics widened with time as the missionaries, exalted by the dream of converting Asia, did not hesitate to use secular means to achieve that end. They actively furthered opening Vietnam to trade with Europe, and more specifically to France, since French missionaries had replaced the Portuguese in importance by the eighteenth century. The missionaries also associated themselves with local political movements which seemed to favor the spread of the Catholic religion, and eventually they were to support French attempts to win political control over Vietnam.

Both the Trinh and the Nguyen therefore took increasingly strong measures against Christians as Catholicism continued to spread throughout their respective realms. The priests were often forced to carry on their missionary activities in secret. However, several rulers were interested enough in what the West had to teach to keep a number of European scientists and doctors (most of them priests) in attendance at their courts.

By the mid-eighteenth century the Catholic Church was not alone in its desire to penetrate the barriers Vietnam had erected against the West. Both English and French merchants and explorers considered establishing a foothold on Vietnamese soil. The French were anxious to get there before the British did and thus to make up for their territorial and trade losses in India. Some Frenchmen went so far as to work out a plan for a military expedition against Vietnam. But the French government rejected it as too expensive, for at that time France was about to move against the British by sending help to the embattled American colonies. The Vietnamese situation, however, seemed to invite foreign intervention—the country was once again at war.

## The Tay Son Rebellion

The war started as a popular revolt against the misgovernment of the regent in the realm of the Nguyen. It was led by three brothers—Nhac, Lu, and Hue—who had assumed the family name of Nguyen because of its prestige in the south. But because they came from the village of Tay Son near Qui Nhon, they were to be known as the Tay Son. In 1773 they captured Qui Nhon and defeated troops sent against them by the Nguyen. The Trinh, quick to profit when they learned of this setback to the Nguyen, sent an army from the north against their old enemy. The northerners crossed the Song Gianh, then forced their way past the Dong Hoi wall, which had held back so many invasions in the previous century, and seized the capital of Hue. Satisfied with this victory, they went no further. They left the field to the Tay Son, who dispatched an expedition to the Mekong River Delta where they again defeated the Nguyen and murdered the reigning prince and his immediate family. Only his nephew, sixteen-year-old Prince Nguyen Anh, survived the massacre.

Nguyen Anh (who was to become the Emperor Gia Long) took over leadership of the resistance to the Tay Son, but his troops seesawed between victory and defeat in the Mekong River Delta. In 1784, when he had lost everything and was close to starvation, he gave his four-year-old son Canh into the keeping of a French missionary, Pigneau de Béhaine, the Bishop of Adran, who held out the hope of military assistance from France. The following year, after another failure against the Tay Son, Nguyen Anh authorized the Bishop to take the boy with him to France and to plead his cause there.

Disorders in the realm of the Trinh, where a crisis over the succession was followed by famine and revolt, played into the hands of the Tay Son. They took over all the territory up to the Song Gianh and then moved on the north. The Trinh prince fled before them and killed himself when he was caught by his own people. In 1786 Nguyen Hue, the youngest of the three Tay Son brothers, entered Hanoi and declared his allegiance to the Le king. The Tay Son then proceeded to divide up the entire country from north to south among the three of them. In an ironic twist of history, the Le king—descendant of the man whose victorious struggle against the Chinese had made him a national hero—appealed to the Chinese for help against the Tay Son. The Chinese expeditionary corps was defeated by Nguyen Hue in 1789, and the last of the Le kings fled with it.

Nguyen Hue, before going to war with the Chinese, had declared himself the new sovereign of Vietnam under the name of Quang Trung, and later received Chinese recognition of his title. Some modern historians, as well as Communist interpreters of Vietnam's history, describe the Tay Son as nationalist and liberal heroes, as opposed to the Nguyen emperors who were to succeed them and who are blamed for the later Vietnamese defeat by the French. But there is insufficient evidence to support this view. During his short reign Nguyen Hue devoted himself to building up his army and demonstrated little interest in social reform. He died in 1792, leaving his throne to a child and effective power in the hands of an unpopular regent. At this time the Tay Son did not control the entire country, for in 1788 Nguyen Anh had won back a foothold in the south in the Saigon area.

This determined prince painstakingly organized his southern base. By giving his people the incentive of exemptions from military service and forced labor, he encouraged them to clear new land and grow more rice. He established his government according to the traditions of the Nguyen, and in 1791 the first literary examination was held to recruit government officials. Austerity was the order of the day, and gambling and witchcraft were forbidden.

Meanwhile, in 1789, the Bishop of Adran had returned from France, where he had signed a treaty with King Louis XVI in Nguyen Anh's name in 1787. This treaty would have brought the prince French aid in exchange for territorial and economic concessions, but the French government decided not to honor the treaty, leaving Nguyen Anh free of obligation to any Western government. The Bishop, however, collected a group of young French adventurers who helped to train Nguyen Anh's troops in the European fashion and to introduce them to Western military techniques and fortifications. Until the Bishop of Adran died in 1799, he played a vital role at Nguyen Anh's side during the long years of the Monsoon War (see Chapter I). The death of Nguyen Anh's son Prince Canh two years later was also the death of the Bishop's dream that a French-educated ruler friendly from childhood to the Catholics would one day sit on the throne in nineteenth-century Vietnam.

In 1801 Nguyen Anh seized Hue. Thus, he returned to the capital of his ancestors twenty-six years after he had been driven from it by the Trinh. When he took over Hanoi the following year, his victory was complete. In 1802 the country for the first time was united from the Gulf of Siam to the Chinese frontier.

# Unity Under the Nguyen Dynasty

Nguyen Anh then became the Emperor Gia Long and founded the Nguyen imperial dynasty. He named the country Vietnam, made his capital at Hue, and began a vast program of national rehabilitation.

The Nguyen had not only to deal with the aftermath of almost thirty years of war—wide stretches of abandoned rice fields and neglected dikes and canals—but they also had to build a state out of separate regions, each with its own local history and special loyalties.

The Nguyen launched a vast program of public works—dikes and canals, roads, ports, and bridges. They constructed citadels in provincial capitals, and such typically Vietnamese features as square towers were grafted onto the architectural style of the French master builder Vauban, a style which the Vietnamese had learned from the companions of the Bishop of Adran. Most important of all, the Nguyen built the Mandarin Road, which symbolized the new unity of the country it linked together. This road climbed the slopes of the Annamitic Cordillera, where steps were cut into solid rock, as it stretched from Hanoi past the capital of Hue to Saigon in the Mekong River Delta.

## ADMINISTRATION

This impressive work of construction was paralleled by achievements in the administrative sphere. Gia Long laid the foundations of the new regime, but it was his son Minh Mang, emperor from 1820 to 1841, who consolidated the state and established a strong central government. Minh Mang was a gifted legislator who had been trained as a Confucianist scholar and had become heir to the throne only after the death of his brother Canh, the pupil of the Bishop of Adran. He was steeped in Chinese culture and therefore profoundly hostile to Western influences which threatened the integrity of the Confucianist state. Within the Confucianist framework, however, he was by no means without originality or vision. It was not he but his father who adopted the curiously backward Gia Long legal code in order to impose on Vietnam a carbon copy of the Manchu legal code of China. This code set aside the code of the Le, whose provisions had been particularly adapted to the special conditions of Vietnamese society. Gia Long presumably was in a hurry to place the country on firm legal foundations after the years of war, and he chose the simplest means of achieving that end.

The administrative system established by Gia Long also bore the marks of improvisation. He left governors-general in control of both north and south, placing only the traditionally Nguyen lands in the center directly under the authority of the Hue government. This loose administration favored the growth of feudal power and separatist tendencies, particularly in the south where Gia Long's old comrade Le Van Duyet ruled as viceroy with the active support of the already numerous Christian community. On Duyet's death, his adopted son, Le Van Khoi, took control, and Minh Mang was confronted with an open revolt that raised the entire south against him. Catholics played an important part in this revolt which received support from Thailand. These events confirmed Minh Mang in his conviction that Catholicism menaced the state. After crushing the insurrection, he took drastic reprisals against the southerners, and many were put to death, including one French priest.

In the northern part of the country, economic problems caused by overpopulation and flood were acute, and the memory of the Le dynasty lingered on. The north was restive under the Nguyen, and Minh Mang had to put down a revolt in the highlands led by the brother-in-law of Le Van Khoi the southern rebel chief.

To counteract the regionalism of the south and to impose his rule on the north, Minh Mang ended the separate status of both and divided Vietnam into thirty-one *tinh,* or "provinces," each administered by a governor who was assisted by two other high mandarins. Supreme authority remained in the hands of the emperor, the Son of Heaven, who ruled by divine mandate in Hue. This Vietnamese imperial city lay athwart the River of Perfumes, protected on three sides by pine-covered hills, the highest of them known as the King's Screen. The courts and pavillions of the imperial palace were in the "Purple Forbidden City," in the shadow of the great citadel called the King's Cavalier. On the outskirts of Hue, the tombs of the Nguyen emperors blended into the hills and pine forests, creating a harmony between nature and the work of man which is distinctive of Vietnamese architecture at its best.

Hue was the center of the imperial cult. Every three years the emperor carried out the awesome rites of the Nam Giao on a sacred hill outside the city. There, in the darkness of the night lit only by torches, he made a sacrifice to the gods of heaven and earth on behalf of his subjects. He was both the religious and the secular head of the nation, and the mandarins had religious and secular powers under his authority. The emperor exercised his power through a cabinet of ministers called the *Co Mat* ("secret council") whose senior members were the four "Columns of the Empire." A corps of censors kept watch for the emperor over the operation of the government in Hue and in the provinces and had the right to report grievances directly to him.

The system of government by officials appointed by the imperial court extended down to the level of the district but stopped there. In the countryside, which has subdivided into cantons, the villages retained the right to choose their own officials, a right which they had acquired in the last years of the Le regime.

The period of the early Nguyen emperors was marked by great literary activity which surpassed previous eras in quality and quantity. The most famous Vietnamese literary work, *Kim Van Kieu,* dates from the reign of Gia Long. Written by Nguyen Du, a mandarin who had served the Le before he reluctantly shifted his allegiance to the Nguyen, this narrative poem expressed the Vietnamese soul so accurately that its harmonious verses are still widely quoted in daily life.

## MANDARINS AND PEASANTS

Under the Nguyen, the Vietnamese came closer than ever before to the Confucianist goal of a ruling class open to all and recruited according to merit. For the first time in the history of the country, mandarins and nobles were stripped of their semi-feudal privileges: they were no longer awarded tracts of land and were deprived of the right to collect taxes for their own use. All they received as payment from the state were salaries and pensions. The five titles of nobility had been carried over from the Le period—*cong* ("duke"), *hau* ("marquis"), *ba* ("count"), *tu* ("viscount"), and *nam* ("baron"). But these titles were bestowed only according to merit and could not be inherited. The nobles and the imperial family, which was governed by its own council, had no special property rights or political power. Along with officials and people of academic rank, however, they were exempted from taxes, forced labor, and military service.

Only the mandarins stood between the peasants and the emperor. Their posts were not hereditary. They came from the people, and their children, with certain limited exceptions, returned to the people. Mandarins were recruited by literary examinations held every three years, and following the democratic precedent of the Nguyen lords these examinations were open to anyone with the necessary educational qualifications. Gia Long founded a National School in Hue which admitted outstanding students from the lower classes, and the government furthered education at the district and provincial levels.

Minh Mang was especially concerned with the role of education in training the future rulers of the country, and he is said to have deplored the limited nature of the subject matter studied. But he made no attempt to change it. Students continued to memorize the Confucianist classics and the ancient history of China, and to learn to interpret them in the orthodox fashion so they could pass the examinations in the traditional subjects: commentaries on the classics, compositions in prose and poetry, and the drawing up of government decrees.

Civil mandarins took precedence over the military, and the Vietnamese inherited from the Confucianist philosophy a contempt for the professional soldier which has survived until today. This Confucianist conditioning also led them to underestimate the importance of nonintellectual occupations like handicrafts and trade, and also to an obsession with the importance of classical literary studies. Students wanted to acquire academic degrees—as many and as advanced as possible—in order to qualify for posts in the governing bureaucracy. Education was the only means to power and influence in nineteenth-century Vietnam. This attitude toward education is still prevalent in present-day Vietnam, where collecting academic degrees is often considered an end in itself.

The absence of a hereditary ruling class gave the regime a popular base, but the failure of any middle class to develop between the mandarins and the peasantry hindered the evolution of the nation. The indifference of Confucianist teachings to science and technology prevented change. An active merchant class could have broken through the stagnation of ideas to help develop the country economically and socially, but although such a class existed in Vietnam, it was powerless to act. In contrast to the political centralization achieved under Minh Mang, the economy of Vietnam remained highly decentralized. It had not progressed much beyond the village level. There was only a small amount of trade between north and south, and with the outside world—in rice, salt, and various products which were carried by river or along the coast.

Although a few bright children of the poor were able to rise to the level of mandarins, the great majority of peasants remained in the rice fields, some owned privately, the rest received on loan from the village. The Nguyen, like their predecessors, were left with no other way to feed the increasing population than to encourage the founding of new villages. They drafted colonists—soldiers, the poor and the homeless, men who had been exiled from their native villages because they had been guilty of various crimes, and prisoners of war—and sent them to clear new rice land and to cultivate it. In regions still occupied or threatened by other peoples who resented the arrival of the newcomers, these settlers divided their time between war and agriculture.

If the well-known aversion of Vietnamese to leaving their homes and the tombs of their ancestors did not prevent many of them from moving southward voluntarily, it was because they moved in groups, in large families or in whole villages, carrying with them the tablets necessary for the worship of their ancestors. Their movement was not only collective but also, generally, state-controlled. Settlers who wished to take over new land or to break away from other villages in order to found their own needed the permission of the government to do so; and it was from their sovereign that each new village received its name. Wherever Vietnamese settled and planted rice fields, they were required to organize themselves promptly into a village on the traditional pattern; and once it was established, the state added it to the administrative rolls of the central government and dispatched an official to collect taxes due the sovereign.

The Nguyen took measures to give more communal land to the village and decreed that it be divided equally among the villagers in periodic redistributions of land (although, with this redistribution in the hands of the village Council of Notables, the state could not do much to enforce such decrees). The Nguyen revived such humanitarian practices as lowering or abolishing taxes when times were bad and maintaining rice stocks to dispense in case of famine. However, the full burden of taxes, forced labor on public works, and military service continued to fall exclusively on the peasantry.

## WAR AND EXPANSION IN ASIA

The government and administration perfected by Minh Mang made Vietnam an important power in Southeast Asia. The Nguyen emperors continued the expansionist policy of their ancestors. Not content with the region already seized from the Cambodians, they struggled with Thailand for control of the Khmer Empire. They even attempted to assimilate it by force until the successor of Minh Mang, the Emperor Thieu Tri, abandoned this effort, and in 1845 Cambodia finally recognized the joint suzerainty of Vietnam and Thailand. Other wars with Thailand broke out when the Thai intervened in local revolts against the Nguyen. The Vietnamese also seized from the Loatians territory extending to the Mekong River, and the Laotian king of Luang Prabang acknowledged the suzerainty of the Nguyen. Even the

Indonesian mountain tribes in the Annamitic Cordillera, whose relations with the Vietnamese were limited to trading their forest products for necessities such as salt, came to Hue to pay homage to the Nguyen.

## THE CHALLENGE FROM THE WEST

Gia Long's relations with the West had been limited to his personal contacts with the Bishop of Adran and his French comrades, whom he had rewarded generously for their help during his years of need. However, he remained deeply influenced by his Confucianist background, and on his death-bed he warned his son against showing special preference to any European country. Minh Mang, in the increasing severity with which he treated foreign missionaries, was simply following the precedent of his Confucianist predecessors.

But the Catholic issue had become linked with problems of trade and empire. Europe was beginning an era of expansion which later forced the opening of Asia and Africa to the West. The Vietnamese might conceivably have been able to blunt the shock of the Europeans' arrival and preserve their independence—as the Japanese, for example, were able to do—but this would have required a degree of adaptation and imagination which was lacking in Hue. The court of the Nguyen extended its anti-Christian hostility to include all things Western. It rejected the offer of commercial treaties with both France and England. An American mission led by Edmond Roberts made two visits to Vietnam but was not received by Minh Mang. The latter reconsidered his position toward the West in 1839, when the outbreak of the Opium War launched against China by the British underlined the danger facing Vietnam. But Minh Mang's reputation as an enemy of Christianity preceded the mission he sent to negotiate in Paris and London and condemned it to failure. He died soon afterward.

Minh Mang was succeeded by Thieu Tri, who ruled from 1841 to 1847. He began his reign by showing tolerance to Catholic missionaries who continued to preach in Vietnam in defiance of governmental edicts against them. But in 1847, when French warships attacked the Vietnamese fleet at Da Nang, he furiously issued a decree condemning to death without trial any European found on Vietnamese territory. He died that same year and was succeeded by Tu Duc, under whose reign the French colonial conquest began.

The considerable achievements of the early Nguyen sovereigns were undercut by weaknesses in the national heritage which they and their court failed to recognize. When the Vietnamese had first emerged from Chinese colonial status, their practice of growing rice in irrigated fields and their social organization had given them a substantial advantage over their Indian-influenced neighbors. Confucianist doctrine had provided the cement to hold this young country together. Almost a thousand years later, however, Vietnamese were still growing their rice in much the same way. The well-being of the nation still depended almost exclusively on the peasant and his rice field. And the Confucianist influence had become an insurmountable barrier to social and economic change, a bar to technological advance. So it was that at a time when Vietnam seemed more powerful in Asia than ever before in its history, it proved less able than ever to defend itself against a foreign invader when, in the second half of the nineteenth century, France took control of Vietnam and made it part of the French colonial empire in Indochina. Once more Vietnam was to be ruled by foreigners.

# The Emergence
# of Modern Vietnam

The villages clung to their old ways after Vietnam became a part of the French Empire, but changes were injected into this traditional society. The country underwent a new development which was shaped by the needs of a colonial economy; the established class structure was altered; and education, once the symbol and the assurance of continuity, broke with the past both in form and content. Vietnamese were poised between two worlds: the static Confucianist world of their ancestors—which, although still an integral part of their lives, had failed them when they needed it most; and the Western world—which, along with technology, brought the seeds of revolution to the conservative backward-looking society of Vietnam.

It might have been possible to achieve a useful synthesis between these two worlds by peaceful means. But to make the leap from nineteenth-century Confucianist monarchy to twentieth-century state, the Vietnamese were in need, above all, of political experience. It was necessary to develop political organizations and parties geared to modern problems, to participate in some form of consultation between the people and their rulers, and to acquire practice in the wielding of political power which alone could create political responsibility. All of these outlets, however, were closed to Vietnamese who were excluded from the government of their country. Poets took refuge in sarcastic verses, but nationalist leaders turned to underground political activity.

As a part of French Indochina, Vietnam became the special preserve of French colonial and business interests. These interests profited from the indifference of much of French public opinion to make their own policy for Vietnam. By refusing to grant concessions and reforms in time, these French interests discredited moderate forces in Vietnam, and by the middle of the twentieth century the Communists seized control of the struggle for independence.

# The French Conquest

In the mid-nineteenth century the imperial court of Hue still chose to behave as if Europe did not exist. Its model was China; its guide, the past. It ignored all overtures designed to open Vietnam to trade with the West. When the court felt it could not ignore Western missionaries as well, it repressed them. This negative policy not only doomed the Vietnamese to an open clash with the West, but left them helpless when that clash occurred.

Determination to protect the Catholic religion was just one of a variety of motives that led the French to intervene in Vietnam. The French conquest of the country, which took place by stages over a period of more than twenty years, did not follow any precise plan. Rather it was a response—sometimes against express orders from the government in Paris—to the pressure of persons and events. If certain Frenchmen were attracted by adventure and some wished to bring Western civilization to Asia, others were fascinated by the possible riches of Vietnam's resources and the proximity of the country to the far greater wealth of China. There was talk of the need for a French base in Asia and a desire—intensified by nineteenth-century competition with Britain for international power and influence—to increase the prestige of France. In the 1880's economic motives became paramount. At that time the French Colonial Minister Jules Ferry insisted on the importance of colonies as a source of new markets and essential raw materials for the expanding economies of Western Europe.

## Conquest of the South

The conquest began in 1858 when a Franco-Spanish expedition commanded by a French admiral seized the port of Da Nang in order to punish the Vietnamese for the murder of missionaries from both nations. This fleet later turned southward following the monsoon, sailed up the River of Saigon, forced its way into the city, and destroyed the citadel. Most of the expedition then left to join the British in a war against China, but a handful of men remained behind. In 1861 Admiral Charner rejoined them on his way back from China and the French conquered three of the six provinces of the south (which the French knew as Cochin China).

While these events were taking place, Emperor Tu Duc,

who had acceded to the Vietnamese throne in 1847, was confronted with a revolt in the north. He agreed to the French peace terms in order to be free to move against the northern rebels, and the treaty signed on June 5, 1862 gave the French the three eastern provinces of Cochin China, as well as the island of Poulo Condore. French and Spanish missionaries were assured freedom of action throughout Vietnam, several ports were opened to French and Spanish commerce, and Tu Duc undertook to pay a large indemnity over a ten-year period. To raise this money he resorted to measures that violated the most prized traditions of Vietnam. He authorized the sale of opium (until then forbidden to Vietnamese citizens) in the northern half of the country, and sold to the Chinese a monopoly on the opium trade. Low-ranking posts in the mandarinal bureaucracy were also put up for sale.

But Tu Duc was not reconciled to the loss of the southern provinces to France, and in 1863 he dispatched his best diplomat, Phan Thanh Gian, at the head of a mission to Paris and Madrid in order to negotiate for their return. This seventy-two-year-old mandarin came very close to success. A treaty which would have enabled the Vietnamese to buy back their territory in exchange for acceptance of a vague French protectorate and a limited French occupation was actually signed in Hue. But French official opinion changed after Gian left Europe, and this first Treaty of Hue was never ratified.

In Cochin China the population launched bitter guerrilla warfare against the French. Admiral Bonard—the first of several high-ranking naval officers to govern Cochin China—had hoped to maintain a protectorate over the three provinces and rule through local institutions. But Vietnamese mandarins and scholars fled rather than serve under him. He was compelled to establish a system of direct administration, and

*The famous poet Tuy Ly was a leader of the anti-French resistance in 1884 and later became regent of Vietnam under Thanh Thai.*

in 1873 the French founded a school in Cochin China to train their own officials. Admiral de La Grandière, who replaced Bonard, greatly extended the domain of the French. In 1863 he declared a protectorate over Cambodia. Four years later, to put an end to Vietnamese guerrilla resistance in the three western provinces of Cochin China, "the refuge of all malcontents, of all agitators, of all the enemies of our authority," he seized these provinces too. Phan Thanh Gian, the governor of these provinces, killed himself, and his sons joined the guerrillas despite the hopelessness of their cause.

Admiral de La Grandière also sent a mission along the Mekong River to explore the route to China. The French thus discovered that the Upper Mekong was not navigable and that only the Red River could provide access to the southern provinces of China. They began to look with interest in the direction of the north, which they knew as Tonkin.

The court of Hue profited neither from the lesson of their defeat in the south nor from the last respite they were to have before being submerged by the French. And yet the country did not lack enlightened citizens who urged reforms on the emperor. One of these was Nguyen Truong To, a Catholic from Nghe An, who had traveled in Europe and Asia. He proposed cooperation with several Western powers in order to balance them off against each other. He also insisted on the necessity of reforming Vietnam's educational system—abandoning the use of Chinese characters, teaching science, sending students abroad, translating European books—and of bringing technicians from Europe to modernize agriculture, to develop industry, trade, and mining, and to reorganize the army. In 1868 Tu Duc did actually try to found a center for scientific and technical education with foreign teachers and textbooks translated from Western languages. But this project came to nothing because of opposition from the queen mother and other important members of the court.

## CONQUEST OF THE NORTH

The French first intervened in the north when a French trader, Jean Dupuis, and his men followed the Red River route from China down to Hanoi and seized the citadel. Admiral Dupré, the Governor of Cochin China who had been ordered by Paris to avoid any involvement in Tonkin, responded to the appeal of the Hue court that he deal with his enterprising countryman by dispatching a French officer, Francis Garnier, at the head of a small number of men to Hanoi. To the dismay of the Hue court, Garnier took over where Dupuis had left off. He captured the city and began the conquest of Tonkin, cut short only by his death at the hands of the "Black Flags," a band of Chinese irregulars who lived by banditry. The Treaty of Saigon of 1874, between

France and the Emperor Tu Duc, returned the north to its previous status under Vietnamese control, but it recognized the French conquest of the three provinces of western Cochin China which the French had held since 1867. In addition, France recognized the "entire independence" of Vietnam but Tu Duc accepted French direction of his foreign policy and conceded trading rights to the French. Tu Duc's acceptance of the treaty led to unrest in the country and to uprisings against him. He later sought in vain for help from abroad against the French—from the Chinese and the British and even from the Americans—but his appeals to France and Spain for revision of the treaty went unanswered.

Ten years after Garnier's abortive expedition, Capt. Henri Rivière repeated the attempt to take Hanoi. With the city in flames and its governor, who had been unable to defend his city, dead by his own hand, the court of Hue called into action the same Black Flags who had defeated Garnier. They came down out of the northern highlands into the delta, and Rivière, like Garnier before him, died in the battle against them. But this time the French had no intention of withdrawing from the north. The year 1883 witnessed the death of Tu Duc—who had accomplished more during his lifetime as a poet than as a ruler. It was the last year of independence for nineteenth-century Vietnam. The French then moved in force on Tonkin. Meanwhile, outside Hue, they bombarded the entrance to the River of Perfumes and imposed a protectorate on the Vietnamese imperial court.

After Tu Duc's death, three young emperors rapidly succeeded each other on the throne. All died under mysterious circumstances. At last, the two regents in control of Hue settled on a fourth emperor, a prince from the south, and in 1884, at the age of fourteen, he became the Emperor Ham Nghi.

The French were now confronted with war on several fronts. Many mandarins refused to accept the treaty of 1874 and led the popular resistance against the invader. China too, the suzerain power of Vietnam during all the centuries of its independence, had sent troops into Tonkin. Events in far-off Cochin China had not disturbed the Chinese unduly, but Tonkin was on the Chinese frontier and its future was a matter of national interest to China. The Chinese went to war with the French in 1883 and were defeated. By the Treaty of Tientsin in 1885 they were compelled to recognize the French protectorate over Vietnam.

The second Treaty of Hue—signed in 1884 between the French and the Vietnamese—spelled out the terms of the protectorate. It left relative autonomy to central Vietnam, to which the French gave the old Chinese name of Annam. An official representative of France was to be stationed in Hue with the right to see the emperor in private audience but with no specific control over him, and Vietnamese were to continue to rule over Annam itself. Only the collection of customs duties was to be in French hands. In Tonkin, French control was to be more direct, and French administrators were stationed in each provincial capital.

The Vietnamese did not accept the protectorate passively, and in 1885 they attacked the French in Hue. Emperor Ham Nghi, the intransigent regent Ton That Tuyet, and the imperial court fled the capital and called on the people to revolt. Throughout Annam and Tonkin, peasants and scholars rose to follow them in a display of unity which deeply impressed their French adversaries. The French replaced emperor Ham Nghi with his more docile relative, Dong Khanh. But Ham Nghi held out against them in the mountains until 1888, when he fell as a result of treachery into the hands of the French and was exiled to Algeria.

*In December 1883 the French captured the fortified village of Son Tay in their drive to conquer northern Vietnam.*

In Tonkin the fighting went on. It was led by one of the country's leading scholars, Phan Dinh Phung, until his death in 1895. Another rebel chief, De Tham, continued sporadic resistance in the northern mountains until the eve of World War I.

Thus, the French established their rule over the country of Vietnam, which was to remain a part of the French Empire for three-quarters of a century.

## The French Colonial Regime

As of 1887, Vietnam had ceased to exist for all practical purposes, except as a memory and a rallying cry to revolt. In its place a French decree of 1887 established the Indochinese Union. This administrative entity was eventually extended to include five regions, plus the small French concession of Kwangchowan in South China. Two of the five were the neighboring countries of Cambodia and Laos. Cambodia had become part of the French Empire in 1863, and thirty years later Laos did the same. As members of the Indochinese Union under French rule, both Cambodia and Laos acquired legal equality with the Vietnamese. The two countries also acquired protection from Vietnam, which they had been unable to achieve by their own means. The French even returned to the Cambodians and the Laotians land which had been seized from them by the Vietnamese under the Nguyen dynasty.

The other three parts of the Indochinese Union—and by far the most populous—consisted of what had been the Vietnamese Empire before it was split horizontally from north to south into the protectorates of Tonkin and Annam and the colony of Cochin China. Annam stretched northward across the traditional frontier of the Song Gianh and the Hoanh Son. It attached the densely populated provinces of Ha Tinh, Nghe An, and Thanh Hoa to the central region of Vietnam, where the Nguyen lords had laid the foundations of their domain. In Annam the mandarinal hierarchy remained in place under the nominal authority of the emperor. But effective power was gradually removed from both. The Vietnamese administration, although owing allegiance to the court of Hue and its ministers, was subordinated in practice to local French officials called Residents. The French Resident Superior was the true ruler of Annam. Another Resident Superior governed Tonkin, where French control over the Vietnamese administration had been established even earlier. The key cities of Hanoi and Haiphong, like Tourane in Annam, were made French concessions administered directly by Frenchmen.

In the south the colony of Cochin China remained under a French governor. After the conquest there was no mandarinal framework left to operate between the people and their new rulers. Therefore the Cochin Chinese came into even closer contact with the French than did their countrymen in the protectorates of Annam and Tonkin. More facilities for acquiring French citizenship were open to the Cochin Chinese, and a number took advantage of them.

A distinctive feature of the French colonial system, which had a good side as well as a bad one, was the use of Frenchmen even in low administrative posts. This had the advantage of bringing a large segment of the population into close contact with the French, thus creating solid Franco-Vietnamese links which have survived to the present. The inconvenience of the system was that it prevented many Vietnamese from acquiring experience in the conduct of their own governmental affairs. The form of government which developed in colonial Vietnam inherited basic weaknesses from the old Confucianist system and perpetuated them. Under the French the country continued to be ruled by an appointed bureaucracy, and the various advisory bodies in which Vietnamese were permitted to sit had no power. As a result, the Vietnamese people—excluded, as they had been throughout their history, from participation in the process of government above the village level—continued to regard government as something imposed on them from above in which they had no share and for which they felt no responsibility.

Ruling over all the different parts of the Indochinese Union was the chief French official in Indochina—the governor-general. His capital was in Hanoi, although he spent part of each year in Saigon. The calibre of French governors in Indochina varied widely from the best, exemplified by Paul Bert, to the worst, personified by Governor-General Martial Merlin. The former, a distinguished scientist, governed Annam and Tonkin in the 1880's with an appreciation

COLONIAL VIETNAM

of their distinctive culture and institutions, while the latter, in the 1920's, tried to impose on Indochina the system of "horizontal education" which had been used by Belgium in the Congo (where natives were trained only to perform subordinate jobs under their white masters).

The power of the governor-general was very great when he chose to exercise it—as did Paul Doumer (1897-1902) who, in violation of the Treaties of Hue, imposed what amounted to direct administration on Tonkin and, to a lesser extent, on Annam. Doumer laid the foundations of French policy for decades to come when he created a group of French "general services" which had jurisdiction over the entire Indochinese

Union. These services dealt with matters ranging from public works to economic affairs. The heads of these services and the commander of the armed forces constituted a sort of ministerial cabinet presided over by the governor-general.

Indirect as well as direct taxes were levied on the Vietnamese, as on the other Indochinese peoples. The colonial regime reaped substantial benefits from the monopolies it had on the sale of opium, alcohol, and salt. It also collected land and personal taxes which in principle were similar to the direct taxes that Vietnamese had long paid to their own government. But the French rulers of Vietnam did not tolerate the practices sanctioned by ancient custom which the villages had used to defend themselves against the onerous demands of the state. Taxes for the first time were not limited to people whose names appeared on the village rolls. They were imposed systematically on the total number of adult men—regardless of their ability to pay—who were estimated by the colonial authorities to live in each village. And the amount of these taxes was not determined by the needs of a regime indifferent to material progress and limited to a village economy as in the past; instead it was determined by an efficiently organized Western administration which was determined to modernize Indochina's public works.

In their program of modernization—more ambitious than any Vietnam had ever seen—the French used contemporary Western engineering techniques to surpass the achievements of past Vietnamese rulers. The French gave Vietnam a network of modern roads and a railroad—the Transindochinese—which paralleled the Mandarin Road as it stretched across the coastal plains to the Chinese frontier. They also developed ports, reinforced and extended the dike system, and built extensive irrigation and drainage works. Public services like hospitals and schools were established, as were scientific and cultural research institutes. The Vietnamese population more than doubled under French rule, benefiting from an extended period of peace and from improvements in public sanitation and in the control of epidemic diseases.

## A COLONIAL ECONOMY

With their strategic position and their control over the administration of Vietnam secured, the French grafted a modern economy onto the hitherto static and self-sufficient economy of Vietnam. The output of traditional crops—rice and corn—was vastly increased. The northern mines were worked on a scale never before known in Vietnam. And the French introduced new crops into the country—notably rubber and coffee. Under French direction Vietnam became a large-scale exporter of agricultural products and raw materials. The country assumed a typical colonial economy.

No emperor or policy of organized colonization had ever opened up so much Vietnamese territory to rice cultivation in so short a time as French drainage and irrigation works did in the Transbassac region of western Cochin China. But the archaic rural life of the country was left unchanged. The Vietnamese peasant continued to plant his rice according to the traditional ways his ancestors had learned from the Chinese more than a thousand years earlier. The result was that the yield of agriculture proved too low for a rapidly increasing population. The country, however, managed to export some million and a quarter tons of rice a year, and Indochina became the third largest rice exporter in the world. The trouble was that these exports came mostly from the newly developed lands in Cochin China. They brought money to private interests and to the Indochinese budget, but they often aggravated the unbalance in food production between the rich, sparsely populated areas of Cochin China and the overcrowded rural areas of Tonkin and Annam. Thus rice could be Indochina's major export at the very time when it was sorely needed within the country. The lack of diversity in food production was another weakness of Vietnamese agriculture. Apart from rice, only corn was produced in large quantities, and this largely for export.

The newly introduced agricultural products like rubber and coffee were grown almost exclusively on plantations owned by French interests and were destined solely for export. First planted in Vietnam before World War I, rubber was cultivated on over 247,000 acres by 1937. All but 4,940 acres were in Cochin China, where plantations were divided almost equally between the "gray lands" near Saigon and the rich "red lands" between the Mekong River Delta and the plateaus of southern Annam and Cambodia. By 1938 Indochinese rubber production (including the substantial amount produced in Cambodia) could have filled France's total needs in rubber—some sixty thousand tons. The success of the rubber plantations was paid for dearly with the ruthless exploitation by private French companies of a new sub-proletariat made up of workers uprooted, often by force, from the northern deltas. Their miserable living conditions have been poignantly described by a number of French novelists and sociologists.

At one time coffee was also an important export crop, but tea—which was native to Vietnam—ultimately proved more successful. Early French attempts to grow coffee and tea in the north were less rewarding than were later attempts to establish plantations on the red lands of the south Annamese plateaus.

Mining and industry were developed on the same colonial pattern as agriculture. It was in keeping with colonial practice to use Vietnam as a source of agricultural products and raw materials while making it a market for French manufactured goods. Mining was concentrated in the north, above all in the anthracite coal mines of north-eastern Tonkin, but only a little bituminous coal was discovered. Well over 2,530,000 tons of anthracite were produced in 1937, and although this represented only a small proportion of all the coal mined in the Far East, Tonkin became the most important Southeast Asian exporter of coal. In 1937 tin and tungsten constituted some 29 per cent of Indochinese mining production. Zinc, which had once been a more important export item than tin, had dropped to 2 per cent because of shifts in the international market demand. The lot of the Tonkinese miners, who worked in gangs under often brutal native overseers, or *cai,* was no better than that of their countrymen who labored on the rubber plantations further south. Their conditions improved only in the last few years of French rule.

During the colonial period, just a few industries were developed. The cement works at Haiphong was one of the first and largest factories the French installed in Vietnam. The French cotton mill at Nam Dinh—which used imported raw cotton—employed more workers than any other factory in the country. Other processing industries included rice mills (which were largely in the hands of the Chinese), distilleries and breweries, and glass works.

## TRADE AND INVESTMENT

As Indochina's foreign trade developed during the colonial period, it shifted from the Far East to France. Foreign interests continued to profit from this commerce. They were French and, to a lesser extent, Chinese. Before World War I Indochina had traded more with the Far East than with France and its colonies. Thereafter France's share in Indochinese commerce became more important, and in 1930 it equaled that of the Far East. France's increasingly protectionist policy, which was applied in Indochina from 1928 on, closed the country even to those Chinese and Japanese products which until then had been available to the Vietnamese. This policy contributed to the growth of Far Eastern tariffs directed, in turn, against Indochinese products, and during the 1930's Indochina had to rely on France as its major trading partner. For the first time, France and its empire bought more from Indochina than they sold there, and Vietnamese rice, corn, rubber, tea, and even coal crossed the ocean to France.

The Vietnamese, for their part, were compelled to depend on the factories of a far-off Western land for fabrics and other manufactured products which were produced according to standards remote from those of the Asian peasant, and at prices much higher than those Indochina would have paid to nearer sources of supply. The Vietnamese were, of course, quite capable of manufacturing at least some of the consumer goods they needed, but in the colonial era such production was discouraged.

In 1938 more than 95 per cent of the foreign investment in Indochina—estimated at some $384,200,000—was owned by Frenchmen. Chinese within the country and outside were believed to have additional holdings of some $80,000,000. The country's economic resources were almost entirely directed by French banks and corporations which had replaced the individual planters who came to Indochina in the decade before World War I. These planters had benefited from the land-grant policy of the colonial government, which handed over to them large concessions formed out of the holdings of local landowners who had fled at the arrival of the French. On these estates they grew rubber, rice, tea, coffee, sugar, and forest products. But by 1918 the Banque de l'Indochine ("Bank of Indochina") had already gained a foothold in the growing trade of the colony. It operated through Chinese middlemen, using the *comprador* system, by which the Chinese dealt directly with the Vietnamese on behalf of the French and pocketed such profits as the French did not take for themselves. Between the two World Wars the Banque de l'Indochine and the Banque Franco-Chinoise ("Franco-Chinese Bank") gained a dominant position over the native economy through their control of credit. French capital was poured into the large-scale production of rice and rubber, and great domains were formed in the south. The majority of these French-owned plantations were controlled not by private owners but by joint stock corporations. They did not specialize in a single crop, or even in agriculture generally, but owned a variety of other economic enterprises in the country. This diversification of investments resulted in an extreme concentration of capital in relatively few hands— virtually none of them Vietnamese.

The Chinese had the organization, the experience, and the capital to monopolize the local rice trade, and generally to act as intermediaries between the Vietnamese peasants and the French. The Vietnamese were unable to compete with either the Chinese or the French. Only a handful managed to gain a foothold at even the lower levels of Western industry and business. In any case, absentee landlordship, speculation in land, and usury required less effort and less risk than industry, and these institutions and practices were the means to riches favored by the new Vietnamese propertied class, which grew up under the colonial regime.

## Social Changes

Throughout the centuries, the growth of large estates worked by a class of landless poor had invariably brought social unrest and violence to Vietnam. For this reason the preservation of a system of widely dispersed land ownership—with each farmer working his own land and without extremes of riches and poverty—has been a continuing problem for Vietnam. Minh Mang was the last emperor endowed with the authority and the wisdom to take action against the accumulation of property in a few hands. In French Indochina the growth of large estates began again—as usual at the expense of the peasant majority which still constituted some 90 per cent of the population. The process by which the gap between rich and poor widened was speeded up by the introduction of a modern capitalist economy into the country. The new importance of money, the emergence of the profit system, the introduction of credit to tide the peasant over from one season to the next, the development of new economic activities under the French, and the colonial administration itself which recruited a certain number of Vietnamese to serve in its ranks—all these contributed to changes in the class structure.

A class of large landowners developed anew even in the Red River Delta which was notable for the considerable proportion of small farmers who worked their own tiny plots of land. In the overpopulated northern deltas, the peasants supplemented their income with artisanal work, but often had to pledge their crop and meager possessions to moneylenders in order to survive—and not infrequently lost to them everything they owned. The French attempted to make credit available to the poor, but the funds provided for this purpose fell into the hands of already wealthy Vietnamese landowners who lent money at exorbitant rates. Thus, a number of large estates owned by Vietnamese emerged in the north, generally acquired through the practice of usury. They were worked by tenant farmers who paid a substantial part of their harvest to their landlords. The country was swept by a wave of land speculation connived in by village headmen and mandarins alike. It affected even communal lands, which in

Tonkin shrank to just one fifth of the total cultivated area, so that it was no longer possible for the small landowner and the tenant farmer to turn to the communal lands on which they used to rely to supplement their insufficient crops.

The concentration of land in a few hands was particularly marked in Cochin China. Vietnamese who sided with the French at the beginning of the colonial era received some of the land the French had taken over in eastern and central Cochin China when they first arrived in the country. In these old provinces, estates, although larger than those farther north, tended to be moderate-sized, and were cultivated, at least in part, by their owners. Quite different was the situation in the west, in the Transbassac, where land had been made fit for rice cultivation under the French, and was then sold in large lots for rapid development—some to Vietnamese who were usually French citizens. Here there was no question of landlords working their own fields. Often they did not even live on their lands. They were absentee landlords, who preferred life in the towns, leaving their rice fields to be worked by *ta dien* ("sharecroppers") and seasonal workers controlled by *cai*. The *ta dien* often paid more than half of their total harvest in money and rice to the landlord, and were forced to borrow from him to make ends meet, so that they constantly labored under a grinding burden of debt. Thus the absentee landlord frequently made even more money from usury than he did from the sale of the rice crop.

Parallel to the development of this propertied class, a new working class grew up during the colonial period which labored on French- and Vietnamese-owned estates in the south and in the various other enterprises established by Frenchmen. In some cases workers were constrained by contracts to remain on the job for years on end at the mercy of *cai,* forced by chronic indebtedness to renew such contracts whether they wished to or not. Abuses of this system led to French reform efforts in the late 1920's directed at improving the conditions of contract labor. Other workers had to wait for the advent of the French Popular Front government in 1936, when labor reforms within France were extended to the French colonies. But the governor-general was empowered to adapt these reforms to local conditions, and labor unions were forbidden. In any event, these reforms were suspended in 1940 with the outbreak of World War II.

It is as difficult to estimate the size of the Vietnamese working class as it is to draw the line between worker and peasant. There was a rapid turnover among laborers, and most returned when they could to their native villages and to peasant life. Others, however, remained uprooted. They were cut off from the security and stability of village life, and became a prey to extremist political agitation.

Thus the economic and social structure of the country was profoundly altered under Western rule. Equally significant was the impact of the French on the educational system and on the cultural attitudes of Vietnam, which had been static for many centuries before the French came.

## Changes in Education

One of the few things on which Vietnamese nationalists and their French rulers agreed was that the traditional educational system was deficient both in substance and in method. For many centuries this system had relied exclusively on the old Confucianist manuals, ignoring the natural sciences and mathematics—which were subjects necessary to the development of modern technology and economics. Students had been taught to rely on memory rather than on observation and analysis, and were indoctrinated in an uncritical acceptance of the past. They had studied Chinese characters by this time-honored system—and with them history and social ethics—as they prepared in public and private schools throughout the country for the triennial Confucianist examinations held by the state to recruit the mandarinal bureaucracy.

The imprint of this traditional education has been slow to die out in modern Vietnam. But the cornerstone of the system was removed with the ending of the examinations and with the adoption of *quoc ngu,* the Romanized script first introduced in the seventeenth century. The examinations were suppressed first in Cochin China, where the French colonial regime had been established longest. In the north, traditions were stronger, and the old system lasted in Tonkin until World War I, and in Annam until the war's end.

*Quoc ngu* served as a vehicle for introducing modern and Western ideas into Vietnam. It replaced not only Chinese, but also the impractical transcription of Vietnamese by means of characters derived from the Chinese, and was taught in schools along with French. In a few high schools standards were the same as in metropolitan France. These *lycées,* created initially for French children, were opened to Vietnamese in increasingly large numbers. The Lycée Albert Sarraut in Hanoi and the Lycée Chasseloup Laubat in Saigon were seedbeds from which emerged many of the leaders of modern Vietnam, Cambodia, and Laos. Many *lycée* students went on to the University of Hanoi but a privileged few were able to go to France to complete their education.

In contact with French culture, the grip of the old traditions and outlook on many members of the educated class was bound to weaken. However, it should be kept in mind that Westernization—largely confined to the urban population—was, and still is, slow and superficial. In many instances it had simply the negative effect of discrediting the past, thus leaving a cultural vacuum which later was often filled by Communist doctrines.

# Nationalist Movements

Throughout the French colonial period foreigners ignorant of Vietnamese history underestimated the depths of Vietnamese nationalist sentiments. They were misled by superficial appearances. They saw young men competing for places in French schools and leading citizens who preached collaboration with the colonial authorities. Until the 1940's most Vietnamese appeared to accept their foreign rulers with docility. But behind this facade of acquiescence, the bulk of Vietnamese society remained nostalgic for its lost independence. The Vietnamese were bound together by an intricate network of loyalties and customs which was closed to the foreigner. The result was that few Westerners understood what was happening beneath the surface of Vietnamese life, and were surprised and outraged when things did not go as they had expected. Signs of an undercurrent of intransigent nationalist activity were evident, however, in the large number of secret societies noted even by the French colonial authorities.

## ROLE OF PHAN BOI CHAU

The great patriot Phan Boi Chau embodied the determination to find in the Vietnamese national traditions the force to produce a new group of leaders able to bridge the gap in technology between the Vietnamese and their Western rulers. He was intent that this ancient Asian society should develop a modern political organization which could achieve independent statehood.

Phan Boi Chau was a scholar trained in the classical

fashion. Because effective reform movements were not tolerated by the colonial authorities, he and other Vietnamese political leaders were compelled to act underground and resort to the techniques of revolution. They looked to the two main Asian powers—Japan and China—for guidance and support. Japan's victory in the Russo-Japanese War in 1905 showed them that a traditional Asian country could reach the level of material power of the West, and soon afterward Phan Boi Chau and Cuong De—a prince of the house of Nguyen—went to Japan, where they were followed by other patriots.

Vietnamese who reached metropolitan France also found —paradoxical as this may seem—opportunities for political action in an atmosphere of freedom which did not exist in Vietnam under the colonial regime. It should be noted that the Vietnamese independence movement, when it became locked in a life-and-death struggle with the colonial authorities, never lacked support among liberal Frenchmen. And books highly critical of the colonial conditions in Vietnam are to be found in French literature.

But China also made a major contribution, not only by harboring and training nationalist refugees, but also by influencing the thinking of Vietnamese intellectuals. Vietnamese scholars first read the works of French and British eighteenth-century philosophers in Chinese translations. The reform movement in China, the founding of a republic under Sun Yat-sen in 1912, and the activities of the nationalist Kuomintang party were followed closely in Vietnam. In keeping with this trend, before World War I, Phan Boi Chau shifted his headquarters from Japan to China. In Canton he gathered those of his countrymen who had succeeded in slipping across the Chinese frontier into the Viet Nam Phuc Quoc Dong Minh Hoi ("League for the Restoration of Vietnam") or Phuc Quoc. His goal was an independent state headed by Prince Cuong De.

In the years leading up to World War I, political agitation in Tonkin and Annam took many forms. It ranged from the educational activities of scholars—prominent among them Phan Chu Trinh—who published a newspaper and books in Hanoi and in 1907 set up a free school to teach science and other modern subjects (a school later closed down by the colonial authorities), to peasant demonstrations and even an attempt to poison the French garrison in Hanoi. A number of men cut off their chignons (knots of hair worn at the back of the neck)—the traditional hair style of Vietnamese men—as a symbol of their desire to modernize the country, and they demanded social reforms.

The imperial court in Hue—where high mandarins were in touch with Phan Boi Chau—was another center of nationalist activity which the colonial authorities did their best to stamp out. The subservient Dong Khanh, whom the French chose to replace Emperor Ham Nghi, had died in 1889. He left the throne to Thanh Thai, a more nationalist-minded ruler, who was deported in 1907 and replaced by his son Duy Tan. The young emperor was only in his teens—as Ham Nghi had been—when in 1916 he and the poet Tran Cao Van led an uprising in Hue. When the uprising failed, the poet was executed, and Duy Tan was deported to the island of Réunion. There were thus three emperors in exile when the colonial authorities put Khai Dinh, a son of Dong Khanh, on the imperial throne. Khai Dinh died in 1925. His heir, Bao Dai, was still a boy when he was sent abroad to continue his studies in France under the close tutelage of a French colonial official.

By the mid-1920's Phan Boi Chau had to accept defeat. He had finally been captured in China and condemned to death by the French. Saved from execution only by a strong show of solidarity by the Vietnamese nation which prevailed on the colonial authorities to pardon him, he renounced all political activity and lived the rest of his life in seclusion in Hue.

## THE VIET NAM QUOC DAN DANG

Leadership in the independence movement then shifted to the Viet Nam Quoc Dan Dang (Vietnam Nationalist Party or VNQDD), which was to be the most important non-Communist party in Vietnam between the two World Wars. Its activity reached a climax in February 1930, when Vietnamese auxiliary soldiers rebelled against the French garrison at Yen Bay. Nguyen Thai Hoc, the party leader, and twelve of his comrades were guillotined. They died with the cry "Vietnam!" on their lips.

This decimation of the Viet Nam Quoc Dan Dang leadership gave the Communist party, which had been organizing secretly, its opportunity to recruit many nationalists. Its founder, the son of a low-ranking mandarin from Nghe An (the province in which Phan Boi Chau and Phan Chu Trinh were also born), used the alias Nguyen Ai Quoc ("Nguyen the Patriot"). He left Vietnam before World War I and did not return there until late in World War II, and, as Ho Chi Minh, he became President of the Democratic Republic of Vietnam.

## HO CHI MINH AND THE COMMUNIST PARTY

A member of the French Communist party in the early 1920's, Ho Chi Minh was also trained in revolutionary methods in Moscow along with other Asians who later became Communist leaders. By 1925 he had left Europe for China, where he remained until the 1927 break between

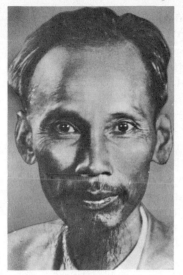

*To the left, Ho Chi Minh is shown as he appeared
prior to the outbreak of the war with France. To the right
is Ngo Dinh Diem the late President of the Republic
of Vietnam.*

Chiang Kai-shek and the Communists. Following in the
footsteps of Phan Boi Chau, he drew on the Vietnamese
colony in the southern Chinese city of Canton to form a
Revolutionary Youth Association, training revolutionaries
who returned secretly to Vietnam to establish Communist
cells. In China and in neighboring countries, Ho Chi Minh
operated as a representative of the Communist International
in Moscow. In 1930, when the Vietnamese Communists were
split into several groups, Ho Chi Minh, in Hongkong,
unified them into the Indochinese Communist party. The
party capitalized on the social unrest which marked the year

1930 when famine occurred. And when violence broke out among the peasants in Nghe An, the Communists took over leadership of the peasant revolt. Two "soviets," or governing councils usually made up of peasants, workers, and soldiers, were actually established in north Annam, but the French put them down by force.

## THE RISE OF NGO DINH DIEM

These same years witnessed the rise to prominence of the man who for nine years was to lead the nationalist opposition to Ho Chi Minh—Ngo Dinh Diem. An uncompromising opponent of French colonial rule, he was one of those who tried to achieve freedom for Vietnam by working within the mandarinal system rather than against it. In 1933, when he was named Minister of the Interior by Bao Dai, newly returned from France, Ngo Dinh Diem demanded a legislative assembly for Annam. The colonial authorities, who had no intention of permitting representative government in Hue, rejected his proposal. Bao Dai accepted their decision, but Ngo Dinh Diem resigned from government service. He went into retirement in Hue, but kept in touch with nationalists inside the country and abroad, waiting for a more propitious time to intervene in the struggle for independence.

## POLITICS AND SECTS IN COCHIN CHINA

Throughout the French colonial era, Cochin China was administered separately from the rest of Vietnam and had its own elected Colonial Council. Living as they did under direct French administration, the Cochin Chinese were closer to the free interplay of French politics than their countrymen in the protectorates of Annam and Tonkin. A number of Cochin Chinese were even permitted to join in or emulate the political activities of French residents. Thus, a mild Vietnamese reformist group, the Constitutionalist party, was founded during the 1920's. It failed, however, to win either concessions from the colonial regime or respect from the population. Instead, some Cochin Chinese joined the secret parties which existed farther north. Others set up local revolutionary movements which were allowed to function openly. In the 1930's, opposing factions of the Communist party, the Trotskyites and the Stalinists, took advantage of the special conditions prevailing in Cochin China to elect candidates to public office there. At this time the Communist party was outlawed in Tonkin and Annam. The talent of the Trotskyite leader Ta Thu Thau as a public speaker won him a popular following which extended well beyond the small number of party members. In 1936, when Leftists came to power in France's first Popular Front government, Communists from Tonkin and Annam as well as Cochin China were active in the movement which organized throughout Vietnam to demand social reforms.

Outside the mainstream of this Western-type political activity, two groups, far more numerous than the others just described, gained strength in Cochin China—the Cao Dai and the Hoa Hao (see Chapter II). These politico-religious sects drew their strength from the reservoir of nationalism in the population as well as from deeply ingrained local practices and beliefs. The Cao Dai, which had been founded in the 1920's, cut across class barriers to include officials and landowners as well as peasants. Some of its leaders looked to Japan and Prince Cuong De to achieve independence in Vietnam. The less influential Hoa Hao, by contrast, was a peasant movement which coalesced just before World War II around the personality of its prophet, Huynh Phu So. Both sects had an organization and activities which extended well beyond the field of religion to make them real political forces in the south.

# The Japanese Occupation

World War II marked a turning point in the emergence of modern Vietnam. The Japanese intervention in Indochina broke the continuity of French rule. And after Japan's surrender to the Allies in 1945, the division of the country into Chinese and British occupation zones prevented the French from reestablishing their control during this crucial period.

With France defeated in Europe in 1940 and unable to defend its Asian empire, the Japanese had moved into Vietnam to exploit its economic resources and its strategic position. They found it convenient to leave the French administration in place—watched over by a small Japanese occupation army—during most of the war. Japan, contrary to the expectations of the minority of Vietnamese who were actively pro-Japanese, was of no immediate help to the nationalist cause and did not interfere when the French repressed nationalist and Communist uprisings in 1940.

However, the presence of Japanese troops in the country—combined with a Japanese propaganda drive among Vietnamese for an "Asian Co-prosperity Sphere" directed by Tokyo—underlined the isolation of Indochina from France. Admiral Jean Decoux, the French Governor-General, was therefore forced into a policy of closer cooperation with the Vietnamese in the administration of their country, and to greater encouragement of native youth associations and cultural groups. Eventually, some nationalist elements were able to resume action under Japanese protection.

Only on March 9, 1945, when faced by a deteriorating military position, did the Japanese seize Indochina outright from France. This forcible eviction of Frenchmen from the government of Indochina marked for many Vietnamese the real beginning of the end of French rule over Vietnam.

But few Vietnamese were convinced by the "independence" which Japan now accorded them under Bao Dai. Not only did the Japanese ignore Prince Cuong De, who symbolized Vietnamese nationalism to many Vietnamese as Bao Dai did not, but they were obviously unwilling to give the emperor real power. Ngo Dinh Diem, to whom Bao Dai sent an invitation to become prime minister which Diem never received, told this author that he believed that the Japanese had deliberately withheld the invitation because they did not intend to allow Vietnam the independence they knew Diem would expect. The Japanese refused to give Bao Dai authority over Cochin China, and then kept it separate from the rest of the country until the eve of their defeat. However, a number of nationalist groups—among them members of the Phuc Quoc, the Cao Dai and the Hoa Hao, and the Communists—emerged to operate more openly in the south after the French were dislodged from power.

In Hue, Bao Dai finally appointed a famous historian, Tran Trong Kim, to head his new government. For support this government drew on Phan Boi Chau's old Phuc Quoc party and on the newly formed Dai Viet party, as well as on a number of officials and intellectuals. It also inherited youth movements, organized by the French, which were ultimately infiltrated by the Communists.

But the Tran Trong Kim government was totally unprepared to deal with the grave problems which now afflicted the country—famine, the breakdown of administration, and the spread of lawlessness. It suffered in popular esteem from the limitations on its power and its territory, and did not survive the August 1945 surrender of the Japanese, who had brought it into existence.

In 1945 General Charles de Gaulle, farsighted about colonial problems, had a nationalist solution for the Vietnamese problem after Japan's defeat. His solution consisted of returning to Vietnam the exiled Emperor Duy Tan—who had become a military leader in the Free French movement during World War II—to head an autonomous government that could rally popular support. But this plan was foiled by Duy Tan's death in a plane crash, and the field was left open to the Communists.

# The Democratic Republic of Vietnam

On September 2, 1945, in Hanoi, Ho Chi Minh declared the independence of the Democratic Republic of Vietnam. He spoke in the name of the Viet Nam Doc Lap Dong Minh Hoi ("League for the Independence of Vietnam"), or Vietminh, which had emerged from the highlands of Tonkin at the end of World War II. The Vietminh had been founded by the Indochinese Communist party in China in 1941, in coalition with other Vietnamese nationalist groups. In the autumn of 1944 Ho Chi Minh had set up his headquarters at Thai Nguyen in the Tonkinese Middle Region. Here his anti-Japanese position brought his followers American and Free French aid and advisers.

The Vietminh took advantage of the power vacuum left by the collapse of the Japanese to gather around a core which consisted of Ho Chi Minh's Communist party, many nationalist organizations, and individuals dedicated to winning independence. Its leaders convinced the population by able propaganda that the Vietminh alone had the support of the victorious allies, and Bao Dai was frightened into abdicating in its favor. He was then named "Supreme Adviser" to the new government set up in Hanoi under Ho Chi Minh—a coalition representing many political opinions, although controlled by the Communists. In Cochin China—not yet effectively united with the rest of the country—a Committee of the South, also Communist-dominated, seized power.

Ho Chi Minh later tried to persuade Ngo Dinh Diem to join his government, but Ho was less successful with Diem than he had been with Bao Dai. Ngo Dinh Diem refused to cooperate with the Vietminh which in 1945 had killed his elder brother. Many Vietnamese who were considered potential contenders for power died at the hands of the Vietminh during this period, among them such well-known men as Pham Quynh, Diem's successor as chief minister at the court of Hue, and the Trotskyite Ta Thu Thau; in Cochin China, Huynh Phu So, founder of the Hoa Hao, was killed in 1947.

The Vietminh, however, was not left alone in control of the government for long. American policy-makers had been unenthusiastic about seeing Indochina returned to French colonial rule. As early as 1943, President Franklin D. Roosevelt had suggested the creation of an American-Chinese-British trusteeship in Indochina. At one point, prior to the Japanese defeat in World War II, the President even went so far as to offer the region to China, the ancient enemy of the Vietnamese—an offer which the Chinese leader Chiang Kai-shek wisely declined. At the Yalta Conference of the great powers in 1945 Roosevelt again brought up the trusteeship idea, but it was firmly rejected by Winston Churchill, the British Prime Minister. Thus, Roosevelt's desire to see Indochina placed under international trusteeship was never implemented. But some Allied force had to supervise the Japanese surrender. This task was finally divided between the British, operating in Cochin China and Annam up to the sixteenth parallel, and the Chinese further north. Troops from both countries arrived in Vietnam in September 1945.

Britain had decided to cooperate with France in Vietnam and, this mission fulfilled, the British made way for the

French who expelled the Committee of the South from Saigon and sent an expeditionary corps into the southern countryside to win back control of the area.

By contrast, north of the sixteenth parallel, it took the French several months to negotiate for the departure of the Chinese occupation troops. Ho Chi Minh profited by this interim to exploit the greed of the different Chinese warlords and whatever feelings of Asian solidarity they may have had, in order to consolidate his regime. Support was also offered to him by a small group of American Office of Strategic Services (OSS) and army personnel who came to Hanoi at that time. (During the war in the Pacific, OSS teams had been engaged in intelligence operations against the Japanese in Vietnam. Just prior to and after the Japanese surrender, Ho Chi Minh and the Vietminh had been in contact with the OSS. The latter cooperated with Ho, for a time, in his operations against the Japanese.) This brief period of American-Vietminh contact proved of little material benefit to the Vietminh and did nothing to impress on Ho Chi Minh and other Vietminh leaders the advantages of United States friendship. In any case, the encounter was unlikely to produce positive results. The orthodox Communist leaders of the Vietminh saw no reason to further the cause of the American presence in Southeast Asia at the expense of a French government in which the Communist party was then represented. In addition, Ho's past experiences did not predispose him to accept the strings attached to OSS aid. The most far-reaching effect of this abortive experiment in American-Vietminh relations was that, for years to come, it generated among the French a distrust of American policy in Vietnam.

In the autumn of 1945 the new Ho Chi Minh government was forced into immediate—and ultimately successful —action to cope with the famine prevailing in the north. It organized the population in rebuilding long-neglected dikes and in the large-scale planting of "dry" secondary food crops. It also launched an effective campaign against widespread illiteracy by sponsoring popular courses in *quoc ngu* throughout the areas under its control.

The Chinese (under Chiang Kai-shek) were not without political ambitions of their own, and they did their best to strengthen such pro-Chinese nationalist groups as the Viet Nam Quoc Dan Dang (VNQDD) and the more recently formed Dong Minh Hoi, at the expense of the Communists and their allies. Nevertheless, the Vietminh profited enormously from the official neutrality of the Chinese and extended its authority throughout the north. In January 1946 it even organized national elections to endorse Vietminh candidates for office in Vietnam's first national assembly.

When the Chinese finally reached agreement with the French to evacuate the north, Ho Chi Minh was left to his own resources. He had to work out a quick understanding with the French before the troops of General Leclerc, commander of the French expeditionary corps, landed in Tonkin. On March 6, 1946, France recognized the Democratic Republic of Vietnam as "a free state" which was to be part of the Indochinese Federation and of the French Union (the postwar term for the French Empire). In exchange, the French were unopposed by Ho Chi Minh when they landed north of the sixteenth parallel.

## FAILURE OF FRANCO-VIETNAMESE NEGOTIATIONS

But when Ho Chi Minh signed the March 6 accord, he was only bargaining for time, well aware that true guarantees of Vietnamese sovereignty did not yet exist in the system he had agreed to join. The March 6 accord was a vague statement of principle which postponed the necessity for both sides to talk frankly with each other about their true intentions. These intentions were laid bare in all their incompatibility at the

conference held during the summer of 1946 at Fontainebleau, near Paris.

The Vietnamese delegation at Fontainebleau, led by Pham
Van Dong (who was to become prime minister in 1955)
and watched over by Ho Chi Minh himself, was determined
on unity—by which they meant uniting Cochin China with
Tonkin and Annam—and independence. They overestimated
the ability—and the desire—of French Socialists and Communists to impose such terms on their government. The
French government, for its part, might possibly have accepted greater autonomy for Tonkin and Annam. But it
would have conceded this only on condition that Cochin
China and the fertile highlands of southern Annam, where
French business interests were concentrated (and without
which the rest of the country was not economically viable),
remained free of Ho Chi Minh's grip.

To assert France's political control over the south at this
time, the French colonial authorities openly encouraged a
separatist movement among the small pro-French Cochin
Chinese propertied class. The High Commissioner (the postwar title of the governor-general), Admiral Georges
Thierry d'Argenlieu, went so far as to recognize the "Republic of Cochin China." The Fontainebleau Conference broke
down specifically on the Cochin Chinese issue. However, a
temporary compromise agreement was signed by Ho Chi
Minh and the French in September, just before Ho embarked
for Vietnam, leaving the door open for resumption of the
conference. But Vietminh leaders had lost confidence in the
immediate success of any negotiations.

THE WAR WITH FRANCE BEGINS

The last months of peace were used by the Vietminh to
consolidate its power over the country by using force to
destroy the troops of armed nationalist groups—notably the

Viet Nam Quoc Dan Dang and the Dong Minh Hoi—which challenged its authority. The Vietminh also increased its military preparedness. In November thousands of Vietnamese were killed in the bombardment of the port city of Haiphong by French forces in connection with a minor customs incident. This tragic event convinced the Ho Chi Minh government that it had no alternative to armed insurrection against the French expeditionary corps. On December 19, 1946, the Vietminh launched a sudden attack against the French garrison in Hanoi. This was the signal for generalized revolt and the beginning of the war with France which was to last until 1954.

## The Bao Dai Experiment

In December 1946 the Vietminh was supported by the majority of the nation because, when it went to war against France, it carried on a nationalist tradition which stretched back to Emperor Ham Nghi. In communism Vietminh leaders found an ideology, a discipline, and a technique of popular organization which helped to compensate for the military inferiority and political inexperience of the national resistance movement they led. But as the Vietminh progressed toward military victory over the colonial regime, its Communist core abandoned the national-front character of the movement to impose a ruthless Communist orthodoxy on the resistance and eliminate nationalist elements to whom it owed the greater part of its initial successes. This policy, by alienating a growing number of Vietnamese, gradually brought support to the Bao Dai government which in the beginning had been only an artificial creation of the French colonial regime.

The "Bao Dai experiment," as it was called at the time, dated from 1947. When it was clear that the Vietminh would not be rapidly defeated on the battlefield, the French had resigned themselves to sponsoring a rival government for the whole of Vietnam in opposition to the Vietminh. The aim of the French was to rally the non-Communist forces in the country, some of which had already broken with the Vietminh by 1947. The French turned to Bao Dai to head this government. He had left Vietnam early in 1946 and had severed his connection with the Ho Chi Minh regime.

To many of his countrymen Bao Dai did not symbolize the cause of independence. It is not unusual in history, however, to find even puppet rulers transformed by the pressure of events into nationalist leaders—and this happened with Bao Dai. In an attempt to counteract the military successes of the Vietminh, the French relinquished more and more of their political authority to Bao Dai until he received far greater concessions than they had ever been willing to make to Ho Chi Minh. Bao Dai returned as Chief of State to Vietnam in 1949 only after France had recognized the unity of Cochin China with the rest of the country. But the "unity and independence" granted to him was more theoretical than actual, and Bao Dai was not the dedicated political leader who could make real the concessions he had won. This hollow independence was welcomed by the successive French governments of the period, whose Vietnamese policy was strongly influenced by the conservative politician Georges Bidault and his Christian Democratic party, the Mouvement Républicain Populaire (*MRP*).

The first stage in the military operations against the Vietminh ended in disaster for the French expeditionary corps under General Carpentier when the French-held towns at the northern frontier—Cao Bang, Lang Son, and Lao Kay—fell one after the other to the fledgling Vietminh army of Vo Nguyen Giap. By that time the victorious Chinese

Communist forces of Mao Tse-tung, having taken over mainland China, had arrived at the Vietnamese border, bringing aid and support to the Vietminh. The war had ceased to be a matter concerning the French and the Vietnamese alone.

The United States, until then, had been disinclined to become involved in what had seemed essentially a colonial struggle. If Washington had not taken a strong anti-colonialist stand in Vietnam, as it had in other regions of the world, this was partly due to its decision that priority should be given to aiding its Western European allies, and partly because of its suspicion of the Communist leadership of the Vietminh. But with Mao Tse-tung in control on the other side of the Tonkinese border, the Communist issue assumed a dominant role. In line with its policy of opposing the spread of international communism, the United States began to send aid to the French forces engaged in fighting Ho Chi Minh. At the same time Washington attempted to use its influence to gain a more genuine independence for the Bao Dai regime, so that it could extend its popular following. However, this policy did not prove either politically or militarily successful. The Bao Dai government claimed to rule over the entire country and received international recognition, but still was unable to form an effective nationalist regime. And even with the weight of the United States against them, the Vietminh continued to increase their power and their prestige.

This situation led the French to seek negotiations with the Vietminh on the basis of independence and neutrality for Vietnam, and early in 1953, at the request of French President Vincent Auriol, a secret mission made overtures to the Vietminh in Rangoon, Burma. The mission was led by Prince Buu-Hoi, a leader of the overseas Vietnamese community who had played an important role in the Vietnamese war of liberation during its national front phase, and Jacques Raphael-Leygues, a French political figure. These overtures were eventually rejected, because the Vietminh was already committed to maintaining a tight alliance with Communist China, and the Chinese intended the war to go on until they could use it as a means of winning a seat at an international conference table. The failure of this mission ended the hope of achieving a unified, neutral Vietnam in the foreseeable future.

## The Geneva Conference

With no prospect left of achieving a political solution acceptable to the entire Vietnamese nation, the Geneva Conference on Indochina assembled late in April 1954. General Giap achieved military victory early in May at Dien Bien Phu, where he captured considerable French forces. This victory marked the end of the French military effort in Indochina, but the French disaster at Dien Bien Phu was not itself of decisive military importance. (Years later, after another long colonial war, France was to concede independence to Algeria without having suffered a single military defeat.) The importance of the fall of Dien Bien Phu was primarily psychological. It completed the disillusionment and dissatisfaction of French public opinion with the war in Indochina and at the same time convinced Vietminh leaders of the effectiveness of their formula for simultaneously winning a colonial war and establishing Communist domination.

A last-minute French appeal for limited American intervention to stave off the collapse of Dien Bien Phu was rejected by Washington, as public opinion in the United States would not have supported such action any more than did its ally Britain. However, the Ho Chi Minh government realized that it risked American intervention if the peace talks broke down. Undoubtedly this realization influenced the government and its Soviet and Chinese Communist allies to accept the French terms at Geneva, even though these terms seemed to deprive the Communists of half the country. The British played a leading part in seeking a compromise during the conference, while the Americans, although present, remained very much in the background. The State of Vietnam (the Bao Dai government) was also represented at the Geneva Conference, as were Cambodia and Laos because the war had long since spread to their territory as well.

Under the cease-fire agreement of July 20, 1954, France and the Democratic Republic of Vietnam agreed to draw a temporary line of demarcation at the seventeenth parallel, leaving the north to the Vietminh, and the south to the French army and the State of Vietnam. Each side was to regroup its troops and evacuate them from the other half of the country. The entry of fresh troops or military personnel and of additional armaments and munitions was forbidden to both zones. Also banned were the establishment of foreign military bases on Vietnamese soil and the adherence of either zone to military alliances. These terms were accepted and signed by the High Commands of the French and Vietminh armies.

In a Final Declaration, the Geneva Conference attempted to fit this military settlement into a political framework. It noted that the line of demarcation at the seventeenth parallel was a provisional one and should in no way be interpreted as constituting a political or territorial boundary. The independence, sovereignty, unity, and territorial integrity of Vietnam were specifically recognized. According to Article 7, the Vietnamese people were to enjoy the fundamental freedoms guaranteed by democratic institutions. These institutions were to be established as a result of free general elections by secret ballot in July 1956, under the supervision of an International Commission (composed of representatives of India, Canada, and Poland, who also constituted the International Commission for Supervision and Control charged with supervising the carrying out of the cease-fire agreement).

In contrast to the detailed implementation provided for ending hostilities and for the *de facto* partition of the country (including the right of each Vietnamese to decide whether he wished to live north or south of the seventeenth parallel), the Final Declaration offered no long-term perspective for a definitive settlement of the Vietnamese question. The method by which the desirable conditions laid down in Article 7 were to be achieved, was not explained. And even this Final Declaration, vague though it was, did not have the approval of either the State of Vietnam or the United States, although both were represented at Geneva until the end of the conference. The United States government announced simply that it would refrain from the threat or use of force to disturb the Geneva agreements and would view any renewal of aggression in violation of them with grave concern and as seriously threatening international peace and security. The situation was further confused by the fact that France, and not the State of Vietnam, was made responsible under the cease-fire agreement for implementing the Geneva accords south of the seventeenth parallel. The French government, however, pledged itself to respect Vietnamese independence and sovereignty, and to withdraw its troops from the south when asked to do so by the Saigon government; and at the request of Ngo Dinh Diem, France had already evacuated South Vietnam by early 1956.

# Political Institutions

The main political problem of Vietnam today is the attainment of stability. In the north this problem appears to have been resolved under a Communist government ruling through Communist institutions. But in the south the stability which was achieved with such difficulty under Ngo Dinh Diem vanished with the destruction of his regime in 1963, and in 1965 the very existence of the state of South Vietnam was in question.

During this period of anarchy in the south, the National Liberation Front emerged as an unseen government. Under Hanoi's supervision, this political organization directed a Communist-led war against the south. It controlled more of the population, territory, and economic life of the country than did the government in Saigon. The South Vietnamese army, although ill-equipped for this ideological war and deeply divided within itself, remained the only faction capable of forming successive, if ephemeral, Saigon governments. With the decline in the authority of the Saigon regime, its right to speak for the south was challenged even by a number of non-Communist factions in the country.

## One State or Two?

Although the practical effect of the Geneva Conference in 1954 was to divide Vietnam into two independent states, the text of the agreements drawn up at Geneva insisted on the essential unity of the country. No one was more emphatic in regarding Vietnam as one and indivisible than the people most directly concerned with the conflict—the two rival governments of Vietnam, each of which demanded unity on terms favorable to itself.

The pretensions of Bao Dai's government in Saigon to rule over the entire country did not correspond to the political and military means at its disposal. The Bao Dai regime, however, failed to accept and exploit the bitter but real possibility of the emergence of two Vietnamese states when France agreed at the peace conference to withdraw its military forces from the north—leaving half the country to the Communists. Saigon simply took refuge behind the juridical device of refusing to recognize the legalization at Geneva of a Communist state in North Vietnam.

The Democratic Republic of Vietnam in the north, fresh from its victory at Dien Bien Phu, also regarded the division of the country as temporary. It removed its forces from Cochin China and the southern half of central Vietnam, as decided at Geneva, but left behind a subversive organization ready to reopen the drive for the conquest of the south when the time came. According to the Final Declaration of the Geneva Conference, the seventeenth parallel was to be the line of demarcation between the two Vietnams only until general elections were held throughout the country in July 1956 to decide on its future status. In the interim, however, two separate states emerged in Vietnam, almost equal in size and population, although not necessarily in political drive, governmental stability, and natural resources.

## North Vietnam

In 1954, nine years after Ho Chi Minh had proclaimed the Democratic Republic of Vietnam at the end of World War II, he left the highlands where his government had taken refuge during the long war against France, and reestablished his capital in Hanoi. During those nine years the Democratic Republic had covered the country with an intricate administrative network. Its grip on many villages dated back to 1945, when it had first begun to expel the old Councils of Notables and establish its own local Administrative Committees which included Communist party members. From the outset, the Ho Chi Minh government had been particularly successful where foreigners had invariably failed. It had imposed its authority at the village level, breaking down the traditional autonomy which had enabled the villages to hold out against the demands of many previous rulers.

The Ho Chi Minh government operated through a pyramid of Administrative Committees of increasing complexity, each subordinate to the one above. Even in regions nominally under French authority during the war, the Communists had interposed their own organs of government between the

*In 1954 many North Vietnamese fled to the south carrying their meager belongings with them. In some instances they were transported by United States naval vessels.*

people and the French-supported Bao Dai regime, ruling with more or less effectiveness in proportion to the ability of the French and their Vietnamese allies to root them out. The Communist network of committees covered the traditional administrative units of Vietnam but added new units of its own. It grouped together villages (*xa*) into intervillages (*lien xa*), each of whose Administrative Committee was subordinated to that of the district (*huyen*), as each district committee was subordinated to that of the province (*tinh*). The provinces were organized into new and larger units, the zones (*khu*), and out of these the Communists had constructed six interzones (*lien khu*) during the war years. The first four of these interzones extended from the Tonkinese mountains to the southern half of central Vietnam. The other two included the regions which the Geneva Conference awarded to the State of Vietnam.

With the coming of peace, the Ho Chi Minh government set about the difficult task of transforming a resistance movement based on the countryside into a full-fledged government able to carry on the multifold functions of administration in town and village alike. To complicate the situation, some 860,000 refugees fled from the north to the south after the Geneva Conference (in contrast to about 100,000—most of them soldiers—who went north). And hundreds of thousands of other northerners who also wished to leave were unable to do so. The northern refugees were mostly Catholic villagers, but they also included many non-Catholics who came from the urban areas. This group included members of the propertied classes, professional people, officials, and a part of the Nung ethnic minority. Their departure was evidence of the refusal of a large portion of the northern Vietnamese population to live under a Communist regime.

For the Ho Chi Minh government, however, the departure of these people had distinct short-term advantages. True, the north lost a certain number of technically trained men who could have been useful in the work of reconstruction and industrialization that lay ahead. But the departure of the refugees eased the economic situation in the north, if only temporarily, for the rice fields they abandoned were divided among the overcrowded population. More significant, their departure removed from the north a hard core of potential opposition to the Communist regime. By mid-1955, when the transfer of population provided for at Geneva came to an end, no organized opposition to the Ho Chi Minh government was left. This was an element of strength in the northern regime—one such element among many which differentiated it from the regime in the south.

## THE LAO DONG PARTY

During the early national front period of the Ho Chi Minh government, political expediency had dictated the temporary effacement of what was then known as the Indochinese Communist party. This organization was ostensibly abolished in 1945 and replaced by a Marxist study group. In 1951, however, it re-emerged as the Lao Dong, or "Workers'" party, and was the dominant political force in the Democratic Republic. It has grown into an all-embracing organization, overlapping, paralleling, and controlling the various organs of government and administration. The tentacles of the party extend to the smallest hamlet and to each city street, and reach to the highest echelons of the central government. The Lao Dong party dominates the life of North Vietnam and has its cells, or local organizations, wherever people live and work in groups, ranging from the army to the factory.

In marked contrast to the regime in South Vietnam, membership in the northern government has changed very little over the years. As of 1965 Ho Chi Minh was still President, and for a while was also Prime Minister. In 1955 he gave up the post of Prime Minister to Pham Van Dong, who had worked closely with him since the establishment of the Democratic Republic. In 1965 General Vo Nguyen Giap still led the army which he founded, and was also Minister of National Defense as well as one of the five Vice–Prime Ministers. Both Giap and Dong were members of the Politburo (Political Bureau) of the Lao Dong party, which, under the presidency of Ho Chi Minh, is the true governing body of North Vietnam.

Because of the concentration of political power in the hands of the Lao Dong party, the government can allow itself a certain amount of non-Communist window dressing. Thus, there are still non-Communist ministers in the Cabinet who have been members of the Ho Chi Minh government since the outbreak of the war against France—men like Phan Anh, the scholar Nguyen Van Huyen, and Hoang Minh Giam, who serve in the government but have no political power. North Vietnam has also maintained the forms of a multiparty system, with Socialist and Democratic parties—both negligible in numbers and influence—represented in the National Assembly.

Truong Chinh, a leading member of the Lao Dong party, was First Secretary of the party at the time it imposed a disastrous agrarian reform program on the north (see Chapter VII). The violent popular reaction against the harshness of that program in 1956 turned against Truong Chinh personally and cost him his post as party leader. But as a member of the Politburo he remains today one of the most politically important men in North Vietnam. After the agrarian reform program, Ho Chi Minh found it advisable to become First Secretary of the party himself for a few years. Younger men, however, who have made names for themselves in the service of the party, have come to the fore in the postwar period. Typical of them are Le Duan, now First Secretary of the Lao Dong party, and Nguyen Duy Trinh, a Vice–Prime Minister who is in charge of economic planning.

## PRO-CHINESE—OR PRO-RUSSIAN?

In the rare moments when the pressure of domestic and foreign events does not impose a unity of views on the

Communist leaders of the north, they are considered to be divided into two groups of almost equal importance—pro-Russian and pro-Chinese. The choice of what stand to take between China and Russia is particularly urgent for North Vietnam because it depends on both countries for aid in its economic development program and in the war over the future of South Vietnam.

The pro-Russian tendency is represented by almost all those who distinguished themselves during the war against the French—notably Pham Van Dong, the closest associate of Ho Chi Minh; Vo Nguyen Giap, the prestigious leader of the army and past master in guerrilla warfare; and above all that long-time Asian representative of the Russian-led Communist International, Ho Chi Minh himself. The best-known member of the pro-Chinese faction is Truong Chinh. Because the Chinese Communists have favored a more active policy in helping revolutionary wars abroad than that urged by the Russians under Khrushchev and his successors, some observers tend to identify as pro-Chinese any Vietnamese Communist who has urged strong military action in South Vietnam. This pro-Chinese label, however accurate and useful, should not be allowed to obscure the personal and local factors which also play a part when Communist leaders assume policy positions on national affairs.

Evidence of successive shifts in the balance of power between pro-Russian and pro-Chinese groups in Hanoi has been noted from time to time. However, Ho Chi Minh has long been the actual as well as the titular leader of the Democratic Republic. He has so far succeeded in maintaining the maximum independence from China possible in a situation where the vital economic and military interests of North Vietnam leave him little freedom of maneuver. The population of North Vietnam, if consulted, would doubtless choose a closer reliance on Russia rather than subservience to their overwhelming Chinese neighbor. They seem to think that the distance separating Russia and Vietnam would ensure them a certain degree of independence. Ho Chi Minh, the already legendary "Uncle Ho" under whose leadership the Vietnamese ended colonial rule, favors the Russian tie and is personally above political controversy in the north. But Ho is now in his mid-seventies, and it is doubtful whether he is still willing or able to control the struggle for power going on within the Lao Dong party. It is by no means certain that his disciple, Pham Van Dong, will be able to match him in ensuring the continuance of his pro-Russian policy.

## THE CONSTITUTION

The constitution of North Vietnam—a document of major importance in the communization of the north—reflects the exceptional position of Ho Chi Minh in the political life of the Democratic Republic. This constitution refers to the "far-sighted leadership" of Ho in its preamble, and in its main text confers far-reaching powers on the President of the Republic. The present constitution is the second constitution of the Democratic Republic, but the only one it has made any serious attempt to implement. The first constitution, which was adopted late in 1946 on the eve of the war with France, operated more as a legal justification of government than as a working constitution. Even the present document, promulgated in January 1960, appears to be transitional in nature, for its declared aims of building socialism in North Vietnam and of achieving national reunification look forward to a future situation which will require a new set of guidelines.

The 1960 constitution proclaims Vietnam a single entity from Lang Son on the Chinese border to Ca Mau, at the southern tip of the peninsula. In Section 1 it emphasizes the multinational character of the country—the fact that Vietnam is one nation composed of several peoples. The various ethnic minority groups are assured equal rights and duties with the rest of the population. They are guaranteed the right to preserve their own customs and habits, to use their own spoken and written languages, and to develop their own cultures.

Section 2 outlines the economic and social system whereby the economy of the country is to be transformed into a Socialist economy. Its professed goal is modern industry and agriculture as well as advanced science and technology. In this transitional period, provision is made for ownership of the means of production not only by the state and by cooperatives, but also by peasants and other working people, and by "national capitalists." The state guarantees to its citizens the right to possess and inherit private property, but only on condition that they do not use this property to disrupt the economic life of society or to undermine the economic plan of the state.

Mention is made of civil liberties, and representative government is assured by the election of a National Assembly—described as the highest organ of power in the Democratic Republic—which may amend the constitution by a two-thirds majority vote. The bulk of the Assembly's power, however, is in its Standing Committee, a permanent executive committee elected by the Assembly. The Assembly elects the President and the Vice-President. It chooses the Prime Minister on the recommendation of the President. And on the advice of the Prime Minister it also selects the five Vice–Prime Ministers and other members of the Cabinet. With the country living under a planned economy, the Cabinet has grown in size since the end of the war with France, and its work has become increasingly technical. The

President, whose powers overshadow those of the Prime Minister and his Cabinet, may preside over and participate in all Cabinet meetings.

The constitution also describes the system of local administration which has been developed in North Vietnam. It makes no mention of interzones but lists both provinces and autonomous zones. The latter are established in areas where ethnic minorities constitute the majority of the population. Each administrative unit from the village upward has a popularly elected People's Council and its own Administrative Committee. The People's Councils ensure the observation and execution of state laws and they maintain order. They elect and may recall both members of the Administrative Committee and the president of the People's Court at their level (see below). The Administrative Committees, as their name implies, direct the administration of their respective areas, and they carry out decisions of the People's Councils as well as decisions made by higher state organs.

Article 100 of the constitution declares the independence of the judiciary, which consists of the pyramid of People's Courts extending from local People's Courts to the Supreme People's Court at the top. However, even in theory (and certainly in practice) the judiciary has no such freedom of action. The local People's Courts are responsible to the People's Councils, and at the summit of this legal edifice, the Supreme People's Court is responsible to the National Assembly or, when the Assembly is not in session, to its Standing Committee. There is also a People's Control Organ, with units at the local levels, which is controlled from above by a People's Supreme Control Organ responsible only to the National Assembly and its Standing Committee. "The Supreme People's Organ of Control . . . controls the observance of the law by all departments of the Cabinet, all local organs of the state, persons working in the organs of the state, and all citizens." The powerful People's Control Organs "bring justice to all cases subject to inquiry, may suspend prosecution and may participate in judicial operations, and may appeal judgments of lower courts to higher tribunals."

This constitution is part of a general phenomenon which is not limited to Communist countries: the more underdeveloped a country is politically, economically, and socially, the more theoretical is its constitution. Some of the provisions listed above are liberal, especially with regard to civil rights and the supremacy of the National Assembly, but they have not been translated into practice. The work of the various organs of government and administration is dominated by members of the Lao Dong party. And popular elections, when they take place, are controlled by the party.

The first elections to the National Assembly under this constitution were held in 1960 and a number of seats were symbolically left vacant for representatives from South Vietnam. When the four-year legislative term ended in 1964 and new elections were held, Ho Chi Minh, Le Duan, and Truong Chinh were each reelected with majorities of over 99 per cent.

## THE QUESTION OF REUNIFICATION

Since 1954, reunification has been regarded by northern leaders as a matter of life and death for the Democratic Republic of Vietnam. In 1955, when the nationwide elections envisaged at Geneva still seemed possible, the Lien Viet, or "United Front" (which had been created during the war against the French to replace the Vietminh), was replaced by the Mat Tran To Quoc, or "Fatherland Front." This organization was presided over by the elderly Communist personality Ton Duc Thang, with Ho Chi Minh as honorary president. Its purpose was to prepare the way for taking over the south.

The Fatherland Front was headed by a twelve-member presidium which included such leading Communists as Truong Chinh, Hoang Quoc Viet, and Chu Van Tan as well as representatives of the five religions existing in the south—the Cao Dai, the Hoa Hao, the Buddhists, the Catholics, and the Protestants. The program of the Fatherland Front was based on the reunification of Vietnam. Separate legislatures in each zone were to choose a provisional national government that would respect the different economic conditions prevailing in the north and in the south.

In 1965 the Fatherland Front was still in existence. But in view of the fact that there were no reunification moves in 1956, most of the activities of this northern organization remained secret. Both national and international attention has been focused instead on another organization, created in the south in December 1960 on the exact model of the old Vietminh national front: the National Front for the Liberation of South Vietnam. This body is the political arm of the Vietcong which has fought to dislodge the anti-Communist regime in South Vietnam. "Cong" is an abbreviation for Communist, and the designation "Vietcong"—that is, Vietnamese Communist—was used by the southern government to avoid the nationalist connotations which the older term "Vietminh" had in the country.

## South Vietnam

In July 1954 the war which had engulfed the country ended, leaving behind a devastated land. This destruction was not simply a matter of rice fields which had been abandoned and public works which had been destroyed. The Vietnamese had dealt with the physical aftermath of war many times before in the course of their history, and in 1954 South Vietnam had foreign friends—both American and French—standing by to offer any economic aid it needed. Far more difficult was the problem of recreating a unified society out of the shattered remnants of the old.

In the north the appearance of unity had been achieved by a regime forged out of a successful resistance movement using an imported Communist system which had been super-imposed, without much difficulty, on the collectivist bureau-cracy-ruled society of Confucianist times. But no such organ-ized political movement nor ready-made political system existed to impose unity on the anarchic patchwork of groups and clans which remained south of the seventeenth parallel.

The Western-educated propertied class—which included members of the liberal professions (who are known in Vietnamese political terminology as "the intellectuals")— was concentrated in the cities where it had lived under French protection throughout the war. Some of its members had collaborated with the French for no other reason than material gain. Many others had remained aloof from the French-supported Bao Dai regime and had been bitterly critical of its lack of nationalism. These people, relying as they did on the French army to preserve their freedom and possessions against the Communists, but unwilling or unable to take up arms in their own defense, had lived in a political vacuum during the war years.

In the atmosphere of intrigue and corruption which had thrived in wartime Saigon, ambitious politicians had formed factions divided more often by personal jealousies than by ideology. They had no power of their own, and there were no broadly based non-Communist political parties. Therefore,

for support they looked to foreigners who did have power—
first to the French, and later to the Americans. Factionalism
and dependence on foreign powers were to burden the nation
even after the end of the war in 1954.

When the Communist network of political control was
withdrawn from the south—or went underground—after the
1954 armistice, the villages reverted to their traditional
isolation and were again cut off from the central administration. Wide areas of the Cochin Chinese countryside were in
the hands of the politico-religious sects. The Cao Dai and the
Hoa Hao, whose influence had been greatly increased thanks
to French government subsidies, had their own private
armies which had served as auxiliaries of the French army
against the Vietminh. Anti-Communist rather than pro-
French, these were feudal movements which had broken with
the resistance earlier than other nationalist groups after
clashes with virulent Communist elements in Cochin China.
And despite the divisions in their ranks and the corruptibil-
ity of some of their leaders, the Cao Dai and the Hoa Hao
were important political groups in Cochin China.

A third group in the south, the Binh Xuyen, which was
more a gang than a sect, had no religious pretensions. In
1954, under the protection of Bao Dai, it had achieved the
profitable position of controlling both the organized vice and
the police of Saigon-Cholon. Its chief, General Le Van Vien,
who had once played a key role in the anti-French resistance,
had later switched sides and been instrumental in destroying
the assassination committees which the Communists had
established in Saigon during the war.

Both the civil service and the army of South Vietnam were
inherited directly from the French. The corps of Vietnamese
who had spent their professional careers in subordinate
administrative posts under the colonial regime were not

trained to assume any greater responsibility, and many of them were devoid of any ideal of public service. The national army, members of which had fought on the side of the French expeditionary corps against the Vietminh, had only recently been formed. Like the civil service, it had not yet had the occasion to identify itself with the nationalist traditions of the country which the Communists exploited so astutely in the north.

Many of the officials and soldiers who gathered in the south in 1954 came from north and central Vietnam. They were joined in Cochin China by hundreds of thousands of Catholic refugees, mostly Tonkinese whose clerical leaders had governed them in virtual autonomy and had formed them into militia to fight off the Vietminh. Their tightly organized communities set them apart, not only from the southern population in general, but even from the Catholic minority in Cochin China which was more tolerant and more French-influenced than its northern coreligionists.

All these heterogeneous elements lived side by side in South Vietnam. Few common ties existed to bind them together. Most of them knew no greater loyalty than to their family or local leader, and contact with people from other regions served only to remind them of the differences which separated southerners from northerners, and people of central Vietnam from both. South Vietnam achieved international recognition as an independent state at Geneva. But south of the seventeenth parallel there was neither social unity nor political direction, and no real state yet existed. This was the country to which Ngo Dinh Diem returned as Prime Minister in July 1954.

## THE RETURN OF NGO DINH DIEM

Bao Dai named Ngo Dinh Diem as Prime Minister in 1954 on the advice of the French and with the encouragement of the United States. Diem had kept his distance from Bao Dai during the series of compromises the latter had made with France since 1947, and had lived abroad—in the United States, France, and Belgium—in self-imposed exile. In 1954, however, Vietnam was on the verge of achieving complete independence from France when Ngo Dinh Diem assumed the post of Prime Minister. Although Diem was a profound believer in the theory of Confucianist monarchy, he had an acute personal distrust of Emperor Bao Dai because of his past experience with him. Diem resolved this contradiction by agreeing to become Bao Dai's Prime Minister only on condition that he would have full civil and military powers when he went back to Vietnam, while Bao Dai, the Chief of State, remained in France.

Ngo Dinh Diem, a man of central Vietnam and a Catholic, arrived in Saigon to be greeted by public indifference and political effervescence. The army and the sects were restive. Army leaders sought a strong government which could assert effective leadership in the country, while the sects wanted to keep the privileged position they had acquired during the war against the Vietminh and to play an influential part in the new southern government.

For the first time, the articulate Western-educated professional class was also astir. To many of them the coming of peace seemed to have opened an era in which they could at last play a part in determining the future of the south and in determining it on Vietnamese, not foreign, terms. The pride which they had derived from the Vietminh victories was intermingled with a rejection of the brutal methods of communism, and with an awareness of the emergence on the international scene of new Afro-Asian states which seemed able to steer a successful course between the Communist and free-world blocs. These sentiments explained the popular yearning for a regime which could assure them peace and protection from communism while avoiding a purely negative anti-communism, the inefficacy of which had already been demonstrated by the failure of the successive governments of the Bao Dai era.

## ALTERNATIVE POLICIES FOR THE FUTURE

Two alternative policies were then proposed in South Vietnam. One would have aimed at reconciliation between the great majority of southerners who, although non-Communist, had sympathized with the anti-French resistance, and those who had participated in the Bao Dai regime and the French colonial administration. This reconciliation was desired overwhelmingly by the Cochin Chinese population which was to provide the grass roots support for the new state of South Vietnam.

Within the country, this first policy would have led to the use of the fleeting respite from political tensions to build up popular participation in administrative and economic institutions. In foreign affairs it called for neutrality and close links with such new Afro-Asian states as India, with the ultimate aim of taking both Vietnams into the United Nations. It is now believed that had such a policy been adopted the general elections envisaged for 1956 by the Geneva agreements would have given the nationalist group an overwhelming majority in the south. But this policy, which was outlined by Prince Buu-Hoi, was rejected by Ngo Dinh Diem and his advisers.

The second policy was that advocated by Washington. Not having experienced the frustration of the French in Vietnam, the American government nourished the belief that it was possible to transform the then weak Vietnamese society, eager only to bind up its wounds, into a spearhead of militant anti-communism in Asia. This belief seemed to be justified by the outstanding success of Ramón Magsaysay after World War II in the Philippines, a success which was due in substantial part to American advice. Unfortunately, however, there were fundamental differences in history, civilization, and the people themselves between Confucianist Vietnam and the largely Christianized, longtime Spanish and later American colony of the Philippines.

Diem was pressed to discard and treat with suspicion both the liberal elements among the educated class and the non-Communist fighters of the resistance. He failed to give a strong nationalist ideology to the army he had inherited from the French, and left it in the hands of opportunists. The southern population had no desire to live under communism as practiced at that time in the north, but neither did it approve of the government's hostility to veterans of the resistance. The Saigon government therefore—to implement its anti-Communist policy—turned to the more militant among the northern refugees who were pouring into the south, and proceeded to build a regime based on the support of this minority. This course of action, chosen under Washington's guidance, caused the state of South Vietnam grave difficulties, most of which are still unresolved today.

## WAR AGAINST THE SECTS

Thus, the first two years of Diem's tenure in power were devoted by him to a costly and, in many ways, sterile war against the sects. True, by playing off the various sect leaders against one another, he succeeded in annihilating their military strength. The Binh Xuyen was expelled by the army from the Saigon area in 1955. The most dynamic of the Cao Dai generals, Trinh Minh The, joined Diem, but almost immediately was killed in action. The Cao Dai pope fled to Cambodia, and after a long campaign the forces of the Hoa

*The late Cao Dai pope Pham Cong Tac is shown here
during an official visit to Paris. Behind him is his successor
who now directs a branch of the Cao Dai from Cambodia.*

Hao were defeated. Their young leader Ba Cut was executed
in 1956. These military successes brought the appearance of
unity to South Vietnam, but at the cost of forcing significant
segments of the Cochin Chinese population into the opposition and eventually, in numerous cases, into cooperation with
Communist subversion. After these successes the absent
Chief of State, the Emperor Bao Dai, was deposed following
a referendum in October 1955 which declared Diem President of the Republic of Vietnam.

THE QUESTION OF ELECTIONS

The date of July 20, 1955, was the date specified in the
Geneva agreements for the beginning of consultations between north and south to prepare for nationwide elections a

year later. The Diem government refused to hold any such consultations on the ground that elections could not be free in the north. It thus missed the opportunity of giving the Saigon regime a definitive legal basis by demonstrating that elections on broad political issues could be held in the south—to the advantage of Asian democracy over Asian communism. Overtures from the north for economic relations and individual contacts between the two zones were also rebuffed, although had the Hanoi government been permitted to exchange its coal and other raw materials for the rice of the south, the north could have reduced its dependence on Communist China and possibly increased its sense of Vietnamese solidarity.

When the month of July 1956 passed calmly without general elections, Ngo Dinh Diem received acclaim from the United States government and the American press. The apparent stability achieved in South Vietnam, the seeming passivity of the north, and the unruffled relations of the Diem regime with American officials all seemed to justify the policy which had been urged on Diem by Washington in 1954. Some persons, however, deplored the fact that two years had been allowed to pass during which the southern population had not been given any sense of identification with its government or any political incentive to defend itself against a future Communist offensive.

## GOVERNMENT IN THEORY AND PRACTICE

On October 26, 1956, the new Republic of Vietnam acquired a constitution which was modeled in essentials on that of the United States, although some features, like the Economic Council, were of French origin. It provided for a presidential system; the separation of powers between the legislature, the executive, and the judiciary; and the election by universal suffrage of the President, the Vice-President, and the single-chamber legislature (the National Assembly). The President was given even stronger powers than the President of the United States, with the right to declare a state of emergency and to rule by decree. He could also call for a referendum with the consent of the National Assembly. The constitution included a bill of rights and duties, and specifically outlawed communism.

Having been inspired by Western political experience and the institutions derived from it, this fairly liberal and conventional document represented a welcome change for Vietnam. Throughout the two thousand years of Vietnamese history, government had been based on the sense of responsibility of the governing elements and the passive consent of the governed who had never participated in the making of policy. The 1956 constitution provided a legal framework within which South Vietnam might conceivably have evolved genuine republican institutions over the years. But the republican institutions envisaged by the charter were not to become a reality.

The government which emerged in South Vietnam was authoritarian and was built around Ngo Dinh Diem—re-elected President in 1961—as the incarnation of the Vietnamese nation. Elections were carried out at the prescribed intervals, but genuine opposition candidates were not permitted. The one exception, courageous Dr. Phan Quang Dan, elected to the National Assembly by a substantial majority in Saigon, was disqualified when he arrived to take his seat in that body.

The truth was that the Diem government found itself confronted with distinctively Asian and Vietnamese problems which could not be solved merely by following the system outlined in the constitution. Along with representative government, the country needed strong leadership, some form of popular organization which could enable the state to defend itself against anarchy and subversion, and a discipline that could unite the members of this demoralized Confucianist society. Diem recognized these needs, but, lacking a doctrine with broad popular appeal, he identified the welfare of the state with the fate of his own government. Therefore the administrative apparatus was paralleled by semiofficial organizations geared to strengthening the government's hold on the country.

These organizations included the Movement of National Revolution which, backed by the various political pressures at the disposal of the regime, became a mass movement, controlling and rallying its members in support of the government. It was later supplemented by the Cong Hoa, or "Republican" Youth, which included well over a million young men and women, and was politically important enough to be headed by Ngo Dinh Nhu, the President's brother and political adviser. Nhu was also the founder and leader of the Can Lao Nhan Vi, or Can Lao, a secret party whose members operated as the agents of the Diem regime and honeycombed the ranks of the army and the civil service, where they wielded great political influence. But these organizations never achieved the same grip on the population and the same efficiency as the Lao Dong party in the north, and the badly led Movement of National Revolution rapidly degenerated into a weak group of opportunistic government officials. The fact that these various organizations were financed by levies collected from commerce and industry throughout the country, led to accusations of corruption directed against many officials.

Political and administrative power was concentrated in the hands of a few people in Saigon under the direct supervision of the President and his brother Nhu. Supervision of the provinces was exercised through regional Delegates. In central Vietnam another brother, Ngo Dinh Can, an ultra-nationalist and a disciple of Phan Boi Chau, governed with ruthless power, but was on closer terms with the population than were other members of his family.

## THE OFFENSIVE FROM THE NORTH

North Vietnam had never accepted the refusal of the south to agree to its terms for reunification of the country. After the general elections had failed to materialize in 1956, the infiltration of Communist agents from the north was re-

*Voters participate in South Vietnam's first national elections under the 1956 Constitution.*

sumed, first on a small scale and then as a spearhead of invasion when it became clear that the Diem government intended to postpone indefinitely discussions on reunification. The agents left behind in the south when the Communists had withdrawn in 1954 were reinforced by Cochin Chinese and central Vietnamese from south of the seventeenth parallel who had gone north after the Geneva agreements. These men were now dispatched secretly to reestablish contact with their wartime comrades in the villages and towns of the south. They obtained their arms from caches where they had hidden them after the armistice, and from a heavy clandestine traffic across the sea and land borders of South Vietnam. Members of this group formed the nucleus of the Vietcong.

Ideologically, they capitalized on the popular feeling that Diem was linked too closely to the United States, and they used the political slogan "My-Diem" against the regime. "My" means United States, and both within the country and abroad the Communists attacked the Diem government as not truly Vietnamese but rather a semicolonial regime under American domination. Tactically, they resorted to a mixture of propaganda and terror adapted to the specific situation and directed sometimes against arbitrary acts by individual administrators and sometimes against the neglect of the government in rural affairs where competent officials were scarce. From murdering local officials in remote villages, the Vietcong went on to attack isolated army outposts to obtain food and military supplies.

SOURCES OF FRICTION

To counter this offensive from the north, Diem attempted to tighten his control over the population and to make clear his independence of his United States ally. In external affairs, in order to assert his independence, Diem sought and obtained the help of his former opponent Prince Buu-Hoi in building a more workable foreign policy which would put an end to South Vietnam's isolation from the Afro-Asian nations. This policy bolstered considerably the international position of South Vietnam, which by 1963 had achieved recognition from the great majority of the nonaligned states of the world.

However, Diem's pursuit of independence in internal affairs brought him into conflict with the United States. In order to assuage the strong nationalist feelings in the country he discouraged direct intervention by Americans at the local and provincial levels both in the administration and in the implementation of economic programs. His insistence on viewing all technical activities in terms of politics clashed with the general American belief that in underdeveloped countries the most effective weapons against Communist subversion are good administration and economic development. Another source of friction with his American advisers was Diem's increasing tendency to give precedence in the nomination of public servants to the loyalty they showed for his regime rather than to their professional capacity. This tendency became more marked after an abortive coup d'etat organized against him in 1960 by paratroop units, and after the bombing of his palace by two air force officers in 1962.

At the same time, Diem insisted on centralizing under his immediate control all economic and administrative activities in the country, even if such action halted or slowed American-supported programs. The uneasiness of the United States was increased by the unpopularity of the Diem regime in the cities, where measures to reform Vietnamese society (such as the forbidding of both polygamy and divorce) were resented as a Catholic attack on traditional customs. Popular dislike for these measures was heightened because they were imposed on the National Assembly by members who were close relatives of the President and whose presence in the Assembly seemed to give substance to accusations that elections were systematically rigged.

At the higher levels of government, the President's refusal to offer posts to any of his critics removed men of value from participation in the affairs of the country. The bulk of the government, however, had been inherited by Diem from his predecessors and was made up of appointed bureaucrats; some of these bureaucrats were dedicated patriots, others were incompetent and corrupt. Most educated Vietnamese still earned their living as members of the governing bureaucracy, but many of these were as reluctant to assume responsibility as the President was to delegate it to them. Often they abused the power they had.

Critical shortcomings of the administration were concealed from the President, and measures which had proved to be unpopular among the people continued to be enforced by overzealous officials. The bureaucracy was overloaded with paperwork, devoid of any sense of urgency, and both sluggish and ponderous as though it represented an old and secure state instead of a very new one whose existence had been threatened from the moment of its foundation. The President himself, in dedicating the new buildings of the National Institute of Administration, had to warn in 1962: "Remember that administrative work is by no means routine desk work consisting of handling files and mechanically carrying out orders. Particularly in the present circumstances, [war and terrorism] do not allow that public administration officials indulge themselves in a nonchalant automatism, in the pursuit of comforts, in dodging their true responsibilities."

*This Strategic Hamlet is located in Darlac Province in South Vietnam. It was one of many such hamlets created to counter Vietcong influence in the countryside.*

## STRATEGIC HAMLET PROGRAM

The necessity for the government to regain contact with the villages remained acute. The government would not risk elections in which the population could choose its own village councils. In 1961 the government tried to increase its hold over the villages with the aid of the Republican Youth. By that time, however, wide areas of the south had been infiltrated by the Vietcong, and many of the best officials in the country had been murdered. Drastic measures were required to halt this trend.

The government inaugurated the Strategic Hamlet program under which peasants were regrouped in villages which were then fortified. Beginning in 1962, this program was applied throughout the country.

The immediate aim of this program was to provide the peasants who lived in each strategic hamlet with either military security or, at least, psychological defenses against Vietcong penetration, and at the same time to deny to the Vietcong guerrillas any facilities for obtaining supplies and recruits from isolated villages. The long-term aim, as defined by the head of the program, Ngo Dinh Nhu, was to promote democratization of Vietnamese society by giving back political responsibilities to the villages while at the same time improving their living standards and bringing the influence of the regime down to the village level.

In its practical aspects, the hamlet scheme was inspired by the successful British experience in Malaya, where villagers had been regrouped to shelter them from exploitation by Chinese Communist guerrillas. The situation in Vietnam, however, was far more complex than it had been in Malaya, because the peasants and the guerrillas belonged to the same national group, and the ties of the Vietnamese to his ancestral village were especially strong. And Malaya, unlike Vietnam, did not have a Communist state just across the border.

As in every other project undertaken in South Vietnam during this period, the necessary ingredients for success of the hamlet scheme were time, dedicated personnel, and peace. The Vietcong, which understood the threat to their cause represented by the strategic hamlets, did their best to prevent implementation of the program. However, although it was overextended and beset by difficulties, the Strategic Hamlet program was carried through successfully enough to justify the optimism in 1963 of the head of the British Advisory Mission, Robert G. K. Thompson, who had earlier directed the victorious Malayan campaign against the Communists.

CLASHES AND MISUNDERSTANDINGS

But meanwhile, the increasing guerrilla offensive in South Vietnam had led the United States in 1961 to increase its commitment to train and aid the South Vietnamese army. However, the views of the Diem administration and of the American government with regard to the war—as well as on many other matters—seemed by 1963 to be diametrically opposed. The Americans envisaged a war of extermination against the Vietcong in which successes could be measured best by the "kill rate"—in other words, the number of Vietcong dead. The Diem government belatedly had come to recognize that the Vietcong, too, were Vietnamese and that the adversaries of yesterday could change sides tomorrow. It realized that there was an ill-defined zone, which was the battle for men's minds, where it was less important to kill Communists than to give them a chance of changing sides— as the Communists themselves made a practice of doing. But Diem's orders to military commanders to avoid heavy casualties led to misunderstandings on the part of foreign observers and to a belief in Washington that Diem had become "soft" in the conduct of the war.

The Vietnamese army, trained by an American mission since 1955 according to American principles for a conventional war, was ill-equipped for the guerrilla warfare used by the Communist aggressors in the south. Psychologically, the army remained a foreign body among the peasants who considered it as a privileged class more likely to impose hardship on them than to render aid. The army medical corps, for example, which comprised most of the doctors available in the countryside, was instructed to keep away from the sick among the peasants, who received greater consideration from the medical personnel accompanying the Vietcong guerrillas.

Ideologically, the Vietnamese army had been trained in the Western way to resent political interference, even though they were fighting an army whose strength derived far more from thorough political indoctrination than from military power. Diem's desire to exercise close control not only over the army but also over military operations, was in the Vietnamese tradition that supreme military command should be in the hands of a civilian and not of a professional soldier. But only a few American officers, like the American commander General Paul Harkins, appreciated Diem's grasp of local military problems.

The frequent clashes and misunderstandings of Americans with the Diem regime, its growing nationalism in relation to its United States ally, the subordination of all activities, whether military or civilian, to politics and personalities, and the alleged prevalence of corruption—all these factors led many United States officials by early 1963 to wonder whether the war could be prosecuted more effectively if there was a change in personnel at the top level of the Saigon government. The gathering tension in Washington's relations with the Diem regime reached a climax with the outbreak of the so-called "Buddhist affair" in May 1963.

## THE ASSASSINATION OF NGO DINH DIEM

During all the centuries that Vietnam had been a Confucianist state, it had known only one official cult—that of the Emperor, the Son of Heaven, who practiced the necessary rites to intercede for the nation with the powers of Heaven and Earth. The Nguyen emperors, as orthodox Confucianists, had kept Buddhism and Catholicism separate from the state. And under the French, although the Catholic community was favored in practice, the colonial administration was officially a secular system, like the government of France itself.

But by the time South Vietnam gained its independence, there was a new ferment in Asia, where nations like Cambodia and Burma had also achieved freedom from colonial rule and had made Buddhism their state religion. In Ceylon, Buddhism became a determining force in the political life of the country. And Vietnamese bonzes who traveled to Japan witnessed there the rapid development of a powerful Buddhist political movement. In South Vietnam itself, Buddhism had steadily grown in strength since 1954 by exerting its influence over the young people who were frustrated by the lack of political freedom. At the same time, a new generation of Buddhist monks was in touch with the world Buddhist movement and dreamed of making their faith the official religion of Vietnam. They were particularly active in the old city of Hue, the metropolis of Vietnamese Buddhism and the home of the Buddhist patriarch Thich Tinh Khiet. At the forefront of the movement in Hue was Thich Tri Quang, a Buddhist monk who had a compelling personality and the talents of a popular leader.

Although it has been established that the Diem government neither persecuted nor systematically discriminated against Buddhists, the same could not be said of some Catholic officials and priests. By contrast, Ngo Dinh Can, a devout Catholic who held supreme power in Hue, had been known for his benevolence toward the Buddhist movement. But the balance that he had deftly maintained was upset in favor of the Catholics when the Vatican named Monsignor Ngo Dinh Thuc, the most important Catholic figure in the country and the elder brother of the President, as Archbishop of Hue. Incidents provoked by overzealous Catholic officials in the provinces intensified the rising tension between the two communities. The explosion came in May 1963 when the display of the Buddhist flag was forbidden on the anniversary of Buddha. This prohibition led to a Buddhist demonstration in Hue, during which eight people were killed.

Unrest spread rapidly to Buddhist communities throughout the country, and culminated in the spectacular act of a Buddhist monk, Thich Quang Duc, who burned himself alive on a Saigon square. By that time the "Buddhist affair" had aroused international concern. Within Vietnam it went beyond religious matters, becoming a political movement and crystallizing discontent in the urban areas against the restrictions and controls brought about by the war. Therefore, when the Diem government reached agreement with the Buddhist hierarchy on purely religious subjects, this agreement failed to settle the conflict. Buddhist demonstrations against the government continued inside the main pagodas of the country, and students and school children participated in them.

Tension reached its climax when in August 1963 government troops raided Buddhist headquarters at Xa Loi pagoda in Saigon and other pagodas which were also centers of agitation. Numerous monks, Buddhist militants, and students were arrested. These events intensified differences between Diem and the United States government which by then had taken the important step of replacing Ambassador Frederick Nolting with Henry Cabot Lodge in an attempt to transform Washington's policy into one of direct intervention in Vietnamese politics.

American impatience with Diem increased when it was learned that his brother Nhu was in contact with North Vietnam and with the Vietcong insurgents, and was seeking an agreement by which Hanoi would let the Vietcong rebellion subside in exchange for a restriction of the American military presence in South Vietnam. These contacts had been encouraged by India's Prime Minister Jawaharlal Nehru and by France's President Charles de Gaulle, who issued a declaration favoring such a policy of neutralization. But Nhu's secret dealings—directed at arranging terms which, in 1965, would have been considered as close to an ideal solution for South Vietnam—were regarded then by Washington as an outrageous attempt to switch alliances.

A last attempt to mediate between the Buddhists and the Diem government was made by Prince Buu-Hoi, who prevailed on the members of the United Nations to agree unanimously on sending a fact-finding mission to Saigon. But when the UN mission had completed its investigation and the Saigon press announced the imminent release of all the arrested Buddhists and students, all this no longer mattered. For on the next day, November 1, 1963, a military coup was staged against the Diem government.

This coup, the culmination of a series of plots and counterplots, had been prepared by a number of army leaders nominally headed by General Duong Van Minh, with the concurrence of American officials. The following day Diem and Nhu surrendered to the insurgents and were both assassinated by their military guards while being taken to army headquarters. Their ailing brother Ngo Dinh Can was later turned over to the new junta by the United States Embassy and was executed soon afterward.

The overthrow of the Diem government marked the end of nine years of stability and relative calm in this turbulent area of the world. His administration, in spite of its mistakes and its failure to promote healthy political life in the country, had finally evolved into a coherent nationalist regime. And Diem's overthrow was considered by his formidable opponents Ho Chi Minh and Mao Tse-tung as marking the end of the attempt to create an independent state in South Vietnam free of Communist interference.

THE SEARCH FOR A NEW STABILITY

For nine years the government and society of South Vietnam had developed around the personality of Ngo Dinh Diem and the institutions created in his name. The abrupt removal of this regime destroyed the framework of authority which, for better or worse, had held the nation together. The immediate result—far from opening an era of popular and democratic government in which the people would unite behind their elected leaders against the Vietcong—was to plunge the country into anarchy. No elections were held to replace the defunct National Assembly (abolished, along with the constitution, by the military junta immediately after the coup) nor to designate a new leader who could supersede the junta which had replaced Diem. In the general disarray, arbitrary purges paralyzed the administration. These purges were accompanied by a collapse of the Strategic Hamlet program and by desertions in the army and militia. In the wake of these developments, the Vietcong extended their control over large areas in central Vietnam which until then had been considered secure. In the countryside Diem's overthrow meant to the still Confucianist population that his policy of resistance to the Vietcong had failed, and that the "mandate of heaven" had passed to the Communists.

Washington's expectation that stability could be restored by handing over power to political parties (such as the remnants of the VNQDD and the deeply divided Dai Viet) which had opposed Diem, rapidly foundered because of factional rivalries among officers and civilians alike, personal clashes within these small groups, and the political parties' lack of a popular base. An era of political instability accompanied by extension of Communist power was opened, and more than two years afterward the end was still not in sight.

In that period nine different governments succeeded each other by a series of coups. No serious effort was made to replace the abolished 1956 constitution, and governmental nepotism and corruption reached unprecedented levels. The regime formed by the military junta which had overthrown Diem, with General Minh as Chief of State and ex-Vice-President Nguyen Ngoc Tho as Prime Minister, lasted only three months and was then overthrown by General Nguyen Khanh. Khanh managed to last a few months longer with tragi-comic episodes of eclipses and reappearances. This anarchic period was marked by violent communal strife between Buddhists and Catholics in Saigon and cities further north; student unrest; and the appearance of "Committees of Public Salvation," organized in central Vietnam under the Buddhist leader Dr. Le Khac Quyen, which tried to prevent Khanh from establishing a military dictatorship.

A civilian government headed by the Cochin Chinese leader Phan Khac Suu, with another southerner, the efficient Tran Van Huong, as Prime Minister, was rapidly overthrown in January 1964 by General Khanh, who was himself definitively ousted by a coalition of army officers. Suu remained Chief of State and named as Prime Minister a northerner, Dr. Phan Huy Quat, a Dai Viet leader whose government was also short-lived. In June 1965 both Suu and Quat were dismissed by a newly formed military junta. The heads of this new junta were General Nguyen Van Thieu from central Vietnam, who assumed the post of Chief of State, and Air Vice-Marshal Nguyen Cao Ky, originally from Tonkin, who became Prime Minister. This government had to face new conspiracies and smashed an attempted coup led by Colonel Pham Ngoc Thao, a Cochin Chinese Catholic leader who had served in the resistance during the war against France. In the background lurked the strong personality of General Nguyen

Chanh Thi, considered as the military spokesman of the nationalist Buddhist movement in Hue.

The earnest efforts of Ky's government to insure stability remained handicapped by the absence of representative institutions which could express the popular will, and by the passive hostility of the Cochin Chinese population. The growing uneasiness of the Cochin Chinese community, which represents two thirds of the population of South Vietnam, reached even into social and religious affairs. Cochin Chinese Buddhists refused to participate in the operation of a unified Buddhist movement, and remained closer to the Cao Dai and the Hoa Hao and even to the southern Catholic community than to the Buddhists from Hue and from the north.

## THE NATIONAL LIBERATION FRONT

As early as December 1960, the Communists had taken into account the uneasiness of the Cochin Chinese when they established an ostensibly Cochin Chinese organization, the National Front for the Liberation of South Vietnam, to lead the resistance against the Saigon government. They chose a Cochin Chinese lawyer, Nguyen Huu Tho, a non-Communist, to act as its president. The Front was directed by an executive committee modeled on the Politburo of the Lao Dong party in the north. This secret body coexisted with an official organization similar to the northern Fatherland Front, in which both Communist and non-Communist groups were represented. Twenty-one of the fifty-one seats in this official organization were to be filled eventually by political figures now in the areas controlled by the Saigon government. The Communist party operated within the Front as the Nhan Dan Cach Mang, or "People's Revolutionary party." The best-known political leader of the National Liberation Front was Nguyen Van Hieu, who held the post of Secretary General and acted as the Front's able spokesman on the international scene.

Officially, the Front envisaged a transitional period during which, inside the country, a provisional state would be formed to carry on until ultimate reunification was achieved, while in foreign affairs, it would assume a Communist-inclined neutrality. During the Diem period, the Front also spoke of creating a "zone of neutrality and peace" with Cambodia and Laos, and emphasized the sovereign and independent status of this provisional state of South Vietnam —concessions to the West which, for all practical purposes, were dropped after Diem's overthrow.

Meanwhile, the Front operated as a government in the south. It had its own army, the Vietcong; levied taxes; and carried on administrative and social functions not only through its own agents but also, occasionally, by persuasion or force, through agents of the Saigon government. In foreign affairs, it sent its own missions abroad, not only to Communist countries but also to neutralist states.

# Economic Institutions

For centuries the most typical sight in the Vietnamese countryside has been the peasant working in the rice field. Wearing a sort of pajama and a wide conical hat to protect himself against sun and rain, he laboriously tills the land, using implements which are not very different from those used by his distant ancestors. Though his farming methods are primitive, they have nevertheless created a rice-growing economy which has enabled the Vietnamese nation to expand across the length of the peninsula and maintain the population at a high rate of increase.

However, rice growing based on primitive methods has not been able to liberate the peasant from dependence on the caprices of tropical nature, or guarantee to him and his family even the simple necessities of life. Thus, after partition in 1954, the governments of North and South Vietnam undertook to enlarge and improve the economic base of the nation by modernizing agriculture and industry.

Since 1954 the Hanoi government has been committed to rapid industrialization of the north, on the pattern of Communist China. To achieve industrialization, it regimented the peasantry and treated agriculture primarily as the cornerstone on which industry had to be built. In the south, by contrast, agricultural development was given priority. But vital reforms in land distribution were neglected, and industrialization was unnecessarily delayed. However, despite errors in formulating and executing policy, the hard work of the Vietnamese people, combined with generous help from abroad, produced a period of unmistakable growth in both zones of this divided country between 1955 and 1963.

The measure of this Vietnamese achievement can perhaps best be appreciated only now, when the destruction of war has wiped out much of this advance. Vietnam, once the richest colony in France's prewar empire, has been transformed by war into the poorest country in Southeast Asia. In many regions, both in the north and in the south, the country is slowly reverting to a backward village economy based entirely on the peasant and the rice field.

# Problems of Independence

The artificial boundary drawn across the center of Vietnam did not alter the essentially agricultural and traditional character of either half of the country. In 1954, after the long armed struggle against the French had ended, the newly independent governments of Hanoi and Saigon fell heir to problems very much like those which had confronted Le Loi in the fifteenth century after his victory over the Chinese, and Gia Long four centuries later after the defeat of the Tay Son. Enormous areas of agricultural land, abandoned during the war years, had to be won back for cultivation. Hydraulic works needed to be repaired, and new ones constructed. And much of the country's communications system had to be rebuilt.

But although these problems were very old, new methods were necessary in 1954 for dealing with them. Even had Vietnam returned to the economic conditions of colonial times (and in the production of some commodities it never did achieve prewar levels), this would not have been enough. No independent twentieth-century Vietnamese government could afford to ignore the extreme underdevelopment of the country, the widespread rural poverty, and the pressure of the rapidly increasing population on available resources. Before World War II the yield of Vietnamese rice production per acre was one of the lowest in Asia. Agriculture had thus been overemphasized at the expense of industry, and commerce at the expense of both. And the economy of the country had been largely in the hands of the French and the Chinese.

Even had Vietnam been allowed an extended period of peace and unity, improvement of these conditions would probably have been a long and difficult process. The great majority of the population still knew no other life than subsistence agriculture, while the small propertied class drew its wealth from absentee landlordship and usury and saw no reason why it should not continue to do so. Only a very limited pool of technically trained Vietnamese existed. As individuals some of them were at least as competent as their counterparts in more developed countries, but because of the unsettled political conditions in Vietnam, many preferred to pursue their careers abroad.

All these problems of reconstruction and development were vastly complicated by the partition of Vietnam. Partition cut each zone off from the resources of the other. The overcrowded north was cut off from the agricultural wealth of the south, just as the south was deprived of the raw materials of the north. Thus, each zone had to waste effort in trying to find substitutes for the resources of the other. Partition also forced both north and south into far greater reliance on their respective allies than would have been the case had the country remained united. Although most of the newly emerging countries have been able to supplement the foreign aid they receive from one of the world's power blocs with aid from the other, Vietnam was not able to do so. Hanoi and Saigon each had to rely completely on one bloc, with all of the resulting problems of political dependence that this situation involved—Hanoi on the U.S.S.R. and Communist China, and Saigon on the United States.

The state controlled economic life, not only in the Communist north, but even, to a considerable extent, in the south. This situation resulted from the underdevelopment of the country; from its Confucianist traditions, which left the initiative in economic matters to the administration; and from the political convictions of its leaders. Differences in ideology and in local conditions affected the manner in which north and south attacked the problem of economic development and caused major variations in approach.

# North Vietnam

After an initial three-year phase of reconstruction, the north launched a three-year economic plan in 1958 under Communist leadership, and in 1961 embarked on a more ambitious five-year plan. Priority was given to rapid industrialization, and especially to the development of heavy industry. But unable to meet its declared goals, the government continued to revise them downward in both agriculture and industry. Even so, the statistics it has issued are impossible to verify and must be regarded with caution.

## THE STRUGGLE FOR FOOD

Economic life in the already overcrowded northern plains was dominated by the high birthrate which led to chronic food shortages; in certain areas the density of the population reached more than two thousand inhabitants per square mile. To feed its hungry population, Hanoi concentrated on improving the yield of cultivated land, and also sought to increase the area under cultivation. Barred by the seventeenth parallel from the underpopulated southern plains, the north tried to develop its own back country which lowland Vietnamese had traditionally regarded as unhealthy and alien. More than half a million people were transferred to the highlands in the back country where they had no choice but to support themselves by raising new crops. At the same time peasants were enrolled in labor battalions to build dikes and dams, thus carrying on the ancient Vietnamese tradition of compulsory labor on hydraulic works. A number of small electric pumping stations were established in the northern delta for irrigation and drainage. Rice output, only about 1.5 tons per 2.5 acres before World War II, rose to about 2.2 tons per 2.5 acres. And improved irrigation and drainage made possible the harvesting of two and sometimes even three crops a year in many areas.

But despite these achievements, productivity remained low, in part because of the shortage of fertilizer. Of more than a million tons of fertilizer required every year to enrich the exhausted soil of the Red River Delta, only some 100,000 tons were available. And yet, more fertilizer than ever was needed because the big hydraulic works increased the drain on soil resources by permitting more frequent rice harvests. Improvement of yield by the use of scientific plant breeding was begun only recently and on a limited scale.

Mechanization, which could also have helped to increase output, was largely confined to some fifty-nine State Farms devoted to raising various crops hitherto concentrated in the south, such as rubber, coffee, and tea; oil-bearing crops, such as peanuts; and livestock. The Communist bloc sent only a small number of tractors and agricultural machines, and the peasant cooperatives—now the usual form of agrarian organization in the north—still had to rely on draft animals. Despite a reported rise in livestock production, as of 1965 these animals still seemed to be in short supply.

The five-year plan at first optimistically aimed at a yield of 7.7 million tons of rice in 1965, or twice the figure achieved ten years earlier. When harvests did not live up to expectations, this goal was lowered to a more modest figure. The escalation of the war soon made all such economic predictions meaningless. The production of such crops as textile plants, sugar cane, and tobacco, was reported to have increased considerably, as was fish culture. But since 1960, food production has been unable to keep pace with the annual rate of population increase—estimated to be as high as 3.6 per cent a year. With barely enough rice to feed its population, and with food grown by government order even in gardens around schools and official buildings and army barracks, the government counted heavily on secondary food crops to supplement the rice supply. Corn, yams, beans, and manioc, none of them liked by Vietnamese, have all become increasingly important in the diet of the people of the north. The recurrent famines which afflicted the poorer areas until

World War II have disappeared. But a decline in living standards has been noted in the cities, particularly Hanoi, where signs of malnutrition have been observed. The government stringently limits the amount of food distributed to each family even with respect to cereals, and there is a permanent shortage of meat and fats.

## LAND REFORM

These difficult conditions did not discourage the Communists from attempting to transform the structure of economic life in the countryside. They began in wartime to alter the pattern of land ownership. The destructive impact on northern society of the 1954–56 land reform program—carried out primarily for political reasons and in disregard of economic conditions—will be described in Chapter VII. The professed goal of this land reform was the seizure of land held by wealthy landlords and its redistribution among the poor peasants. But this goal had little economic meaning in a region where, before World War II, more than 98 per cent of the landowners had holdings of less than 12.3 acres, and private holdings larger than 123 acres accounted for only one fifth of the total cultivated area of Tonkin and just one tenth of that of Annam. By 1954, most of the rice land north of the seventeenth parallel had long since been subdivided into tiny parcels, and the real problem was not one of too few small landowners but one of too many small landowners to permit efficient farming.

The total amount of land confiscated and redistributed to the peasants under the agrarian reform program is uncertain. According to a Soviet estimate, 1,733,940 acres were divided among 1,500,000 families who would thus have received about one acre each. A more recent Hanoi figure—2,000,000 acres for 2,104,100 families—would bring the share of each down to a little less than one acre. In any case, the ultimate result of Communist agrarian policy was not an increase in private holdings but rather their absorption in cooperatives as a step toward the total collectivization of northern agriculture.

The cooperative system was also applied to other branches of individual and family activity ranging from fishing to handicrafts, and even extended to the mountain regions occupied by the ethnic minority groups, where more than four fifths of the population was reported organized into cooperatives. In semi-socialized agricultural cooperatives the members, in addition to compensation for their labor, received a small sum in proportion to the amount of land they had contributed to the common holdings. In the fully socialized cooperatives this land payment was discontinued.

Although the North Vietnamese agrarian reform program was originally inspired by the example of Communist China, Hanoi did not go as far toward collectivization as its northern neighbor. The Vietnamese· stopped at the cooperative stage and made no attempt to organize communes on the Peking model.

## INDUSTRIALIZATION AND FOREIGN AID

The chronic food shortages in the north acted not as a brake on industrial development but, on the contrary, as a spur toward industrialization. The north never regarded the seventeenth parallel as a permanent boundary between the two Vietnams and looked to the agricultural riches of the south to complement its industrialization when the country was reunified. In the meantime, the building of heavy industry, considered as the only means to end underdevelopment, took precedence over attempts to raise living standards.

But the hardworking northern population, which included

*The Hon Gay coal mine is one of the few anthracite coal mines in the world which is in the open air.*

many skilled artisans, had to acquire technical knowledge and experience before they could operate and develop the mining and industrial enterprises inherited from the French. As new industries were built, with substantial economic aid and technical assistance from the Communist bloc, workers had to learn to operate them. And there was little margin for the frequent mistakes and delays which usually attend a policy of rapid industrialization imposed on a backward agricultural society.

The mining industry was reorganized with generous U.S.S.R. and Eastern European help. Industries which were carried over from the colonial period and then expanded included not only the Hon Gay coal mines and metal ore mines in the northern highlands, but also the Haiphong cement works and the cotton mills at Nam Dinh. A number of new plants, whose manufactures ranged from plastic objects to processed food, tobacco, and tea, were built by the Chinese and the Russians. Both Moscow and Peking made major commitments to help in carrying out the five-year plan, and important technical assistance came from East Germany and Czechoslovakia. In the field of heavy industry, the most impressive enterprise—which was constructed with Communist bloc aid—was the iron and steel complex in the Tonkinese Middle Region at Thai Nguyen. Several other development centers were built north of Hanoi; these included the industrial installations at Uong Bi and the electrical and chemical complex at Viet Tri, whose plants produced such varied commodities as refined sugar and antibiotics. The north hoped it would be able to diminish its dependence on foreign aid to only 15 per cent of the budget by 1965. However, this and many other hopes were dimmed by escalation of the war.

Industrial development was made possible by the enormous amounts of coal available in the north. Most of this coal was located in the Quang Yen basin and was easily accessible, either to barges for transport along inland waterways to the new industrial centers, or to seagoing ships for transport abroad. Coal production was reported to have reached 3,520,000 tons in 1964. Iron ore, too, was not lacking and pig iron is already in production at Thai Nguyen. But no steel had been produced at Thai Nguyen by 1965, although the plan called for 220,000 tons. Extensive deposits of apatite, out of which fertilizer is made, were also part of the north's wealth. Other mining products were wolfram, tin, chromium, and zinc. Cement production, still one of the basic elements of northern industry as it was during the colonial period, was said to have reached almost 6,600,000 tons in 1964.

Even without the destruction caused by the war, it would have been impossible to achieve the goals set forth in the five-year plan without a parallel development of electrical energy and the construction of a better communications network. Progress in both these essential fields was announced in 1964. More technical workers were also trained but not yet in the numbers required by the ambitious industrialization plans of the north. It was claimed that light industries (such as textiles and paper) supplied 90 per cent of current consumption needs. However that may be, it is important to emphasize that these needs were kept to the barest minimum.

The Communists put an end to private industry and commerce in the north, leaving only so-called "state and private joint enterprises," in which the former owner managed the enterprise for the state. All French investments in North Vietnam were expropriated. Eleven years after the Geneva Conference the only economic link remaining between North Vietnam and France was a small amount of trade. About 80 per cent of northern commerce was with the Communist bloc. The rest was divided largely among Japan, Hongkong, and various countries of Western Europe. Under an annually renewed commercial agreement, France imported 110,000 tons of coal per year from North Vietnam and also granted Hanoi use of five-year credits for purchases of machinery and trucks. North Vietnam exported products of its mines, forests, and agriculture, and cement, light goods, and handicrafts. However, these exports left a sizable gap between what the north could earn abroad and its import requirements for fulfilling its industrial plans.

The north had to rely heavily on the Communist bloc for

aid, first for reconstruction and then for economic development, and grants and loans thus received are estimated to have already gone beyond the billion-dollar mark. More quantitative help may have been given by Peking than by Moscow, but the U.S.S.R. and Eastern Europe provided most of the vitally needed machine tools, electrical equipment, and modern means of transport. There were conflicting reports as to whether Moscow withdrew technical assistance promised in connection with the five-year plan when North Vietnam sided with Peking in opposing the nuclear test ban treaty in 1963. Reports also conflicted as to what extent this policy was reversed after escalation of the war, if indeed it was a policy at all. In any case, Hanoi signed additional economic agreements in July 1965 with both Moscow and Peking.

Despite the aid Hanoi received from the Communist bloc, the inferior quality of North Vietnamese finished goods hampered efforts to exchange them for foreign currency, and in 1963, when a poor harvest compelled Hanoi to seek food abroad, it could not afford to pay for Australian wheat. Foreign aid never reached sufficient proportions to meet the excessively ambitious goals of the five-year plan. The overburdened workers were left struggling to achieve industrial goals imposed on them by a government which had not made allowances for their limited technical experience and insufficient material equipment.

## South Vietnam

When President Diem took over the government of South Vietnam in 1954, the economy was not his most urgent concern. In addition, the 1955 resignation of the talented Minister of Economy, Nguyen Van Thoai, and his team of

*During the colonial period rubber became one of Vietnam's most important industrial products. Shown above are workers in a modern tire-recapping plant near Saigon.*

experts, further slowed the beginning of economic development in the south. When this development was finally undertaken, it was hampered by the contradiction between the necessity for the state to manage certain sectors of the economy, and the necessity for adherence to the free enterprise system which was basic to the American economic aid program, the main source of economic revitalization.

An American aid program based on minimum interference

by the state in the conduct of business affairs had been highly successful in postwar Western Europe. But this method, which had worked so well within the framework of the Marshall Plan, proved inadequate in an underdeveloped Asian country just emerging from colonial status, where industry was practically nonexistent and the economic life-lines were controlled almost entirely by foreigners. The attempt to reconcile the free enterprise system urged on Saigon by the Americans with the need for drastic action by the state itself, in order to place the economy on more balanced foundations and to encourage its growth, led to halfway measures; and forceful measures necessary to speed up the country's economic development were postponed.

In spite of these limitations, two five-year plans, one begun in 1957 and the other in 1962, were introduced and carried through—until the deterioration of the military and political situation which followed the death of Ngo Dinh Diem put an end to economic planning. At first the emphasis had been simply on raising the level of agricultural production. This, it is true, was no small task. But growing concern in government circles over South Vietnam's extreme and continuing dependence on American economic aid led to a policy of encouraging the growth of light industry and mining, with the declared goals of filling more of the country's needs out of local production and reducing imports of consumer goods.

Agriculture in the south made great strides after 1954, and by the end of 1963 it was estimated that almost half the land suitable for agriculture was being farmed. Much of the additional five to six and a half million acres which could still be opened to cultivation was located in the area of the High Plateaus. But since 1963, intensification of the war made it increasingly difficult for the peasant to harvest his crops, still more difficult to ship his surplus to the cities, and impossible to open new lands to cultivation; and many fertile lands were abandoned.

## RESETTLEMENT

When the French first arrived in Vietnam in the nineteenth century, they found two small Vietnamese colonies in the central highlands. But it was only after 1954, under Diem, that settlement of the highlands became a major concern of the government. It was a favorite project of President Diem, who took special pride in the new provinces which were carved out of the wilderness in the mountains and in the sparsely settled or uninhabited areas of Cochin China. Saigon could not afford any delay in opening new lands to agriculture because the northern refugees who streamed into the south in 1954 and 1955 had to be resettled and rapidly integrated into the country's economic life.

These skilled and hardworking farmers from the north were resettled in Cochin China and on the High Plateaus where they set about increasing the agricultural resources of their new land. In Cochin China, in the area of Cai San alone—a development project which benefited from substantial American aid and became a showplace of the regime—they reclaimed some 190,000 acres of rice land and produced some 110,000 tons of rice a year. In the border regions, as in the unsettled expanses of the highlands and the plains, these refugees offered an additional advantage to the state by forming a barrier against Communist infiltration.

The new settlers in the central highlands were not only northerners but they also included people who had been born in the poor and overcrowded plains of central Vietnam south of the seventeenth parallel and had been sent to land-development centers in the plateau regions. Here, virgin land was cleared by bulldozers. At first the colonists were provided with rice by the government and they grew only secondary food crops and crops for industrial uses. But after a while the colonists became rice growers, too, and by 1959 had already produced almost 110,000 tons of this basic component of the Vietnamese diet.

# The Problem of Agrarian Reform

The resettlement program was one of the more spectacular successes of the southern regime. But the plight of the local peasantry, families born and raised in Cochin China but possessing no land, remained unsolved. Even before World War II an estimated 45 per cent of the cultivated area of Cochin China had been concentrated in the hands of 2.5 per cent of the population, with holdings ranging from just over 123 acres to well over a hundred times that amount. An estimated two out of three farmers possessed no land of their own and struggled hopelessly against the grinding burden of exorbitant rents and usurious interest on their debts, living entirely at the mercy of their landlords. During the war against France, when many of the owners of large estates fled the countryside, the Vietminh had encouraged tenants and agricultural workers to take over their land for themselves. But after 1954, when the Vietminh had ostensibly evacuated the south, many landlords were able to regain possession of their land and began to collect back rents. Thus, the classic problem of Vietnamese society reappeared —the concentration of rice fields in a few hands and the growth of a landless class of tenant farmers and agricultural workers. Throughout Vietnamese history this condition had presaged agrarian unrest and political revolution.

The southern government tried to deal with this situation

by stages. In 1955 land rentals were lowered from the 40 per cent or more of the principal crop which had been customary in the past, to 15 to 25 per cent. The landlord-tenant relationship was defined in a written contract to avoid abuses. And credit was made available to the farmer on moderate terms so that he would not have to turn to the usurer. But the core of the program was the 1956 decree which limited private holdings of rice land to 247 acres. The surplus was to be bought up by the government and sold to the landless, who were to pay for it in six annual installments.

Almost 1,729,000 acres of land came within the scope of the program. Land in excess of 247 acres was held by 2,033 Vietnamese, totaling some 1,048,750 acres. (The remainder, which was in the hands of French citizens, was acquired for redistribution by Diem's government with funds provided by France.) By July 1961, the Vietnamese government had taken over 1,027,132 acres of rice land, and more than half that amount—574,154 acres—had been transferred to 109,438 tenants.

But in spite of these achievements, the agrarian reform program in the south remained handicapped both by its timing and by the methods used to implement it. Measures which would have been liberal in prewar Cochin China were regarded in a very different light by Cochin Chinese farmers who had already been told by the Vietminh that they might keep the land they had occupied during the war years. These farmers now saw no reason either to rent or buy what they regarded as already theirs. As a further complication, the implementation of the program was often entrusted to the landowners themselves, members of the southern government and administration, who were reluctant to recognize any need for the concessions required of them by law. There was no sense of urgency about carrying out land reforms.

Thus, when the Vietcong started its subversion in the south, it was able in many areas—where the Vietminh had been active before—to reassert its control over the very peasants whom a drastic and effective agrarian reform program might previously have won over to the legal government.

## PROGRESS IN AGRICULTURE

Despite these handicaps, as well as the halt in the building of agrovilles (agrarian towns designed to concentrate rural life into large centers in order to ease the life of the peasant) and the revolution in village life caused by the rapid development of the Strategic Hamlet program in 1962 and 1963, the southern regime continued to achieve agricultural progress during the Diem period.

Irrigation works were built to return regions to cultivation, to open up new lands, and to improve the yield of the older settled areas of South Vietnam. Some regions, plagued by water heavily charged with salt and alum, were drained and irrigated by a network of canals; and a few fields began to produce two crops a year. Although spared the dramatic overcrowding and fragmentation of farmland which afflicted the northern plains, South Vietnam, too, had to grapple with population problems caused by its soaring birthrate. Diem, in the last year of his life, looked to construction of new hydraulic works to improve irrigation in the central Vietnamese plains and to extend the small area already producing two harvests a year in Cochin China.

Improved water control, the beginnings of mechanization, and better farming techniques—principally the growing use of fertilizer—combined to improve the yield of rice production. Output reached 5,858,600 tons in 1963. However, even in time of excellent harvests the rising domestic demand for food limited exports, and the country never resumed its prewar position as a major exporter of rice. Natural disasters and wartime conditions pared down still further the amount of rice available for sale abroad. In 1964, Vietcong activity made it impossible to transport large quantities of grain to the cities, and by 1965 South Vietnam, paradoxically, was compelled to import at least 200,000 tons of rice from the United States to feed the besieged urban areas.

To diversify its agricultural resources, the south under the Diem administration grew a variety of secondary food crops —starchy roots (sweet potatoes, yams, and manioc), fruits, vegetables, maize, peanuts, and soya, from which the sizable vegetarian contingent of the population derived its main source of protein. Coffee, tea, and tobacco were also grown. The production of livestock and poultry increased, and ducks, which thrived in the canals and rivers, represented a significant source of exports—the bird itself, its eggs, and its feathers. The production of hogs, which provide the favorite meat of the Vietnamese, also increased for local consumption and export. New fisheries were established and some of their frozen products were shipped abroad as far as France.

Notable results were also achieved in such crops for industry as sugar cane and the textile plants (kenaf, ramie, and jute) which were grown for the first time on the High Plateaus. Silkworm culture was renewed, and the production of another essential raw material for traditional handicrafts, lacquer, was introduced in the south for the first time in the form of lacquer tree plantations.

Significant as were these moves toward diversification, rubber remained the country's major cash crop. With the help of government loans to plantation owners, the area planted in rubber almost doubled between 1954 and 1961; and improvements were made in rubber culture. Almost all the rubber produced was exported, and in 1963, for example, out of a total production of 79,000 tons, 67,000 tons were sold abroad. It will be a long time before such figures are achieved again because beginning in 1964 many of the large plantations were devastated by aerial bombings of rebel positions; and any sizable amount of rubber still being produced could not reach the city because of dangerous conditions that prevailed on the roads. Some of the big plantations closed down entirely.

## TRADE AND AID

Despite attempts to diversify agricultural production and grow industrial crops which might some day find new and more lucrative markets abroad, rice and rubber represented close to 90 per cent of the value of South Vietnam's exports annually. France was still the main purchaser of Vietnamese products during the first decade of independence. These strong commercial ties were explained by the traditional trade links which survived between France and its former colonies, as well as by the substantial investments retained by Frenchmen in South Vietnam after 1954.

The injection of massive American aid into the southern economy gradually destroyed this pattern of trade even though the United States was unable to replace France as the main market for Vietnamese goods. In 1964 France bought about one third of the total value of South Vietnamese exports, mostly rubber and tea—both grown largely on French-owned plantations. But France's already diminishing role as a source of imports dropped sharply that year as a result of anti-French measures taken by Saigon early in 1964 in retaliation against President de Gaulle's stand in favor of neutralization of Vietnam. The United States, whose importance in the Vietnamese market as a source of supply (but not as a customer) continued to grow, provided 42 per cent of its imports, and was followed by Japan and Formosa.

At no time since 1954 was South Vietnam able to pay for even half of its annual imports by selling its own products abroad. In 1960, a peak period, its trade deficit was $155 million; in 1963, with imports at $286.2 million and exports at $77.2 million, its deficit had risen to $209 million and its exports covered only 27 per cent of its imports. These deficits were paid for by the American economic aid program. Since 1961 United States financial aid was no longer available to subsidize imports from nineteen industrialized countries, including Western European countries and Japan, and South Vietnam was compelled to buy from the United States many goods which it could have acquired at prices 15 to 20 per cent lower from Japan. This departure from natural commercial practices increased the already unavoidable dependence of the Vietnamese economy on United States financial aid.

As of June 30, 1964, American economic aid had reached $2,155.4 million of which all but $93.7 million were grants. The amount of military aid has been kept secret since 1963 and therefore its repercussions on the economy cannot be accurately estimated. American aid financed not only the major part of Vietnamese imports but also the budget deficit, which generally represented about a half of total government expenditures. Only 10 per cent of the South Vietnamese government's revenue was derived from direct taxes. Because of the unsettled conditions prevailing in the country for many years, the census of taxable citizens is very inaccurate, which accounts for the fact that perhaps only one hundredth of the Vietnamese population paid any taxes at all.

With so much of the American aid funds devoted to commercial imports and to government expenditures, it was not surprising that the economic structure of the country inherited from colonial times changed only slowly. Under Diem the Chinese were excluded from eleven major commercial and business activities, and pressure was put on them to become Vietnamese citizens. However, these measures did not produce any sizable degree of assimilation. The Vietnamese were as unable to compete with the Chinese as they ever had been. They watched helplessly as Chinese businessmen, operating through their well-organized trade circuits in Hongkong, Macao, and Singapore, began to reap profits from the American program of commercial aid. The Chinese also continued to profit from their control over local commerce in general and the rice trade in particular.

The Chinese were more interested in trade, banking, and usury than in industry. Many French commercial firms, however, with their assets frozen and threatened with further interference by the state, did invest in industry. By 1965, French investments were divided largely between industry and agriculture (notably rubber, tea, and coffee plantations, where French interests still dominated), and amounted in all to some $320 million. Frenchmen remained important in foreign trade, land and sea transport, public services, and real estate. The Banque de l'Indochine, which had once dominated much of the Vietnamese economy, now had only 2 to 3 per cent of its total holdings in Vietnam, and was supplemented by other French banks. Thus, the French were able to handle a substantial part of South Vietnam's banking activities. This portion was estimated by Vietnamese sources at more than one third of the total in 1964.

## BUILDING NEW INDUSTRIES

The war brought to a halt a number of industrial projects in the south, but it is still interesting to record the progress made in this field since 1957 when the first five-year plan went into effect. American economic aid and technical assistance were indispensable in carrying out both five-year plans. But because of rigid Washington policy, only a relatively

*The United States A.I.D. program has helped to create modern plants such as this one in South Vietnam.*

small part of this economic aid could be assigned to specific large-scale industrial or agricultural projects. Unlike the Sino-Soviet assistance to the north, which was given directly to individual projects, American "commercial aid" released dollars to private Vietnamese importers for buying goods abroad. The sale of these goods in Vietnam generated a "counterpart fund" of piastres (Vietnamese currency) that enabled the Vietnamese government to meet its expenses. Vietnamese importers, left to their own devices, saw no advantage in investing these funds in industrial or technical equipment. The consumer goods which they preferred to buy brought them easy profits and gave a false appearance of rising living standards to South Vietnam, at least in the cities. But the country as a whole did not experience the basic industrial development necessary for meaningful and lasting progress.

The efforts of the government to attract private Vietnamese capital into industry were frustrated by bureaucratic procedures and by the partiality of the small Vietnamese propertied class for the rapid profits that could be made through commerce, speculation, and the construction of luxury buildings in the cities. The Diem administration, therefore, was eventually forced to take the initiative in fostering industry. The Vietnamese state was anxious to limit the power of foreign groups which had dominated the economy in colonial days and was also unwilling to give other foreigners a chance to replace them. The state therefore became a partner along with local and foreign capital, required foreign investors to establish "mixed" firms with Vietnamese or—as it did for the Nong Son coal mines and the Ha Tien cement works and cane sugar refineries—set up state-managed industries. As in the north, industrial development was hampered by the shortage of technically trained workers. At the same time, unskilled labor, of which there was an overabundance, crowded into the congested urban areas. An estimated one tenth of the two million people in Saigon-Cholon were either unemployed or underemployed.

Important new manufactures were added to the industries inherited from the colonial era. The sugar industry was developed; new plants were installed to make plastic goods, glassware, and rubber products; and an embryonic pharmaceutical industry was created. The rapid growth of a textile industry (formerly nonexistent in the south), which benefited from a special priority given by the American aid authorities, led to expectations that more than four fifths of the domestic requirement for cotton cloth could be supplied locally by 1965.

All of this development was accomplished despite the shortage of industrial raw materials and energy in South Vietnam. Total production of electrical energy reached 398 million kilowatt hours in 1963. A program for production of hydroelectric power, aimed at easing the acute power shortage, resulted in the Danhim dam project financed by Japan's reparations for war damages and constructed by Japanese engineers. The first stage of this project was completed in 1963. But the spread of insecurity in the countryside after Diem's death greatly reduced the utility of the project which is located in the High Plateaus and requires long and vulnerable transmission lines crossing strongholds of Vietcong territory. A plan for building an atomic reactor in the Saigon-Cholon area, drawn up by the Vietnam Atomic Energy Office under Buu-Hoi and expected to be financed by a loan from the International Monetary Fund, was abandoned after Diem's assassination. By 1965 Saigon-Cholon had to rely on thermal plants using imported fuel to produce electric power.

The production of low-quality coal in the Nong Son mine near Da Nang—which had risen from 2,311 tons in 1956 to 114,400 tons in 1963—has been jeopardized by intensification of the war after 1963. For the same reason, the first industrial complex of South Vietnam in Anh Hoa near Da Nang is neither completed nor in operation. Constructed with both French and West German aid, this complex was geared in its first stage to produce fertilizer, basic chemicals, and electricity. The first cement works in the south was inaugurated at Ha Tien, on the Gulf of Siam, in 1964. It had a capacity of 330,000 tons and was built by French industry with French financial aid. But the contribution of this plant to the Vietnamese economy—like that of many smaller establishments—has been considerably reduced by the breakdown of security throughout the country.

# Social Institutions

A thousand years of Vietnamese history were enacted in the area stretching from the overpopulated, dike-crossed plains of the Red River Delta in the north to the generously abundant Mekong River Delta in the south. The small but densely peopled communities which spread across the length of the peninsula like beads on a string were often cut off from each other by geographic barriers and sometimes by political frontiers as well. Vietnamese colonists encountered not only a changing physical environment as they moved southward, but other peoples as well, notably the Cham and the Khmer. But wherever the Vietnamese settled, they brought with them two institutions which for countless generations remained unchanged regardless of regional differences—the family and the village. They also carried with them their literature and the legends, poems, and stories of their people's history which bound the nation together.

Today, however, neither the family nor the village can offer the same protection it once did. A long and drawn-out war—since 1945 the Vietnamese have known only a few brief spells of peace—disrupted the static society of Vietnam which had maintained its equilibrium by closing itself to alien influences. But the war itself was the result of historical developments—the opening of the country to Western influences, colonial rule, and the introduction of communism—which exposed that society to new pressures. Although still entrenched in the country, the traditional Vietnamese way of life has already been eroded by prolonged contact with the West, and it is now threatened with complete extinction by Marxist communism.

# The Family

The family more than the individual was the basic unit of Vietnamese society. It embraced the dead as well as the living, tying past generations to those still alive and those yet to come. Each member in death as in life was assured his place in this scheme of things, according to his rank. The family included all those who were directly descended through the male line from the same ancestors.

In Vietnam there are few surnames, perhaps three hundred in all, and, as in other Asian lands where the family has been regarded as so much more important than any single member, the family name precedes the given name. In some villages whose inhabitants may all have had a common ancestor, everyone is called Nguyen—the most common surname in the country. Other common names are Le, Tran, Pham, and Phan. To help to indicate lines of ancestry, a middle name was placed between the surname and the given name. In strongly Confucianist families, a boy was also given a pen name at birth, to be used only in signing any literary works he might produce during his lifetime.

It is Vietnamese practice to refer to a person by his given name, preceding it with a variety of terms ranging from the somewhat contemptuous *Thang* (which means "that fellow") to, in rare instances, *Cuu* ("excellency") for a man who has earned the title by a life of honor and distinction. Often the formal *Ong* ("Mr.") or the more personal *Anh* ("elder brother") are used. The designation of a man by his family name is a sign of exceptional respect, and in recent times this form has been used for only two Vietnamese leaders: Ho Chi Minh and Ngo Dinh Diem, both of whom had also earned the title *Cuu*.

The Vietnamese society was traditionally a patriarchal and polygamous one, although in practice women exercised more rights than foreigners have generally thought. The authority of the father, however, was close to absolute. Filial piety was taught by the Confucianist classics and ordained by the Gia Long legal code which, with certain modifications, controlled Vietnamese life until it was superseded both in the north and in the south after independence was achieved. No personal humiliation was considered too great in carrying out filial obligations. Children were made to study the book called the *Nhi Thap Tu Hieu,* adapted from the Chinese, which taught "the twenty-four acts of filial devotion."

So important were obligations to the family, which extended even to remote cousins, that obligations to the state assumed a secondary place. Thus, the favoritism Vietnamese showed to relatives when making appointments to official positions was regarded not as offensive but as a natural form of social solidarity. According to a Vietnamese proverb, "To produce a mandarin is a blessing for the entire family."

The Vietnamese father, in his immediate family, not only expected and received the obedience and respect of his children throughout his life, but also carried out the ceremonies honoring his own father and ancestors, as his eldest son would do after him. At the level of the larger family (which included several generations and more distant relatives), this role was filled by the first son of the eldest male's branch of the family, who was also expected to care for the ancestral tombs. The family held in common the property where the tombs were located, and contributed funds to provide for their upkeep and to allow the head of the family to honor the ancestors according to established rites. Among the sophisticated and educated the ancestor cult was simply an elaborate extension of filial piety. To the simple people it was religion, and they worshipped their ancestors as divine beings who could offer them protection and help. Even in the poorest house, where the floor was beaten earth and the family lived crowded together in one or two rooms, a large space apart was reserved for the ancestors. Rich families kept a separate building for this purpose.

The family also held other property in common that might be used to help the poorer members or to educate the deserving young. This family solidarity eased the rigors of the struggle for existence, as did the village institutions described below. Otherwise, most Vietnamese had little interest in aiding people in need, and neither Buddhism, which regarded the individual's days on earth as simply a period of expiation for acts performed in another life, nor Taoism, which stressed non-action, encouraged them to assume any responsibility for the well-being of their neighbors.

*For all Vietnamese families, rice and vegetables form the basic parts of any meal.*

The family system cut across classes and to some extent blurred the distinction between rich and poor, but by the twentieth century it began to break down as members of the family moved away from the village. Some left their homes in the north to go south; others went to live in the city, where the authority of the father, as well as other bonds which held the family together, was weakened by contact with urban civilization and Western influences.

In North Vietnam as in China, the Communists speeded up this process of change, and the shocking spectacle of sons appearing before the "people's tribunals" to denounce the real or imaginary crimes of their parents has not been uncommon. In a country where the first and overriding duty of children was to their parents, this practice struck at the very foundations of traditional society.

The geographic and political division of the country under two regimes has divided many families, leaving close relatives on opposing sides, sometimes even in high positions in both governments. Foreigners often forget that for the Vietnamese, the enemy is not only one of his own countrymen, but may also be his cousin or even his brother. By 1965 family ties had already been weakened by years of separation, as well as by the grinding ideology of the northern regime, and it can be assumed that if the division of the country continues for any substantial period of time, the cult of family ties will finally disappear.

## The Village

Vietnam has few cities. Only a handful have populations of more than 100,000: in the south, Saigon-Cholon, Da Nang, and Hue; in the north, Hanoi and Haiphong. During the war for independence the French held all of these centers; they never had to surrender a single one of them until the Vietminh surged out of the mountains and rice fields to take over one half of Vietnam and lay claim to the rest. Even the enormous size of Saigon-Cholon, swollen to more than two million by refugees from the Communist government in the north and from the Vietcong-threatened countryside, does not alter the fact that the strength of Vietnam, as well as its weakness, still lies in its villages.

The villages form the social and political background of the Vietnamese people and are the guardians of the country's most ancient traditions. They have survived wars, numerous dynastic changes, and even the dissolution of the Vietnamese empire itself. According to an old saying, "The law of the sovereign gives way before the custom of the village," and few rulers have succeeded in altering the organization of the Vietnamese village, although many have tried. Most recently, with the short-lived Strategic Hamlet program, the government of South Vietnam attempted to impose changes at the village level as the Communists had done before them. Thus, it is unlikely that the pattern according to which the villages have lived for many centuries will persist in the future. Already in North Vietnam, control of the village has been shifted to Communist party activists.

But to understand the continuing significance of the village in Vietnamese life, it is necessary to go back in time to the period when the country, or at least a part of it, was under the rule of the Nguyen emperors. This period ended only after Vietnam was divided in 1954. It is true that the disruptive pressure of Western colonization and a quarter of a century of unceasing war destroyed much of what was good in the village system. But if the system described below no longer exists in its totality in any of the villages, all of them have retained something of this traditional structure, which varied only in degree from one village to another. It is one of the tragedies of present-day Vietnam that where the collective social services of the village have broken down, no alternative, except the Communist system, has emerged to replace them.

At the top of the traditional Vietnamese governmental pyramid, power was concentrated in a few hands. Below the imperial court (which during the time of French rule was, of course, subordinated to France's colonial administration), the largest administrative unit was the province, which was subdivided into districts, all of them governed by appointed officials responsible only to the central government. But beneath the district the system changed sharply and became widely decentralized, first at the level of the cantons, each of which was headed by an official chosen from among the local population, and second in the hamlets, grouped together to form villages which were the basic administrative unit of Vietnam and were probably its most distinctive institution.

Even in the south, where the villages had plenty of land over which they could spread, they were usually surrounded by hedges of bamboo or some other protective foliage which, when regarded from close up, appeared to blend with the landscape. The village inhabitants were thus concealed from raiders and wild animals and from the inquisitive eyes of strangers. These hedges were a source of pride to the inhabitants, and the emperor used to punish a village which had permitted the entry of bandits, by having its hedge razed.

Each village was composed of a very limited number of families, sometimes only a single family, and the great majority of villages were inhabited by peasants. In the northern deltas, however, there existed villages of artisans. Each village was devoted to a single craft, such as pottery making or metal work, and these skills were passed on from father to son. It was not unusual to find one village just raising silkworms while another spun the raw silk and still another wove it into cloth. And on certain rivers floating villages are still found—despite government attempts to abolish them because of the danger they represent to public sanitation—where communities of fishermen are organized in much the same fashion as their land-based countrymen. Their huts, however, are erected on rafts.

Officials of the central government dealt with the village as a unit through the village's own chosen representatives. To the state, the village owed taxes and manpower for military service, as well as labor on public works. In South Vietnam today these various obligations of the village are often abused both by the Communist guerrillas and by their nationalist adversaries. In the past, the central government determined the quota of payment, whether in rice, money, or men, sometimes after long and difficult negotiations with village headmen. After the quota was determined, it was up to the village leaders to decide how it would be met.

The village governed itself through its own Council of Notables composed, in theory, of those whom Confucianists regarded as the natural leaders of the community: scholars who had passed the literary examinations held by the government, retired mandarins, people who had held office in the village and in the canton, and the elderly. However, this Confucianist criterion for the choice of wise and just officials was often ignored. A few men, perhaps with the assistance of relatives who had jobs in the district administration, by intermarriage within the village, by bribery, or by force, were sometimes allowed to take over an entire village and run it to their own profit.

The Council of Notables normally chose its new members according to its own standards. It appointed the *ly truong,* who was the intermediary between the national administration and the village, transmitting the orders of the one and the requests of the other, collecting taxes, and in general performing the duties of chief administrative officer of the village. The *ly truong* also had police functions, for the village policed its own territory.

The Council of Notables decided how the tax burden should be divided among its fellow citizens. It also directed the very important distribution of rice fields held in common by the village. These fields were the property of the village and could not be sold to individuals, but they were periodically divided among the taxpayers for their temporary use to supplement their private land holdings. Other village lands were earmarked for special purposes: to feed the poor; to help the old, the sick, and the widowed; to care for families while their men were away in the army; to support students so they could continue their studies.

Although the village looked after its own members, it did not do so because of a belief that they were all equal. The village was profoundly hierarchical in social structure, and a man's life, in all the many practices and rites that knit the village together, was determined in infinite detail by his rank and function in the society. Great care was taken to establish the rules of hierarchy, which varied from village to village and in some were reported to have included as many as twelve separate categories. But all rules gave preference to the elderly, the scholar, the mandarin, and the local official. In the nineteenth century, these favored groups were exempted from taxation, and, along with the rich and those who had once been rich, they were inscribed on the village register as entitled to the full rights of citizens, including a share in the communal lands. The number of these citizens was fixed at a given figure which could not be changed. An eligible man not already included could become a citizen only when a vacancy appeared on the village register.

The heart of the village was the *dinh*, or "community house." It was the meeting place where the notables sat, where administration was carried on, and where justice was meted out. It was also the temple to which the inhabitants came to worship the village genie, who might have been the founder of the village or one of its respected citizens or even a great man from elsewhere in the country whom the village had chosen as its own and who watched over the villagers' destinies. The village had its pagoda, too—frequented particularly by women—and sometimes its church. Catholics tended to group together, and some of the villages were entirely Christian. Temples might also be erected to Confucius, where only scholars were permitted to carry on the cult. Villages with long military traditions had temples devoted to the cult of military personalities. In other temples villagers worshipped the genie of the earth or some other agrarian spirit.

Within the limits of the village the inhabitants were also bound together in an intricate network of private societies. Some of these were organizations of people who had some experience in common, such as having earned an academic degree or having studied under the same teacher. Other societies were organized for a specific purpose, such as lending each other money or land, or providing for the free burial of members.

More secret groups also might exist behind the closed exterior of the village, maintaining a clandestine resistance against governmental authority. This resistance could take violent and brutal forms, and it often contained at least one ingredient of agrarian revolutionary protest. Thus one can see that the village-based Vietcong guerrilla movement of our times is based on very old traditions.

On occasion, several villages found it advantageous to join forces. They did so to strengthen their security or to combat such natural disasters as epidemics or perhaps to build a school. Some villages joined together simply because their protecting genies happened to be brothers.

It would be wrong to romanticize the remarkable Vietnamese institution of the village, as some observers, both Vietnamese and foreign, have done. Relatively autonomous and long virtually self-sufficient as economic, social, political, and even religious entities, their unique cohesiveness was their weakness as well as their strength. If it was difficult for outsiders to break into a village, it was even more difficult for new ideas to do so. These village bastions of the past, while preserving much that was vital in the Vietnamese heritage, barred the way to progress at every level, whether intellectual or technical.

At the same time, the intensively organized collective life within village boundaries bred the habit of dependence among its inhabitants, whose entire world was the village which minutely regulated their behavior and left them few decisions to make for themselves. If ever the umbilical cord binding them to this ordered and closed community was cut, the villagers were thrown abruptly on their own resources for the first time in their lives, with few personal standards of responsible social or political behavior which might have served them in the anarchic world outside. The Vietnamese, in his quest for security in the organization of his daily life, may have succeeded in developing a culture remarkable for its emphasis on stability and continuity, but he did so only within his family and his village. When the power of these institutions to protect him was destroyed, as has happened widely in recent years, the entire fabric of his society crumbled. Then many Vietnamese were left rootless and uncertain in an alien world against which little in their past experience had equipped them to defend themselves

## Literature and the Arts

The Vietnamese were not great builders like the Khmer of neighboring Cambodia who constructed the Angkor temples, or the Cham who raised their temples in the plains of central Vietnam at a time when the Vietnamese people were still concentrated in the northern part of the country. Well-preserved Vietnamese monuments are rare. They are limited now to some Confucianist and Buddhist temples in the north, the buildings in the Citadel of Hue, and the tombs of the Nguyen emperors outside Hue. Many of these edifices do not differ notably in style from the Chinese models that inspired them. But Chinese art and culture never entirely submerged the other elements which combined to create a distinctively Vietnamese civilization. Thus, the curving roofs still to be seen on certain very old northern temples—which differ from the straight geometric lines of the later temples of the Nguyen period—derive from an ancient Vietnamese architectural tradition. Some statues and altars reveal the influence of India, whose great legacy to Vietnam was Buddhism, and of the Cham, who were absorbed into the Vietnamese nation during its "march to the south."

But the Vietnamese, unlike the Japanese, for a long time did not pay much attention to the visual arts or architecture, even though they excelled in such minor arts and handicrafts as wood sculpture and lacquer work. Under the influence of contacts with the West, however, a contemporary school of excellent architects, such as Ngo Viet Thu, and painters, such as Mai-Thu and Le-Pho, appeared. These artists often successfully adapted the modern techniques of the West to Vietnamese traditions. However, Vietnamese culture remains primarily literary. And the Confucianist respect for the scholar and for the written word is ingrained in the Vietnamese people.

Over the centuries Vietnamese literature and history reached even the most ignorant peasant by word of mouth. Minstrels retraced in song the history of the nation and the feats of notable sons of the province. In Hue, during the long nights of the hot summer, boatmen on the River of

Perfumes still sing nostalgic songs about the emperors Ham Nghi and Duy Tan and how they resisted the French during the colonial period and were defeated. Companies of actors traveled through the countryside performing plays adapted from the Chinese to depict episodes of Vietnamese history and literature. In recent times the popular Cai Luong lyric theater developed spontaneously in the south, free of Chinese influence, and moved northward. This was unusual in a country where the north for many centuries had been the historic center from which the national culture radiated southward. During the resistance against France, as today, roving bands of entertainers were used by the Communists to carry their doctrine to the people.

## A NATIONAL POEM

Poetry is part of the daily life of the Vietnamese, whatever their level of education. They like to make up poems when they get together. Even the illiterate memorize verses of the national poem, *Kim Van Kieu,* to which they turn for quotations when in a romantic mood, for comfort in difficult situations, and for good or bad omens to foretell the future. This novel in poetry was composed by Nguyen Du (1765–1820) during the reign of Gia Long.

*Kim Van Kieu,* although its action ostensibly takes place in China, is profoundly Vietnamese in its richly varied language and in the society it depicts. It tells of the beautiful Thuy-Kieu who renounced the youth she loved and sold herself to another man in order to win her father's freedom. In the course of fifteen years she had many adventures and suffered greatly—as a courtesan, a servant, the wife of a warrior-poet, and, after the poet's death, a Buddhist nun—before she was reunited with Kim-Trong, the Confucianist scholar who had been her first love. Nguyen Du has one of his characters explain that Thuy-Kieu thus purged before heaven the sins she had committed in an earlier existence. But despite this Buddhist-inspired doctrine of reincarnation which provided the poet with the theme of his story, he was not much interested in religion. His insistence on the importance of duty and filial piety is pure Confucianism, as are his concluding lines which state that there is no point in blaming heaven for our sufferings, for "the root of goodness lies within ourselves." To this day new commentaries on *Kim Van Kieu* continue to be written in Vietnam, and the poem has appeared in several French translations.

Other lesser but still popular narrative poems are *Cung Oan Ngam Khuc,* the lament of a neglected favorite of the king, which dates from the eighteenth century, and *Luc Van Tien,* the adventures of a young Confucianist scholar written by a Cochin Chinese poet in the mid-nineteenth century. Although women rarely received the same education as men, some female members of the aristocracy. and of the well-to-do class were exceptions to this rule., Two of Vietnam's greatest poets were women—Ho Xuan Huong, who lived during the late eighteenth century, and another lady known to posterity simply as the wife of the subprefect of Thanh Quang, a contemporary of Minh Mang. A tradition of lively satiric poetry also existed in Vietnam and was carried on by such outstanding writers as Nguyen Cong Tru (1778–1856) and Nguyen Khac Hieu (1889–1939). In Hue—a capital of culture since the days of Gia Long—Ung Binh, who died only recently, wrote numerous enchanting books of verse and plays under the pen name of Thuc Gia.

Poetry also played a role in rallying popular support to the resistance movement during the war against France. This period was marked by an outpouring of free verse which broke through traditional poetic forms and was associated

*Reproduced here is part of a particularly lyrical passage from Kim Van Kieu. It describes the sentiments aroused in the viewer by contemplation of a sea landscape. The passage above is in* chu nom *and that below is in* quoc ngu, *The numbers refer to the verses, of which there are 3,254.*

| | |
|---|---|
| 3 | Trước lầu Ngưng-Bích khóa xuân, |
| 4 | Vẻ mây xa, tấm trăng gần ở chung. |
| 5 | Bốn bề bát ngát xa trông, |
| 6 | Cát vàng cồn nọ, bụi hồng dặm kia. |
| 7 | Bẻ bàng sương sớm đèn khuya (sương) |

(X.ch. 914)

| | |
|---|---|
| 8 | Nửa tình nửa cảnh như chia tấm lòng: |
| 9 | Tưởng người dưới nguyệt chén đồng, |
| 0 | Tin-sương luống những rày mong mai chờ. |
| 1 | Bên trời góc bể bơ vơ, |
| 2 | Tấm son gọt rửa bao giờ cho phai! |
| 3 | Xót người tựa cửa hôm mai, |
| 4 | Quạt nồng ấp lạnh những ai đó giờ. |

with such authentic bards of the resistance as To Huu. Popular poems and plays frequently have been set to music, and the development of Vietnam's music is inseparable from that of its poetry and its theater.

## FROM CHINESE CHARACTERS TO QUOC NGU

In the domain of written prose, the Chinese language was used far more widely than Vietnamese until the nineteenth century. Thus the annals of the reigns of successive rulers—the main historical source in the country—were written in Chinese, as was the oldest surviving treatise on geography written by a Vietnamese. Its author was Le Loi's friend and comrade Nguyen Trai, to whom are also attributed some of the oldest writings to survive in the Vietnamese language. A particularly interesting work of Vietnamese fiction in Chinese is the *Vast Collection of Marvelous Legends* by another Nguyen Du who lived in the early sixteenth century, almost three hundred years before the author of *Kim Van Kieu.* These legends offer a fascinating picture of life in Vietnam during a troubled period. Their skeptical Confucianist author regarded Buddhism and Taoism as superstitions, noted the growing importance of traders (who even if they had money, did not have education), and studded his stories of love and demons with portraits of corrupt officials and a rebel general. He wrote with such immediacy that it is difficult to remember while reading these legends that they were written more than four hundred years ago.

Even when scholars wrote in the vernacular language, they had to rely on *chu nom*—the system of transcription derived from Chinese characters—until the adoption of *quoc ngu*. In late nineteenth-century Cochin China the development and enrichment of *quoc ngu* was carried on by Truong Vinh Ky (Petrus Ky) and others.

After World War I it became clear to the new generation of Vietnamese intellectuals who had grown up under French rule that only in Western civilization could they find the secrets of technology and the key to power. Between the two World Wars Hanoi, Hue, and, to a lesser extent, Saigon were alive with renewed intellectual activity catalyzed by the impact of Western culture on traditional values. In Hanoi the *Nam Phong* ("South Wind"), a magazine written half in Chinese characters and half in *quoc ngu,* served as a bridge between the older and younger generations. Pham Quynh was an important contributor to this journal and was its editor. His leading competitor, Nguyen Van Vinh, became famous for his translations of French classics into Vietnamese. In Hue the nationalist leader Huynh Thuc Khang founded a famous politico-literary newspaper, *Tien-Dan* ("The Voice of the People"), which influenced the thinking of an entire generation of nationalists before World War II, as did the satiric newspaper *Phong Hoa,* published in Hanoi during this same period.

Scholars continued to produce historical treatises even though the language in which they wrote changed from Chinese to Vietnamese. The Vietnamese historian or annalist was traditionally also a student of linguistics. This has also been true of such twentieth-century historians as Tran Trong Kim, Le Thuoc, and Hoang Xuan Han. In the French language a valuable historical source available to students of Vietnam is the *Bulletin des Amis du Vieux Hué* ("Bulletin of the Friends of Old Hue"), which appeared from 1914 to 1944 and included a number of articles by Vietnamese as well as by French scholars. Work of major significance on the history and archaeology of Vietnam, as of Laos and Cambodia, has been produced by scholars attached to the Ecole Française d'Extrême-Orient ("French School of Far

Eastern Studies"), a research organization established in Indochina during the colonial period by the French government and now located in Paris. In other fields the talent of Vietnamese in assimilating foreign languages is shown by the writings in French of such men as Tran Duc Thao, a noted Marxist philosopher; Pham Duy Khiem, an author of folk tales; and the novelist Pham Van Ky.

Although Vietnamese writers have been prolific since the establishment of the states of North and South Vietnam in 1954 and a large amount of printed matter has been produced, its literary quality has steadily declined along with its intellectual level. This decline is clearly a reflection of the political tensions prevailing in the country.

## THE SHORT LIFE OF THE HUNDRED FLOWERS

The decline of Vietnamese culture produced a reaction among some of the leading writers in North Vietnam. In Hanoi, which was struggling to remain a cultural center of the country, intellectuals were restless under the Communist dictatorship. The U.S.S.R., under former Premier Khrushchev, had already repudiated many abuses of the Stalinist period when in May 1956 Communist China launched the Hundred Flowers policy, "a policy of freedom to criticize and freedom to answer criticism." This freedom did not last very long in China. In the autumn of 1956 it spread across the border to North Vietnam where it proved even more short-lived.

Leading members of the Hundred Flowers movement in Hanoi were Phan Khoi, the only Confucianist scholar to survive the agrarian reform program, and Tran Duc Thao, the Marxist philosopher. The movement operated mainly through two publications, *Giai Pham* ("Literary Selections") and a new critical journal *Nhan Van* ("Humanism"). Both attacked North Vietnamese Communist orthodoxy, the party bureaucracy, and the brutal excesses which had been com- mitted in the name of agrarian reform. Tran Duc Thao called for freedom of the press, speech, and assembly. One writer turned to science fiction with his study of the robot poet who in the year 2000 was found to be more effective and reliable than any human poet and could be counted on to turn out reams of verse including such words as "red flags . . . beating drums . . . worker's hands . . . enthusiasm . . . Forward!" Another story in the form of a legend told of how God sent giants to earth to help men fight the devils who had made their life miserable. The giants succeeded in routing the devils, but they also killed many men because the giants had been constructed without hearts. The analogy with the Communists was obvious.

Five issues of *Nhan Van* appeared before it was closed down by the North Vietnamese government in December 1956. Leaders of the movement were arrested and some were condemned to years of manual labor in the malaria-infested highlands.

# Science and Technology

In the Confucianist world of the Nguyen emperors there was not much interest in science or technology. During the colonial period the University of Hanoi was established—the only university in the country—but this was only a collection of technical schools which taught such subjects as law, medicine, and applied sciences, unlike the situation in British India where genuine universities existed with facilities for higher education and research. Not many Vietnamese were admitted to the university, and very few were permitted to go abroad for more training. Nor did traditional values, which were mostly ethical and political, seem to predestine the

Vietnamese to distinguish themselves in science and technology. But with the liberalization of the colonial regime before World War II, Georges Mandel, a farsighted French Minister of Colonies, broke down the barriers against study abroad and enabled Vietnamese students to go to France in greater numbers. Although the scientific atmosphere they found in the West was new to them, these students proved surprisingly gifted in many fields of science.

A recent analysis of the number and quality of Asian contributions to scientific literature ranked small Vietnam directly after Japan and India. These contributions are being made at the present time almost entirely by Vietnamese living abroad. Among these men is Buu-Hoi, considered one of the distinguished living organic chemists who is also credited with fundamental discoveries with regard to the origins of cancer and the treatment of leprosy and tuberculosis. In another domain the biochemist Nguyen Van Thoai is a known expert on enzymes. In the field of fundamental medicine, the surgeon Ton That Tung is one of the world's leading specialists in the delicate surgery of the liver. Many other Vietnamese scientists are now engaged in basic research in even more abstract domains such as mathematics and nuclear physics. Vietnamese have also made their mark in several fields of technology. The engineer Bui Nhuan is an internationally known expert on the technology of natural textile fibers. And Vietnamese living abroad now represent a sizable source of technological manpower. They are working on French programs concerned with the development of the hydrogen bomb and the supersonic jet.

A few Vietnamese scientists have been able to exert a direct influence on the development of their country. In the north Dr. Ton That Tung was the head of the Vietminh medical corps which operated efficiently during the battle of

Dien Bien Phu. In the south Buu-Hoi created the Vietnam Atomic Energy Office to investigate the manifold uses of nuclear science in an underdeveloped country. He also inspired a program for the eradication of leprosy, a program which functioned effectively for several years during the Diem regime. In the north promotion of scientific work is carried on in Hanoi by the Science Committee of the Government, which coordinates the activities of scientific workers and provides links with scientific organizations in the Communist bloc. In the south encouragement of science is left mainly to private initiative through which such organizations as the Vietnam Medical Association and the Vietnam Chemical Society have been formed.

## Education

Despite the country's rich literary traditions and the accomplishments of individual Vietnamese in science and technology, Vietnam is still burdened with its history of underdevelopment which is particularly evident in the basic fields of education and health.

Modern Vietnamese leaders have always been preoccupied with the problem of widespread illiteracy, and by 1946 the Vietminh had already begun teaching *quoc ngu* on a large scale. It is now claimed—by Hanoi, Saigon, and the Vietcong —that illiteracy is on the way to disappearing in the areas under the respective control of the three. In addition, adult education classes in the north are said to be attended after working hours by some 1,300,000 people a year. In the south progress in this field, which had once been rapid, was slowed down by the war.

Both north and south have made a considerable effort at the elementary school level, and well over 2,500,000

*At Dalat, this Atomic Energy Center which was designed by Ngo Viet Thu is an example of contemporary Vietnamese architecture.*

children in the north and 1,500,000 children in the south are said to be attending school. However, the curriculum used by each regime has been the target of justified criticism: in the north the emphasis on political indoctrination leaves little room for other subjects, while in the south the course of study is old-fashioned and not yet adapted to the necessities of modern times.

In contrast to the north, where all education is state-controlled, private and semi-private schools (which are subsidized by the state) are still important in the south, especially at the high school level. There is great competition in South Vietnam to enter schools maintained by the French government's Cultural Mission and by Christian missionaries, where standards are generally higher than those prevailing in the Vietnamese public school system. In the field of technical education there are now a number of establishments—among them the Hanoi Polytechnic School, the Phu Tho National

Technical Center near Saigon, and various agricultural schools. But the need for more and better technical education is generally recognized.

Although the north claims to have a number of institutions of higher education and the south claims to have three, only those at Hanoi and Saigon deserve the name of university as we know it in the West. There are said to be about 26,000 students at the university level in the north and about 20,000 in the south. All teaching in the north is done in the Vietnamese language. In the south French is still used in at least some technical schools. The two main foreign languages taught in the south are French and English; in the north they are Russian and Chinese.

Additional training is provided in the north by sending students abroad to Peking and Moscow and, to a lesser extent, to Eastern European Communist countries. Southern students often come to the United States, although in the past many went to France. As in many underdeveloped countries, there is often a problem in getting these students to return to their homeland once they have completed their studies abroad. In North Vietnam this problem is easier to solve than in the south because North Vietnamese students are automatically returned home once they have finished their studies. But students from South Vietnam, like those from some other non-Communist Asian countries, often tend to remain abroad and are absorbed into the pool of technically trained manpower of the country in which they happen to be living.

## Health

The maintenance of public health has always proved a difficult problem for Vietnam, partly because it is a tropical country and partly because war has disrupted the country for so many years. Vietnam lacks clinics and hospitals, as well as medical personnel. The number of medical doctors in both north and south was among the lowest in Southeast Asia, and since 1954 efforts have been made to increase their number. In the north several medical faculties and schools for medical technicians have been established. The practicing of traditional Sino-Vietnamese medicine, which relies on the use of local plants and minerals, has been encouraged, along with Western medicine. The total number of doctors and technicians in the north is said to be 7,000.

In the south, apart from the Faculties of Medicine in Saigon and Hue, schools for training medical technicians also exist, and there is a sizable number of foreign doctors. As of 1965, it was said that there were more than 8,000 rural health workers in South Vietnam. But only 200 doctors were listed in the national health service in 1964, and there were only about 600 other doctors in all of South Vietnam. In the south the coexistence of Western medicine with traditional medicine and with quackery also poses a serious problem which has so far resisted attempts at solution. As for hospitals, those in the main cities of North Vietnam are more important than hospitals in the south in quality, number, and size.

Efforts at improving health conditions led to claims by the north that it had wiped out malaria in several regions. Meanwhile, a comparable program in the south, which had begun to produce results, was jeopardized by Vietcong terror directed against the government malaria-eradication teams working in the villages.

There is still a very high incidence of tuberculosis in both North and South Vietnam—one of the highest in any underdeveloped country. The control of tuberculosis would necessitate, at least in the south, the launching of a government

*In this photograph a Vietnamese nurse works in one of the health centers in the central Vietnam highlands.*

program based on free medical care and free distribution of medicines, similar to the program carried out under Diem with regard to leprosy. The incidence of leprosy in Vietnam is estimated at 3.5 per 1,000 in the lowlands, and considerably higher than this among the ethnic minorities in the mountains. Another important disabling disease is trachoma, which is propagated widely by poor conditions of hygiene and by insects. In addition to these endemic diseases, cholera and bubonic plague continue to present serious problems in the south. The prevention of epidemics of both depends on the work done at the various Pasteur Institutes founded by the French during the colonial period, which are still in operation.

# The Role of Women

In the *Analects* of Confucius it is written: "The Master said women and people of low birth are very hard to deal with. If you are friendly with them, they get out of hand, and if you keep your distance, they resent it." The Master, it can be seen, did not think much of women, and civil codes like the Gia Long code, which derived more from Chinese than from Vietnamese practice, gave women few rights. Just as they were subjected to their father's authority when children, so as wives they were placed under the control of their husbands and as widows under that of their sons. The system which relegated women to a position of legal inferiority usually condemned them to an inferior education as well, because Confucianist academic training was reserved exclusively for men.

The Vietnamese woman, however, retained great influence within her family circle. She very often managed the finances of the family. And her moral authority over her grown sons—and their wives—could be considerable. Although the practice of polygamy enabled a man to marry second-rank wives and to acquire concubines, the first wife—whose consent was required before other wives could be taken—exercised control over these other women. The children of second-rank wives and concubines were brought up to regard the first wife as their legal mother. Divorce was infrequent under this polygamous system.

Most Vietnamese women limited their activities to family affairs, but others were active in public life, in literature, and even in war. Women have played the best and the worst roles in Vietnamese history. In ancient times a matriarchal tradition may have existed among these people who trace their origins to one of the hundred sons of the legendary Queen

*In the Vietnamese tradition, militia women in Hanoi volunteer for service in the North Vietnamese army in 1965.*

Au Co. Women have fought on the battlefield since the heroic days of the Trung sisters and Trieu Au some two thousand years ago. During the Diem period the attempt of Madame Ngo Dinh Nhu to set up a paramilitary woman's organization received little sympathy from Western observers, and her movement collapsed with the overthrow of the Diem regime. The Communists, however, did not underestimate the courage of their countrywomen, and in 1965 some women held important posts in the Vietcong army fighting in the south.

The 1960 constitution of North Vietnam guarantees equal rights to women, and polygamy no longer exists in law, even though it sometimes survives in practice. In South Vietnam, Madame Nhu, not content with constitutional provisions guaranteeing equality to all citizens and protection of the family, prevailed on her fellow deputies in the National Assembly to pass a Family Law (now abolished) which forbade divorce without the president's express consent and also forbade polygamy. Later she sponsored a Law for the Protection of Morality which forbade a wide number of practices including prostitution, dancing, spiritualism and occultism, and boxing. Certain provisions of these two bills would probably have been enacted by any independent government. Others, however, such as the ban on both polygamy and divorce and the outlawing of spiritualism and occultism (both widely practiced in the south under the influence of Taoism, Cao Daism, and Hoa Hao) were unacceptable to the public. And in general, the high-handed manner in which she imposed these measures on the country and her verbal excesses in attacking the Buddhists in 1963 brought unpopularity to the government and contributed to the ill-feeling which preceded the overthrow of the Diem regime.

But whatever the vicissitudes of governments, the status of the Vietnamese woman has markedly improved. Girls now have a greater opportunity for equal education with their brothers than ever before in the history of Vietnam, and in both north and south they are taking advantage of it. In the future, women can be expected to play a role of increasing importance both in government and in professional life in Vietnam.

## A Society in Transition

The intrusion of the West into Vietnam, which began even before the French arrived in force in the nineteenth century, discredited many traditional values and introduced pressures for change into an essentially static society. The subsequent eagerness of Vietnamese nationalists to use the material and intellectual means of the West to emancipate themselves from France's colonial rule further weakened the old system, although by no means ended it. But at the time when many among the more politically aware Vietnamese were beginning to question the classic values which had proved inadequate against the Westerner, a new and potent instrument of change was imported into Vietnam—the doctrine of communism.

## NORTH VIETNAM

Marxist communism, in principle, was as alien to Vietnam as was the political democracy for which Westerners have looked there in vain. But, unlike democracy, communism found a fertile field of activity in Vietnam. The long war against the French under Lao Dong party leadership gave such a boost to the implantation of communism that in 1954, after nearly eight years of fighting, the Communist framework could be clamped down on the traditional institutions which still survived north of the seventeenth parallel.

In this formerly colonial nation which had barely emerged from an exhausting war, the division of society into classes according to Marxist terminology was entirely artificial. In north and central Vietnam particularly, no one class owned important means of production either in industry or agriculture, and society tended to be divided primarily between the relatively privileged urban population and the rural peasantry. The economic exploitation of the Vietnamese by their fellow countrymen still existed in individual cases, but that could easily have been wiped out through the ordinary processes of government and administration bolstered by the overwhelming prestige of the Communist leaders. Instead, however, the Communists for their own purposes preferred to introduce an ideology and a machinery for creating the conditions of class struggle even where these were not normally to be found.

Years before the war with France ended, the Communists had already imposed drastic taxes on land and agricultural output and on private business. But when landowners and tradesmen, faced with what amounted to confiscation of their property, sought to make a gift of it to the Ho Chi Minh government, they were usually rebuffed. The reason was wholly political: the party required landowners and businessmen out of whom it could later make an example. In 1953 the Communists were sure enough of themselves to undertake more drastic measures, even though it was still wartime. Party blacklists were drawn up and included the names of many people who were neither wealthy nor what the Communists called "reactionary." Public denunciations and executions of many of these people followed, and a wave of terror swept through the Vietminh-controlled countryside turning even against party members, many of whom were denounced in their turn as reactionaries. Among those accused at that time was a nationalist member of the Ho government who was driven to suicide by the denunciation.

By 1953 Vietminh leaders had decided to reproduce in Vietnam the agrarian reform program of Communist China. For that purpose the entire rural population was classified according to five major categories—landlord, rich peasant, middle peasant, poor peasant, and wage earner or landless worker. The system of classification was also applied to the city populations where professional people, artisans, and others were labeled in a similarly artificial way. Under this new caste system, the poorer people were accorded a higher position than were the wealthier people. Thus, when the daughter of a rich peasant married into the family of a poor peasant, she had to wait a year before being admitted to her husband's class—a politically superior one according to Communist doctrine. But when the daughter of a poor peasant married into the family of a rich peasant, she was allowed three years' grace before she had to enter his class—a politically inferior one under the Communist system.

The absurdity of this classification became evident when members of the five classes had to be identified and listed in each village even when the difference between the holdings of the richest and poorest man in that village might be only a quarter of an acre. But there was nothing absurd about the use to which the party put these new labels. When the Communists introduced what they called the Rent Reduction Campaign of 1953 and 1954 and moved from that to a land reform program in 1954, the category to which a man was assigned came to mean literally the difference between life and death for himself and his family.

In the first stage the Communist party concentrated on eliminating the well-to-do and those labeled "reactionary" in each village. When these people were out of the way, the land reform program was directed against the so-called rich and middle peasants until, in the end only the "poor peasant" and the landless were safe. In each case party militants, the *can bo,* worked to whip up popular hysteria, turning the villagers into lynch mobs. Public denunciations, public trials before "Special People's Tribunals," torture, and executions were commonplace occurrences in the fear-ridden countryside. Some 50,000 people were believed to have been killed in the name of agrarian reform. The program took an enormous toll of veterans of the resistance and party members who did not happen to have been born in the poorest classes of the population. Many of these men were killed, and 12,000 party members (the figure was later admitted by the party) were jailed. Thousands of people committed suicide, and countless others—the families of the executed and the imprisoned—died of starvation because it was forbidden to give them food.

These excesses led Ho Chi Minh to call a halt in August 1956 to the program with a statement that "errors" had been committed. This was the signal for a Rectification of Errors campaign marked by the resignation of Truong Chinh, then the Lao Dong party Secretary General and architect of the land reform program. The popular General Vo Nguyen Giap was asked, as the spokesman of the party, to denounce some of these errors. They made a formidable list and ranged from ignoring the resistance record of some to executing "too many honest people." Giap stated that ". . . seeing enemies everywhere, [we] resorted to terror, which became far too widespread. While carrying out our land reform program, we failed to respect the principles of freedom of faith and worship in many areas. In regions inhabited by minority tribes we have attacked tribal chiefs too strongly, thus injuring, instead of respecting, local customs and manners. When reorganizing the party, we paid too much attention to the notion of social class instead of adhering firmly to political qualifications alone . . . Worse still, torture came to be regarded as a normal practice during party reorganization." With the Rectification of Errors campaign, many people were finally liberated from prisons and concentration camps.

It has been suggested by some observers that even the excesses of the land reform program were deliberately planned in order to break the independent spirit of the peasants and to make them more malleable in Communist hands. However that may be, it would seem that the authors of the plan did not anticipate the disorders which followed. Party members who had been released from prison came home to take revenge on the people who had sent them there and who had replaced them on party committees; physical clashes between "old" and "new" party members were frequent. The continuing violence led to unrest in many parts of the country. In the province of Nghe An it flared into open revolt. In November 1956, peasants of this province, where in 1930 other peasants had risen against the French, now rose against the North Vietnamese government. As in 1930, the revolt was put down by the army, but in 1956 these troops were not French soldiers but members of the North Vietnamese People's Army.

Under communism the peasants remain far more important in numbers than in political power. An industrial proletariat had already existed under the French, working in the factories and mines concentrated in the north, notably the Hon Gay coal beds and the Nam Dinh textile mills. The impetus given to industrial development by the Communist regime greatly increased the numbers of these workers and conferred on them a privileged political position. However, even the workers are not necessarily entrusted with the task of governing North Vietnam. In place of the Confucianist-trained mandarins who had long administered the country are Lao Dong party members operating through a network of administrative committees.

More representative of the peasant population than the Lao Dong party, which constitutes an official class, is the "People's Army." As is characteristic of Asian communism, this army has been trained to identify its interests with those of the peasant masses. Despite the great prestige of General Vo Nguyen Giap, the commander who led it to victory against the French and as of 1965 was still head of the armed forces, the army in the north apparently has not sought to play an independent political role. This reluctance to become involved in politics is in marked contrast to what military men have been doing in South Vietnam since the overthrow of the Diem regime.

The top political leaders in the north have come from families which under French colonial rule had already risen above the level of the poorer peasants, and included mandarins and scholars who belonged to the middle and lower echelons of the ruling class of Confucianist Vietnam. The fathers of both President Ho Chi Minh and Prime Minister Pham Van Dong were men who held official rank under the Nguyen emperors. As is being done in China, Ho and Dong have been building a Communist state on the ruins of a society which was once organized according to the ethical and political ideas of Confucius. These and other older Communists, having come of age and attended school under French rule, have had practical knowledge of the West. Although most of these men did not have an opportunity to live in Western Europe, as did Ho Chi Minh, they have been familiar with the principles of the French Revolution as well as with those of Marxist-Leninism. But these older leaders are now greatly outnumbered and have already been frequently outvoted by younger men whose knowledge of the outside world is limited to what they have been allowed to learn from Communist China and, in far fewer instances, from the U.S.S.R. and Eastern Europe.

SOUTH VIETNAM

No totalitarian screen obscures the reality of the breakdown of society south of the seventeenth parallel. Nine years of existence of a separate South Vietnamese state under Ngo Dinh Diem failed to unify the heterogeneous elements of the population. Since his overthrow, as before, each of these social, religious, and racial groups continues to live its own life in its own microcosm, the group which enjoys power at any given time trying to impose its views on the rest. The peasant population, exhausted by the long war of which it has borne the major burden and having received scant benefit in exchange for all it has been called upon to suffer, appears superficially to be amorphous and dispirited. However, when efficiently indoctrinated, the peasantry has produced dedicated government soldiers or, very often, redoubtable Vietcong fighters.

The army is the one mass organization in the south which is drawn from virtually all elements of the population. At one point it might conceivably have proved a stabilizing force in this transitional society. Instead, having been minutely organized in the Western fashion, it runs the risk of segregating itself from the peasants because of its privileges and its higher standard of living. In contrast, the success of the Vietcong guerrillas in competing with the government's army for the sympathy and allegiance of the peasants is largely due to the guerrillas' ability to mingle with the peasants at all levels. Ngo Dinh Diem recognized this disparity between army and peasantry, a recognition which led to his recruiting local defense units made up of village militia and, later on, the "Republican Youth." The downfall of the Diem regime, which was followed by massive desertions from the militia to the Vietcong, ended the efficiency of most of these units.

Because of the insecurity in the countryside and the disparity in standards of living and development between town and village, the urban population is now totally cut off, both socially and spiritually, from the peasantry. The towns have other problems, too. Deep internal dissensions exist among members of the propertied class, and these prevent them from forming a common front for resistance to communism and for development of the country. Saigon-Cholon has become a huge, uneasy metropolis surrounded by a large-scale rural rebellion.

In the period of French colonial rule, workers had already

started to drift from their villages into southern cities in search of jobs. Then they were absorbed into the light industries which had been established by the French. This group of urban workers increased vastly in numbers during the war for independence, when many more found work with the French army and administration. And it grew even larger as a result of the population transfer in 1954 and 1955 and the general insecurity which came with the outbreak of Communist guerrilla activity. These workers are now employed in old and new industries, on the docks, in private transport (pedicabs, taxis, and buses), and as servants in private homes, Vietnamese as well as foreign.

Another element of the heterogeneous population is composed of a class of men who act as intermediaries between powerful foreigners and the Vietnamese. In the early period of France's conquest, the men who served as intermediaries between the newcomers and the local people were Vietnamese who interpreted for the French. These people became a privileged class in the colonial society. The poet Tu-Xuong described this class contemptuously as "those who do not need academic degrees to have a diet of champagne in the evening and cow's milk in the morning." (Milk was then a rarity in Vietnam.)

Today the presence of Americans in South Vietnam, with their important economic aid program and their large army, has created a new class of men who act as intermediaries between the Americans and the Vietnamese. This new class has appeared on the scene and moved up the social scale thanks to the increase in wealth and power they derive from their relations with the Americans. The emergence of such privileged minorities has inevitably created resentment among the majority of their countrymen, resentment which is easily turned against the West.

# Modern Vietnam and the World

Vietnam, a small country by Asian standards, has been divided into antagonistic halves since 1954. The armed conflict between North and South Vietnam which erupted after the partition has since threatened the peace of Asia and the world. For the Hanoi government and its southern satellite, the National Liberation Front—as well as for their Chinese Communist allies—the struggle was not waged only to unify Vietnam under Communist leadership. It also provided an occasion and a battlefield for expelling American power and influence from the shores of continental Asia. The United States government came to understand these aims and therefore lent its support to the Saigon government.

However, because Washington did not address itself to the

task of helping Vietnamese nationalism express itself coherently it failed to encourage movements in South Vietnam which could successfully check the Communist advance. As a result of this failure the United States was drawn into combat against the Vietnamese Communists, a course it had tried to avoid since 1954. As of mid-1965 United States forces were engaged in a full-scale war on the Asian mainland in Vietnam.

# The Background of the Vietnamese Struggle

Many Western policy-makers look back to Geneva with nostalgia as though the secret of peace were somehow to be found in the series of documents drawn up in that Swiss city more than a decade ago. The Geneva accords, however, were workable only to the extent that they represented the desire of the French to end an unpopular colonial war and the willingness of the Vietminh to accept France's armistice terms. For this reason only the specific provisions for the cease-fire between the French and the Vietminh were clearly outlined and finally implemented.

The desire for democratic institutions and general elections in Vietnam as expressed in the accords proved meaningless. The foreign powers which had drawn up the Geneva agreement had neither the means nor the intention of imposing their wishes upon the Vietnamese people. They were especially reluctant to act at a time when one half of the country, North Vietnam, was about to be placed under the rule of a Communist regime, and the other half, South Vietnam, was on the verge of anarchy. In addition the United States and

South Vietnam had refused to approve the Geneva accords. Thus, although the Franco-Vietminh war was ended at Geneva in July 1954, a political solution for Vietnam was postponed to some unspecified future date.

The agreements outlined at Geneva (see Chapter IV) thus contained few if any provisions for their long-term execution. They were a series of desires for the future, drawn up by the conference participants. France was given the responsibility of applying the accords south of the seventeenth parallel prior to the general elections. But the French had not brought one long and onerous war to a close just to assume new responsibilities which might involve them in another. They welcomed the opportunity to evacuate the South by 1956 and avoid any further obligation to bring about a Vietnamese political settlement, which they felt would be fraught with difficult and long-term problems.

By 1956 the only foreign organization with commitments under the Geneva agreements to remain in Vietnam was the International Commission for Supervision and Control (I.C.S.C.), composed of Canadian, Indian, and Polish delegations. Appointed to oversee the implementation of the cease-fire agreement, this Commission was to remain indefinitely in existence when general elections—intended to end the armistice period by establishing definitive institutions for Vietnam—failed to materialize. South Vietnam agreed to tolerate the I.C.S.C.'s activities even though the Diem government had not accepted the Geneva accords. And ultimately, when the Commission found conditions of life and work in the Communist north too restrictive for its operations, it set up headquarters in Saigon. Its tripartite military teams were stationed in the demilitarized zone at the seventeenth parallel and at key points throughout North and South Vietnam.

In theory, the Commission was present to prevent such breaches of the Geneva cease-fire agreement as imports of war material, introduction of foreign military personnel, and hostile acts between North and South Vietnam. But any action the I.C.S.C. might take and any influence it could exert depended on the cooperation of the Hanoi and Saigon authorities, both of whom regarded it as an intruder. These governments were understandably far more preoccupied by their own political and military needs than by any hypothetical duties owed to the Commission. Thus they either concealed breaches of the Geneva accords from the Commission or ignored I.C.S.C. protests when concealment proved impossible.

Such protests were rarely very strong because the Commission was compelled to operate by unanimous vote, and unanimity was difficult to achieve. The Polish delegate supported the Communist north, and the Canadian backed the Western-oriented southern government. As for the Indians, the Diem regime during its first years was suspicious of countries which were nonaligned rather than militantly anti-Communist. Relations with New Delhi were strained, and the Indian delegation was believed by Saigon to favor the Ho Chi Minh regime. But as time passed and Ngo Dinh Diem felt more assured of his standing as the nationalist leader of Vietnam, contacts between his government and the Indians improved.

In 1962, the Indian and Canadian delegations made an important report to Britain and the U.S.S.R., the co-chairmen of the Geneva Conference, in which they joined in declaring that North Vietnam was guilty of acts of aggression and subversion against South Vietnam. The Polish delegation, however, refused to accept this view of the situation. This same report also accused South Vietnam of violating the

Geneva agreements by receiving increased American military aid and accepting what amounted to a military alliance with the United States. By mid-1962 all three members of the I.C.S.C. noted the gravity of the situation in Vietnam, and they recognized the threat of increasing and open hostilities. At that time they admitted their complete impotence to deal with the situation.

A similar impotence had already been obvious on the part of the Southeast Asia Treaty Organization (SEATO). This organization had been founded by the Pact of Manila in September 1954 on the initiative of the United States Secretary of State, John Foster Dulles. Its purpose was to prevent the extension of Communist influence in Asia after the collapse of the French military position in Indochina. South Vietnam, like Laos and Cambodia, although prevented by the Geneva accords from joining any military alliance, was declared to be within the area to be protected by SEATO. But both in its conception and in its membership, this SEATO coalition was ill-equipped from the start to cope with the kind of aggression which was soon to take place in Vietnam.

Although SEATO was supposed to be a regional body, five of its eight members—the United States, France, Britain, Australia, and New Zealand—were not Asian countries, and a sixth, Pakistan, was geographically remote from Southeast Asia. This left only Thailand and the Philippines, both small and weak countries with no military forces to spare for foreign wars, to represent Southeast Asia in SEATO. Neighboring states, which might have joined a genuinely regional organization, seemed more fearful of this American-dominated military alliance than anxious for its protection. The Manila Pact had a twofold effect on Communist China. On the one hand it persuaded Peking that Communist China was being encircled by the West. On the other hand, the disparity between American military power and the extreme weakness of SEATO—which not only lacked a unified military command, but even proved unable to agree on a common program of action—persuaded Peking that SEATO was, after all, only a paper tiger.

In any case, the capacity of SEATO to protect South Vietnam was never put to the test because of fundamental differences among its members, although it can be argued that the very existence of the organization discouraged Hanoi from an open invasion of the south. Vietnamese Communists, however, had been committed to taking over the entire country since 1946, and neither their temporary setback at Geneva—where they were stopped at the seventeenth parallel —nor the Manila Pact deflected them from this goal. On the contrary, these developments merely led them to seek other means of achieving reunification. By the early 1960's North Vietnam, as the International Commission for Supervision and Control had discovered, was already fighting a war in the south. But an old-fashioned military alliance—even one which had been more united and better rooted in Southeast Asia than SEATO—could offer South Vietnam no defense against Vietcong techniques of infiltration and subversion.

## North Vietnam and International Politics

North Vietnam emerged from the war with France irrevocably committed to the Communist bloc. Years earlier—in 1945 and early 1946—northern leaders, because of the weakness of their hold on the country, had been willing to accept non-Communist allies. As we have seen, they tried to achieve a balanced foreign policy by maintaining apparently cordial relations with then Nationalist China and even with some Americans, while at the same time they attempted to reach a political agreement with France.

## COMMITMENT TO THE COMMUNIST BLOC

But after the Vietminh's elimination of organized nationalist parties as early as 1946 and after the consolidation of Communist control over the resistance, these balanced policies were no longer necessary. The Democratic Republic of Vietnam adopted such an orthodox Communist line that in 1950, when it enthusiastically welcomed diplomatic recognition from Mao Tse-tung's China and Stalinist Russia, it scornfully rejected a similar move from Tito's Yugoslavia, whose nationalist tendency had made it a pariah in the international Communist movement. And by the time the Geneva Conference ended the war with France, Hanoi's diplomacy was almost exclusively oriented to the Communist world. It established diplomatic missions in almost all of the Communist countries. Ideologically, it sought to steer a middle course between Communist China and the U.S.S.R.

This middle course, which was followed with ease as long as Sino-Soviet relations remained good, became difficult when ideological conflict broke out between Peking and Moscow and led to an open rift between them. But Hanoi was able to remain on good terms with both, and on several occasions Ho Chi Minh even tried to act as a peacemaker between his two great-power allies.

## CHANGES IN POLICY

For Ho Chi Minh and his long-time associates, Moscow was still the center of the world Communist movement, for they had first come to know communism through the Soviet Union. But in the 1960's, the type of leader open to Western trends within the Communist movement, strikingly represented by Ho Chi Minh, began to lose ground in North Vietnam. Younger elements came to the fore, determined to

*In 1956 Communist Chinese Premier Chou En-lai paid an official visit to North Vietnam. President Ho Chi Minh greeted him at a banquet given in Chou's honor.*

use the numerical weight of the peasant masses to impose communism at the most primitive level of society by following the pattern and leadership of Peking. Instead of suspecting Peking's aims, they derived comfort and encouragement from the overwhelming presence on their frontiers of a China grown vastly more powerful than it had ever been during Vietnam's troubled history.

The influence of this pro-Chinese group greatly increased when the war in Vietnam—formerly confined to the south—engulfed the north as well. An intensive propaganda campaign stressed the solidarity of Communist China with North Vietnam and made use of slogans easy for the people to understand, such as "North Vietnam and China are the teeth and the lips of the same mouth" and "When each Chinese gives up one bowl of rice, North Vietnam can eat for a month." These Peking-inspired slogans turned the North Vietnamese population from the historic fear of their former rulers and gave them a new feeling of racial solidarity with the Chinese in their struggle against the West.

## DIPLOMATIC RELATIONS

Hanoi has followed the Chinese pattern of lending support to leftist governments through the establishment of diplomatic missions, especially in the newly emerging countries of Africa. The first North Vietnamese embassy to be established outside the Communist sphere was in Conakry, the capital of Guinea, after that former French West African colony had broken relations with Paris in 1958 and had adopted a revolutionary anti-Western line. When Mali, under the leadership of a leftist government, seceded from its federation with Senegal, North Vietnam set up its second embassy in Africa in Mali's capital city of Bamako. A third mission was opened in Algeria during the leftist administration of former Algerian President Ahmed Ben Bella. However, Hanoi's attempts to extend its diplomatic activities in Africa were frustrated by the preference accorded to South Vietnam by the great majority of African nations. This preference lasted until the period of anarchy following Diem's death caused African nations to reevaluate the relative standing of North and South Vietnam.

North Vietnam's adherence to the Chinese brand of communism was also evidenced by its activities in the Western Hemisphere. From its diplomatic base in Cuba, Hanoi helped the Chinese to hammer away at the theme that the methods of Asian communism are more suitable than those of the West or of the U.S.S.R. in solving the problems of underdevelopment in Latin America.

North Vietnam's diplomatic standing in Asia has fluctu-ated since the establishment of the Democratic Republic of Vietnam. At first, North Vietnam benefited from consider-able prestige among the noncommitted nations after its victory over the French. This was evident at the first confer-ence of the Afro-Asian bloc at Bandung, Indonesia, in 1955. Subsequently, however—both because of excesses at home during the agrarian reform and because of the rigidity of its foreign policies—Hanoi steadily lost ground to Saigon in such countries as India and Burma, where both Vietnams were represented by consuls general. By contrast, in Japan, which had not recognized North Vietnam, Vietnamese Com-munist propaganda made steady advances in business circles which were eager to trade with North Vietnam, and among both leftist intellectuals and trade-union groups. In other key areas of Asia, such as Cambodia and Indonesia, the balance between north and south was abruptly upset in favor of the north under the impact of the November 1963 coup in South Vietnam. Cambodia, already on strained terms with Saigon, severed relations definitively with South Vietnam, and Indonesia broke diplomatic ties with Saigon and allowed the North Vietnamese consulate general to be promoted to embassy level.

Closer to home, Hanoi was not content with diplomacy and exerted a direct influence on the internal affairs of the king-dom of Laos by placing its military strength behind the pro-Communist Pathet Lao faction. This support enabled North Vietnam to be one of the fourteen countries (South Vietnam among them) summoned to another Geneva Conference which in 1962 established a neutralized status for Laos. Across the Laotian frontier in Thailand—the headquarters of SEATO and a firm ally of South Vietnam—the influence of the north is exerted through a large colony of Vietnamese expatriates, who are almost entirely committed to furthering the subversive intentions of Hanoi.

The neutralization not only of Laos, but also of the other Indochinese states—the two Vietnams and Cambodia—has been consistently advocated by successive French governments from that of Pierre Mendès-France to that of General Charles de Gaulle. France originally had recognized only the Saigon regime as the legitimate government of Vietnam. Nevertheless, to keep open the possibility of neutralization of North Vietnam, however remote, France granted *de facto* recognition to the Hanoi government and established a permanent delegation there. The Communist north was then granted the right to set up a commercial mission in Paris with the initial task of facilitating economic relations with France. With the passage of time, however, the scope of this mission became increasingly political.

In 1965 South Vietnam broke diplomatic relations with France, culminating a period of tension between Saigon and Paris which began after the death of Diem. As a result, the Communist commercial mission in Paris became the only Vietnamese group which had access to the higher levels of the French Foreign Ministry. This change in status was considerably facilitated by the prestige which the Hanoi government had always enjoyed in French intellectual and political circles, and by the existence in France of a large Vietnamese colony, the great majority of whose members favored the north. And recently several Hanoi missions have visited Paris.

## South Vietnam and International Politics

The Republic of Vietnam came into existence handicapped by the contradiction from which the Bao Dai regime had previously suffered. Saigon's juridical independence from France was theoretically complete by 1954, but until the Geneva Conference it had been represented abroad almost entirely by French personalities and French groups, while at home it had depended for its existence on the French army. Many of the people in the uncommitted nations of Asia and Africa, like many people in the West, were dazzled by the Vietminh's successful anticolonial struggle, but they did not believe too strongly in South Vietnam's ability to create an independent state because of its long dependence on French support. They underestimated the potential popular basis of the new southern regime because they were unaware of the historical necessity for the Vietnamese people to have a nationalist state independent of China.

## FOREIGN INFLUENCE

The attitude of the Diem government right after its accession to power did little to dispel the impression, even among its own people, that South Vietnam had ceased to be a French puppet only to become a puppet of the United States. This impression was particularly strong in the brief 1954–55 period during which a cloak-and-dagger struggle took place in Saigon between French and American partisans. Those Frenchmen, who belonged to an army and administration on the verge of departure, were loath to leave South Vietnam in the hands of Vietnamese leaders reputed to be anti-French. Against the orders of their own government, they intrigued with the two politico-religious sects and with the Binh Xuyen (see Chapter V) to plot for the overthrow of Diem. But they lost this undercover battle for power to American officials who supported Diem because his known sympathy for the United States made him appear particularly amenable to American suggestions. Diem's American partisans gained Washington's backing for him despite the adverse report of his ability to lead the country made by the United States ambassador in Saigon, General Lawton Collins.

This dramatic struggle between two groups of foreigners as to who should rule in South Vietnam obscured the strength of Vietnamese nationalism both in the eyes of the people within the country and those abroad. Diem, who was above all a nationalist, found himself in the awkward position of having to justify to skeptical foreign opinion the very existence of South Vietnam as an independent nation.

At first, Diem had been too preoccupied with other problems to pay much attention to foreign affairs, and Saigon's diplomacy was hampered by poor advisers and a lack of understanding of the international scene. This was the period when other newly independent countries, deeply marked by their colonial past, turned to nonalignment as an indication that they did not wish to become pawns of any of the great powers. They relied on the influence of one of the world's power blocs to alleviate any pressure from the other. As successors to the late Secretary of State John Foster Dulles came to realize, the nonaligned nations were by no means indifferent to the issues which divided the Communist bloc from the West; they simply did not want to join one or the other side. But Saigon shared Dulles' conviction about the intrinsic wickedness of nonalignment. At the Bandung Conference in Indonesia in 1955, South Vietnam made a rabid denunciation of neutralism, and the other participating nations attributed the denunciation less to a misunderstanding of the philosophy of nonalignment than to a vocal exercise by what they regarded as a new American puppet state. Years after Bandung, denunciations of nonalignment published during this early period in Saigon were still displayed in Africa as evidence that South Vietnam was not an independent Asian country.

The impression thus created during the mid-1950's

harmed Saigon's image not only with leading Asian countries like India—which otherwise would have had every reason to help South Vietnam—but even with the French. France's conviction that its former "Associate State" of Vietnam had become an American satellite combined with an anti-French campaign inspired by the Saigon regime to delay negotiations for French aid and settlement of important economic problems pending between France and South Vietnam. The anti-French line taken by the Saigon government also served to alienate the influential Vietnamese educated class which had always been able to disassociate its great debt to French culture from the struggle against colonial rule. The Vietnamese, it should be noted, see no contradiction in being both anticolonial and pro-French.

This slowness in evolving a distinctively South Vietnamese foreign policy brought its share of difficulties to the already overburdened Saigon regime at home and abroad. Particularly unfortunate was Saigon's participation in a plot—attributed by the Cambodian government to Americans—directed at the overthrow of the neutralist government of Prince Norodom Sihanouk in Cambodia. The impact made by this incident ·later played an important part in Sihanouk's decision to give discreet support to the Vietcong rebellion.

## DIPLOMATIC RELATIONS

The humiliating isolation of South Vietnam on the international scene, the experience acquired by Diem during visits to various Asian countries and to the United States, and the need for the Diem government to consolidate its power over the country—all these factors led Diem to seek improvement in South Vietnam's standing in the world community, a standing which was more in line with his own strong nationalist convictions.

*Prince Buu-Hoi (in national costume) became
Saigon's first ambassador in Africa. He is shown
here with Ivory Coast President Houphouet-Boigny.*

This new independence in Saigon's diplomacy was put
into operation by a group of young and able diplomats led by
Prince Buu-Hoi, who himself became ambassador-at-large to
several countries and to various United Nations bodies.
Working against the heavy odds presented by the bureaucracy
and the nepotism that had paralyzed the operation of South
Vietnamese diplomacy, this new policy, begun in 1958,
rapidly succeeded in building abroad a new image of an
independent and dynamic South Vietnam. Its most notable
successes occurred in the Afro-Asian countries.

Within a short time, Saigon successfully established diplomatic relations with more than twenty African and Middle
Eastern states, and embassies were opened in key countries of

the Arab world and in French-speaking Africa. Through these missions and the exchange programs they initiated, the Afro-Asian countries came to consider sympathetically the problems of South Vietnam and to appreciate in its people many of the qualities they had hitherto identified only with more developed Asian countries such as Japan. Their sympathy was shown by the frequent exchange of high-level official visits and by the warm support regularly given South Vietnam in the specialized agencies of the United Nations (Vietnam is represented in these specialized agencies only by South Vietnam) and in other international forums. A striking example of this trend was the election of a South Vietnamese to the Board of Governors of the International Atomic Energy Agency in Vienna, in preference to a representative from Formosa, the United States candidate.

This display of independence by Saigon also led to a gradual improvement in relations with France under President de Gaulle, which permitted the final settlement of economic problems outstanding between the two countries and the granting of French long-term credits to aid Saigon's industrialization program. Relations with India also greatly improved, to the extent that Indian President Rajenda Prasad's visit to Saigon in 1959, in return for earlier visits by Diem and his brother Nhu to New Delhi, took place in a particularly cordial atmosphere. Prime Minister Jawaharlal Nehru, who in 1954 had been insulted by a government-organized mob during a stopover in Saigon, now sent South Vietnam one of his best diplomats, Ambassador R. Goburdhun, as chairman of the International Commission for Supervision and Control.

South Vietnam's improvement of its position abroad and its successful containment of Vietcong subversion at home enabled Diem's political adviser Ngo Dinh Nhu to enter into an exploratory exchange of views with Hanoi officials in the spring of 1963. They discussed the possibility of reaching a mutually acceptable agreement between North and South Vietnam which could have been very similar to the *de facto* cease-fire that prevails most of the time between Formosa and Communist China.

France showed its support of this policy of accommodation between the two Vietnams when, in August 1963, President de Gaulle expressed the wish that Hanoi and Saigon might settle their differences in a context of national independence and international neutrality. India also made clear its support for the policy. On the Communist side, and for different reasons, both Moscow and Peking favored the idea expressed by President de Gaulle. The U.S.S.R., already embroiled in an ideological conflict with the Chinese Communists, did not wish the struggle between the two Vietnams to become more serious. Mao Tse-tung, for his part, had no desire to see an intensification of guerrilla warfare which might lead to the establishment of permanent American military bases along the South Vietnamese coast.

But Diem's tragic inability to solve the Buddhist crisis, which reached its climax just as these new developments in the relations between North and South Vietnam were taking place, soon brought about his downfall. His assassination ended any prospects for an immediate settlement of the conflict between the two Vietnams and for political stabilization of the Indochinese peninsula.

AFTERMATH OF THE COUP

Ngo Dinh Diem, despite the lack of skill he had often shown in handling his countrymen, was nonetheless a widely respected symbol of Vietnamese nationalism. His death in 1963 under such unsavory circumstances raised the justified suspicion abroad that a new period of instability had begun in South Vietnam. It also precipitated the collapse of Saigon's hard-won diplomatic position throughout the world.

Some Afro-Asian nations, either pro-Western (for example, the Ivory Coast) or nonaligned, refused to recognize the new Saigon regime. Other nations, such as Morocco and Senegal, refused to accept the nomination of new South Vietnamese ambassadors to their countries. In still other countries, such as Nasser's Egypt, Sukarno's Indonesia, Mauritania, and the Congo-Brazzaville, recognition of South Vietnam was withdrawn, and ambassadors from Hanoi were installed in place of the South Vietnamese ambassadors. The U.S.S.R. and certain other countries even went as far as to grant quasi-diplomatic status to missions accredited by the rebel National Liberation Front of South Vietnam.

Subsequent repercussions of the November 1963 events in Saigon reached far beyond the sphere of Vietnamese affairs and contributed to the deterioration of the international situation. For example, Prince Sihanouk of Cambodia, fearful that a similar attempt might be made to bring about his downfall, renounced American aid, expelled American officials, and turned to France and Communist China for military aid.

The French government viewed the Saigon coup as an American move partly directed against France's influence in Asia, and in retaliation stepped up negotiations leading to the recognition of Communist China. Paris also removed itself, for all practical purposes, from membership in SEATO and henceforth sent only an observer to its meetings.

Finally, the massive increase in Washington's involvement in the Vietnamese war, the establishment of powerful American sea and air bases in South Vietnam, and the presence of American ground troops there—necessary to prevent the collapse of the country and a deterioration of the United States position in the Far East—was certain to increase the pace of the military programs and the subversive schemes of Communist China. Prospects of a settlement of the problems dividing Peking and Washington thus became more remote than ever.

## The Future of the Two Vietnams

Eleven years after the Geneva Conference of 1954 had recognized the independence of Vietnam, that country was still divided, and it looked as though it would remain divided for some time to come.

As of late 1965, it appeared that reunification could become feasible only in the event of one of two equally improbable developments. The first of these would be the recognition by the Vietnamese Communist party of the fact that nationalism, not Hanoi communism, is still the only force which can unite North and South Vietnam into a single nation. The other development would be a decision by the United States to withdraw its forces from Vietnam, a decision which would endanger the entire American position in the Far East. However, as 1965 drew to a close, there was as little likelihood that Hanoi would abandon its Communist ambitions for the south as there was that Washington would withdraw its forces from the embattled country.

Indeed, instead of withdrawing from South Vietnam in 1965, the United States began intensive bombings of North Vietnam. From a political standpoint the aim of these bombings was to produce popular unrest and anti-government feelings which might cause the Communists to relax their stand. However, the extremely austere conditions under which the northern population had lived for the previous twenty years had hardened the people to ordeals, and thus the raids did not have their desired effect. The northern leaders, for their part, were unable to utilize these bombings to create an upsurge of nationalistic feeling against the United States. Their verbal reactions to the raids were so heavily tinged with Communist propaganda that they could not stir the fatalistic and apathetic population of South Vietnam.

And so, at the end of 1965, the future of the war and of North and South Vietnam was still in doubt. But perhaps an indication of what the future will bring can be found in an analysis of the basic assets and liabilities of the two Vietnams.

## THE NORTH

The major asset of the North is its people. The North Vietnamese are industrious and capable of great dedication. They have a contempt for death and an ability to fight in conditions of extreme material hardship—an ability which makes them among the best guerrilla fighters in the world. They have succeeded in establishing an unusually effective chain of leadership in their society. They have a refuge when they need one, provided by their extensive mountainous hinterland. Because their industry is more a political instrument than a vital part of their economy, they are willing to sacrifice it if necessary—notably in the case of destruction by United States air attacks.

These eighteen million disciplined people are regimented by the ruthless Lao Dong party, which is totally committed to a victory that would establish its hold on the entire Indochinese peninsula. Such a victory, if it occurs, would help to alleviate the inferiority complex which Asian Communists feel in the face of the great strides in science and technology made by Western Communists. A North Vietnamese victory would demonstrate the power of human masses—the main weapon of Asian communism.

The north's greatest liability is its blind pursuit of victory at any cost. This drive causes northern leaders to act like sleepwalkers unaware of the course of history in the second half of the twentieth century. This course of history derives its basic impetus not from the sacrifice of individuals or masses but from the ever-growing importance of scientific methods, tools, and weapons.

Associated with this North Vietnamese rejection of the realities of the twentieth century is a refusal to consider political compromise and peaceful negotiation. Thus, all peace proposals and calls for negotiation launched from the West according to Western logic have invariably failed in the past, and may be expected to fail in the future. Difficult as it may be for Americans to understand, it nevertheless is likely that the most generous United States offers to North Vietnam to raise the population's living standard or to build public works after peace has been made are meaningless to Hanoi.

A consequence of this way of thinking on the part of the North Vietnamese leadership is the marked advance toward control of North Vietnam achieved by Communist China. By encouraging existing trends of thought among Vietnamese Communists, Peking is shrewdly using Hanoi's intensely emotional commitment to serve as the "vanguard of the revolution" in order to further its own coldly calculated plan for the conquest of Asia. One obstacle to extension of Chinese influence in the north has already been removed by the effort of more than a decade to break down the traditional institutions of the family and the village, institutions which had preserved Vietnam as a separate nation over the centuries.

What Chinese imperialism had failed to accomplish in

centuries past, Peking may be able to achieve in alliance with Asian communism, that is, to bring North Vietnam irreversibly into the new Chinese Empire. Only the reassertion of Moscow's leadership in world communism would make it possible for North Vietnam's present rulers to maintain a Communist state independent of China.

## THE SOUTH

In the South, the existence of a state free of Communist control—if not of Vietcong infiltration—was provisionally saved by the massive intervention of United States armed forces during 1965. These forces succeeded in halting the deterioration of the military and political situation, which had continued uninterruptedly since Diem's death in 1963. But this halt will prove only a useless and costly respite if it is not used to achieve a new, lasting political stability in South Vietnam.

Grave handicaps to the stability of the state exist in the south—notably the lack of Vietnamese leadership. This lack is particularly serious because of the contrast it presents with the north. There, Ho Chi Minh and many of the same men who, with him, started the war against France in 1946 are still in office. Although numerous changes in northern administrative and political personnel have occurred, they were made gradually and only in the interests of efficiency, either for the party or for the state.

Many men who might have become leaders in South Vietnam, among them some of the most outstanding men in the country, joined the Vietminh a long time ago. Of these men, a large number either would not or could not break with the Hanoi regime after 1954. Other well-qualified political and managerial personnel participated in the southern administration in good faith during the nine years of the

*Despite the increasing modernization of Saigon, open-air markets are common sights in the Saigon-Cholon area.*

Diem regime. After Diem's death, however—notably during the rule of General Khanh—these leaders were either excluded from government service or persecuted because of personal jealousies and antagonisms unrelated to either their patriotism or their competence.

American errors of judgment widened the leadership gap. It is difficult to understand how United States officials could have assumed as great a responsibility as they did in encouraging the coup against Diem without making any provision for filling the political vacuum inevitably created by that coup. The period of demagogy ushered in by General Khanh's coup d'etat against the military junta which replaced Diem completed the disruption of what had remained of the southern administration. Khanh's rule, which was openly and clumsily supported by Washington, proved the most unpopular and disruptive of all the different regimes which have appeared since the November 1963 coup.

The Diem regime, however, must also bear a significant part of the blame for creating the present gap in southern leadership. Rather than develop and train future leaders, it discouraged their emergence. In certain cases, it deliberately discredited men who were ready and able to serve their country. Thus an entire political generation was lost to South Vietnam.

The great problem of this leadership gap was further complicated by a number of even more deeply divisive factors—racial, regional, and religious. The racial problem is due to the occupancy of a large region in the central highlands—which happens to be the most promising area for future economic development—by ethnic minorities which took advantage of the general unrest in the country to further their separatist tendencies. This separatism, which is encouraged by the Vietcong, represents a major danger to the unity of South Vietnam. Although a timid effort was made under Diem to bring these minorities into Vietnamese political life by allowing them representatives in the National Assembly, this effort was successfully countered by the Communists, who assassinated the two most prominent pro-Saigon leaders among these mountain-dwelling ethnic minorities. Subsequently, the deterioration of the military situation led to repeated armed revolts on the High Plateaus, directed by FULRO (the Unified Front for the Struggle of Oppressed Races), a group which enjoys the active support of the Vietcong and the sympathy of neighboring Cambodia.

Even among the racially homogeneous majority population of South Vietnam there is unrest. A permanent undercurrent of tension and suspicion separates the Cochin Chinese from other South Vietnamese who were born in northern and central Vietnam. The unresolved antagonism between the Catholics, the Cao Dai, the Hoa Hao, and the Cochin Chinese Buddhists on the one hand, and the militant Buddhist movement which originated in Hue on the other hand, contributes to governmental instability. This antagonism-based instability was demonstrated by the successive overthrow of the Tran Van Huong government (supported by the first group and opposed by the second) and the Phan Huy Quat administration (favored by the second group and attacked by the first). The political strife among the various factions contending for power is paralleled by similar antagonisms in the army, which in 1965 was the main source of organized authority in the country.

Last, but by no means least of the difficulties besetting Saigon's political life, is the lack of incentive among potential leaders to assume political and administrative responsibility. They are convinced that the ultimate source of decision over the life of the country lies entirely with the United States, and they are therefore reluctant to join a government in which they will have little voice.

But against this formidable array of liabilities can be ranged positive factors which, although few, ought nevertheless to be sufficient to keep alive and eventually to promote the development of a non-Communist, independent, and prosperous state of South Vietnam. These positive factors include the agricultural riches of the south; a relaxed, life-loving, courageous, and highly intelligent population; the continuing rise in political influence of a dedicated, politically aware elite of young army officers; and, above all, the undaunted spirit of nationalism and thirst for independence which, despite all calamities and reverses, has enabled the Vietnamese to survive for two thousand years.

# Glossary

For the reader's convenience, the Vietnamese words and names used in this book have been written without the accents which alone would make them intelligible to a Vietnamese. The phonetic transcription given below can only be approximate because the Vietnamese language uses diphthongs which do not exist in English.

**agroville** (*a*-gro-veel)—an agricultural town created in the southern delta by the Diem regime prior to the Strategic Hamlet program. Its purpose was to insure security.

**animism** (*an*-i-mizm)—the belief that natural phenomena and objects have souls, and the worship of them as supernatural beings.

**bonze** (bonz)—Buddhist monk.

**cai** (kie)—overseer.

**can bo** (kan bo)—formerly a Vietminh official charged with carrying out the party's directives among the population. Today, an organizer or propagandist working for a political party.

**Can Lao Nhan Vi** (Kan Lou Nyan Vee)—the secret party which Ngo Dinh Nhu modelled on the Lao Dong party in the north.

**Cao Dai** (Kow Die)—a politico-religious sect in the south, divided into a number of branches with a wide nationalist following.

**chu nom** (tyoo nome)—the system of writing the Vietnamese language in characters derived from the Chinese.

**dinh** (din)—the village community house, center of the village administration and seat of the cult to the village genie.

**don dien** (don dyen)—one of the military and agricultural colonies by means of which the Vietnamese took over central and south Vietnam.

**Hoa Hao** (Wah How)—a politico-religious sect in the south similar to, but less numerous than, the Cao Dai.

**huyen** (hew-yen)—district, an administrative division.

**Indochina**—can be used to indicate the entire peninsula, but in this book designates only the eastern part of the peninsula, formerly French Indochina, now North and South Vietnam, Laos, and Cambodia.

**junk**—a variety of flat-bottomed vessel with sails, used for sea navigation and found on large Vietnamese rivers.

**Lao Dong party** (Low Dong)—Workers' party. The Communist party in North Vietnam.

**ly truong** (lee trung)—the chief village administrative official.

**mandarin** (*man*-da-rin)—one of the appointed officials who administered Vietnam under its kings and emperors.

**Minh Huong** (*Min* Hew-ong)—a person of mixed Chinese and Vietnamese blood.

**nepotism** (*nep*-a-tizm)—the practice of favoring one's relatives, especially in appointments to desirable positions.

**nuoc** (noo-ark)—water, liquid.

**nuoc mam** (noo-ark mum)—fish sauce, a savory and highly salted liquid used in Vietnam to flavor most foods.

**pagoda** (pa-*go*-da)—a Buddhist, Taoist, or Confucianist temple where people come to worship.

**quoc ngu** (kwuk ngyuh)—literally "national language," used to designate the system of transcription of spoken Vietnamese by the Roman alphabet. Accents indicate a variety of sounds as well as tones by which words, otherwise pronounced the same, are distinguished from each other.

**ray** (ray-ee)—land cleared by the slash and burn system which is used mostly by mountain tribes.

**sampan** (*sam*-pan)—one of a variety of small boats used in the harbors and rivers. It is rowed but sometimes has a sail.

**song** (shong)—river.

**ta dien** (ta dyen)—sharecropper.

**thich** (thik)—reverend, the title of a Buddhist monk.

**tinh** (tin)—province.

**Vietcong** (Vyet-cong)—an abbreviation of "Vietnamese Communist," used by the Saigon government to describe the Communist-led subversive movement in the south after 1954.

**Vietminh** (Vyet-min)—abbreviation designating the Communist-led political front presided over by Ho Chi Minh, which led the war against the French.

**xa** (sa)—village or community, often including several hamlets.

# Bibliography

French is the only Western language in which almost all the important studies have been written on the history, geography, and culture of Vietnam, as well as on the colonial period. The following list, which is by no means an exhaustive one (and in which little space has been allotted to the inevitably growing body of literature on the Vietnamese war), is limited to English-language publications. Wide variations in the reporting of facts, as in their interpretation, are inevitable when Westerners are abruptly confronted with the complications and perplexities of an Asian situation and Asian personalities. This factor should be noted by the reader who wishes to pursue the subject further.

Bouscaren, Anthony Trawick  *The Last of the Mandarins: Diem of Vietnam*  Pittsburgh: Duquesne University Press, 1965
> An analysis of the Diem era by a political scientist.

Browne, Malcolm W.  *The New Face of War*  Indianapolis and New York: The Bobbs-Merrill Co., 1965
> An American journalist's account of the war in Vietnam.

Buttinger, Joseph  *The Smaller Dragon*  New York: Frederick A. Praeger, Inc., 1958
> A history of Vietnam from the origins of the country until the end of the nineteenth century.

Cady, John F.  *The Roots of French Imperialism in Eastern Asia*  Ithaca: Cornell University Press, 1955
> An historical study which deals mostly with the period between 1841 and 1861.

Cole, Allan B., ed.  *Conflict in Indochina and International Repercussions*  Ithaca: Cornell University Press, 1956
> A documentary history of the 1945–55 period.

Fall, Bernard B.  *The Two Vietnams, A Political and Military Analysis*  New York: Frederick A. Praeger, Inc., rev. ed., 1964
> A detailed study of North and South Vietnam by a French student of revolutionary warfare.

Hammer, Ellen J.  *The Struggle for Indochina*  Stanford: Stanford University Press, 1954
> The period covered by this politico-historical account is primarily 1939–53, with background material.

Hickey, Gerald Cannon  *Village in Vietnam*  New Haven: Yale University Press, 1964
> An ethnological study based on field research.

Hoang Van Chi  *From Colonialism to Communism, A Case History of North Vietnam*  New York: Frederick A. Praeger, Inc., 1964
> An informative account by a Vietnamese author who has lived under the North Vietnamese Communist regime.

Honey, P. J.  *Communism in North Vietnam*  Cambridge: M.I.T. Press, 1963
> An analysis based on extensive research in North Vietnamese sources.

Lancaster, Donald  *The Emancipation of French Indochina*  London: Oxford University Press, 1961
> A history by a former member of the British legation in Saigon.

Mecklin, John  *Mission in Torment*  Garden City: Doubleday & Co., Inc., 1965
> "An intimate account of the United States role in Vietnam" by a journalist who was chief of the United States Information Service in Saigon.

Nguyen Thai  *Is South Vietnam Viable?*  Manila: Carmelo & Bauerman, 1962
> An inside view of Vietnamese affairs by a sometime official of the Diem government.

Robequain, Charles  *The Economic Development of French Indochina*  London and New York: Oxford University Press, 1944
> A classic work by a French scholar.

Roy, Jules  *The Battle of Dienbienphu*  New York: Harper & Row, Publishers, 1965
> A dramatic account and analysis by a French writer who served in the French Expeditionary Corps in Vietnam.

Sacks, I. Milton "Marxism in Vietnam," Frank Trager, ed., *Marxism in Southeast Asia, A Study of Four Countries* Stanford: Stanford University Press, 1959
  A monograph by a longtime student of Vietnamese Marxism.

Scigliano, Robert *South Vietnam: Nation under Stress* Boston: Houghton Mifflin Co., 1963
  The author is a student of Vietnamese politics and has written several articles on the subject of Vietnam.

Thompson, Virginia *French Indo-China* New York: The Macmillan Company, 1937
  An extensive survey by one of the first American historians to visit Vietnam.

Tran Van Dinh *No Passenger on the River* New York: Vantage Press, Inc., 1965
  A novel by the former South Vietnamese chargé d'affaires in Washington which gives an idea of the atmosphere in South Vietnam at the time of the November 1963 coup.

United Nations, *Report of the United Nations Fact-Finding Mission to South Vietnam* New York: United Nations General Assembly A/5630, 7 December 1963
  A detailed account of the interviews conducted by the UN mission to South Vietnam in regard to the origins and evolution of the "Buddhist affair" in 1963.

Vo Nguyen Giap *People's War, People's Army* New York: Frederick A. Praeger, Inc., 1962
  General Giap's analysis of revolutionary war in Vietnam.

Warner, Denis *The Last Confucian* New York: The Macmillan Company, rev. ed., 1964
  An account of the Diem era by an Australian journalist, with additional chapters on related subjects.

West, Morris *The Ambassador* New York: William Morrow and Co., 1965
  A perceptive and illuminating novel concerned with the events leading up to the November 1963 coup d'etat, in which the president of South Vietnam is portrayed as a composite of Ngo Dinh Diem and Ngo Dinh Nhu.

# Credits

The format for *Vietnam* was designed by Robert Sugar. The cover was prepared by Leah Ice. The maps were drawn by Donald T. Pitcher.

We would like to thank Jean Vons who executed some of the photographs for *Vietnam*, and the Centre d'Etude et de Documentation sur l'Afrique et l'Outre-Mer which supplied a number of others.

For the photographs on the following pages we gratefully credit:

| | | | |
|---|---|---|---|
| 8 | Eastfoto | 205 | A.I.D. |
| 10 | A.I.D. | 212 | A.I.D. |
| 20 | A.I.D. | 233 | A.I.D. |
| 26 | Ewing Galloway | 235 | Eastfoto |
| 129 | A.I.D. | 252 | Eastfoto |
| 148 | A.I.D. | 259 | Photo Information Côte d'Ivoire |
| 168 | A.I.D. | | |
| 172 | A.I.D. | 267 | Fujihira from Monkmeyer Press Photo Service |
| 195 | A.I.D. | | |

# Index